Supervision of Music Therapy

D0165333

Supervision of Music Therapy discusses the theoretical bases underlying approaches to supervision in music therapy, as well as focusing on the distinctive aspects of music therapy supervision from both clinical and conceptual perspectives.

In this book leading music therapy supervisors and researchers demonstrate how music therapy trainees and practising clinicians can be supported through supervision, allowing them to develop confidence and authenticity in their work. Contributors discuss supervision of clinical work with a variety of patients in a range of settings, from special education to forensic psychiatry, including work in schools, children's services and a dedicated music therapy centre. A chapter on the academic supervision of music therapists undertaking doctoral research is provided, together with an overview of the history and continuing development of the field.

Supervision of Music Therapy contributes to current debates about approaches to supervision in music therapy and offers the reader fresh perspectives on the subject, making this a book of value to practising therapists, supervisors and students alike.

Helen Odell-Miller is Director of the MA in Music Therapy at Anglia Ruskin University, and a head music therapist and research specialist in the Arts Therapies Service in the Cambridgeshire and Peterborough NHS Partnership Mental Health Trust.

Eleanor Richards is a Senior Lecturer in Music Therapy at Anglia Ruskin University, and a senior music therapist in the Cambridgeshire and Peterborough NHS Partnership Mental Health Trust.

Supervision in the Arts Therapies
Series Editor: Joy Schaverien

'This splendid series breaks new ground in its depth, breadth and scope, guided by Joy Schaverien's recognition that the time is right for a comprehensive, multi-faceted study of supervision in the arts psychotherapies. With each volume, the reader is invited to imagine, explore, and reflect on the expressive qualities of a particular art form in clinical supervision, turning special attention to art, music, dance, drama, and sandplay through contributions by leading experts from different parts of the world. These five volumes will make a lasting contribution as essential reading for supervisors and supervisees across the psychotherapies. The series also contributes towards a deeper understanding of the mentor–student relationship and the healing power of the arts.'

Joan Chodorow, Jungian Analyst and former President of the American Dance Therapy Association

'This new series of *Supervision in the Arts Therapies* is both timely and necessary. Now that all the arts therapies are established as state-registered professions in their own right, there is a lack of resources that can support both the more advanced practitioner and the student. The writers of these individual titles are leaders in their respective fields both as researchers and practitioners. These publications make very important and innovative steps, and should be read by everyone in related fields of work.'

Dr Sue Jennings, Consultant Dramatherapist and Supervisor

This innovative series comprises five edited volumes, each focusing on one of the arts therapies – art, music, drama, dance or sandplay – and reflects on the dynamic nature of the presentation of that art form in supervision. The series reveals similarities and differences encountered in the theory and practice of supervision in each modality and within a range of contexts, and with diverse client groups.

Supervision in the Arts Therapies makes a timely contribution to the literature and will be essential reading for experienced practitioners and students of the arts therapies, as well as psychotherapists and other professionals engaged in supervision.

Titles in the series

Supervision of Dance Movement Therapy
Helen Payne

Supervision of Art Psychotherapy
Joy Schaverien and Caroline Case

Supervision of Sandplay Therapy
Harriet Friedman and Rie Rogers Mitchell

Supervision of Music Therapy
Helen Odell-Miller and Eleanor Richards

Supervision of Dramatherapy
Phil Jones and Ditty Dokter

Supervision of Music Therapy

A Theoretical and Practical Handbook

Edited by Helen Odell-Miller and Eleanor Richards

Routledge
Taylor & Francis Group

LONDON AND NEW YORK

First published 2009 by Routledge
27 Church Road, Hove, East Sussex BN3 2FA

Simultaneously published in the USA and Canada
by Routledge
270 Madison Avenue, New York, NY 10016

Routledge is an imprint of the Taylor & Francis Group, an Informa business

Typeset in Times by Garfield Morgan, Swansea, West Glamorgan
Printed and bound in Great Britain by TJ International Ltd, Padstow, Cornwall
Paperback cover design by Sandra Heath

British Library Cataloguing in Publication Data
A catalogue record for this book is available from the British Library

Library of Congress Cataloging-in-Publication Data
Supervision of music therapy : a theoretical and practical handbook / edited
by Helen Odell-Miller and Eleanor Richards.
 p. cm.
 Includes bibliographical references and index.
 ISBN 978-0-415-41125-7 (hardback) – ISBN 978-0-415-41126-4 (pbk.) 1.
Music therapy. I. Odell-Miller, Helen, 1955- II. Richards, Eleanor (Eleanor
Gurney)
 ML3920.S93 2008
 616.89'1654–dc22

                                                    2008014134

ISBN: 978-0-415-41125-7 (hbk)
ISBN: 978-0-415-41126-4 (pbk)

Contents

Contributors

Sandra Brown trained as a music therapist at the Nordoff–Robbins Music Therapy Centre, London. She currently holds the post of Senior Music Therapist at the Nordoff–Robbins Centre, and Senior Clinical Tutor on the City University Master of Music Therapy (Nordoff–Robbins) degree programme. She has also trained as an analytical psychologist with the Society of Analytical Psychology, London, and works in private practice as both analyst and supervisor. She has published a range of papers in books and journals relating to music therapy practice.

Alison Davies is a music therapist and a psychotherapist. She trained at Roehampton Institute and the Philadelphia Association in London. Her clinical work has been mainly in psychiatry, working in NHS Trusts in Cambridge and Lincoln. Group work has been of special interest to her and she runs the experiential music therapy groups for trainees at the Guildhall School of Music and Drama, London and at Anglia Ruskin University, Cambridge. She currently has a private psychotherapy and supervision practice in Cambridge.

John Glyn is a psychoanalytic psychotherapist working at The Cassel Hospital, Open Door Young People's Consultation Service, and in private practice. He worked for 10 years as a music therapist in forensic psychiatric settings and continues to supervise music therapists.

David John is a psychoanalytic psychotherapist working in private practice, and a member of the British Association of Psychotherapists. He has worked as a music therapist in the NHS adult mental health service in Cambridge for over 20 years, where he is currently professional lead for arts therapies. David supervises music therapists and other arts therapists and co-ordinates clinical placements for arts therapies trainees in his NHS role. He has published and presented papers on supervision in music therapy and on the connections between music therapy, psychotherapy and psychoanalysis.

Nicolas Krueckeberg graduated as a music therapist in 2004. Before this he worked for many years in residential childcare, special education and also with young adults with learning disabilities. In his present job he works with children on the autistic spectrum and their families. He is also currently training as a systemic psychotherapist.

Helen Odell-Miller is Head of the MA Music Therapy programme at Anglia Ruskin University, Cambridge, UK, and has worked as a clinician, researcher and manager in the NHS for over 30 years in adult mental health. She is an adviser to the Association of Professional Music Therapists (APMT) and has been an adviser to the Department of Health on music therapy. She has led three major research projects looking at clinical outcomes, including music therapy for older people with dementia, and arts therapies in the adult mental health field; recently for her doctorate studies at Aalborg University, Denmark, she looked at links between diagnosis and clinical method in music therapy across five European music therapy centres in psychiatry. Helen has lectured and published widely around the world and was a founder member of the European Music Therapy Committee. She was also a founder of the APMT supervision scheme. She has also published chapters about the relationship between psychoanalysis and music therapy, and music therapy group work.

Amelia Oldfield has over 27 years' experience as a music therapist. She currently works at the Croft Unit for Child and Family Psychiatry and at the Child Development Centre, Addenbrooke's Hospital, Cambridge. She was the joint initiator of the MA Music Therapy course at Anglia Ruskin University, where she has been a part-time lecturer for the past 13 years. She is an approved APMT supervisor and has supervised music therapists and music therapy students for the past 17 years. She has completed four research investigations and a PhD. She has written three books as well as a wide range of articles and chapters on various aspects of music therapy. She has also produced six music therapy training videos. She has run workshops and given papers all over Europe and in the USA. She is married, has four children and plays the clarinet in local chamber music groups in Cambridge.

Inge Nygaard Pedersen is a professor in music therapy at Aalborg University, Denmark. She has qualifications in Guided Imagery in Music and Relaxation Training, and her PhD examines the concept of countertransference in music therapy. Since 1995 she has been head of the music therapy clinic at Aalborg University and Aalborg Psychiatric Hospital. She was founder and head of the masters programme in music therapy between 1982 and 1995. She has worked in clinical practice in psychiatry as a music therapist and counsellor for over 25 years, and is co-author of four books. She has published more than 50 articles and book chapters in Danish, English and German. She is currently establishing a postgraduate supervisor training course for professional music therapists in Denmark.

Eleanor Richards trained in music therapy at Roehampton Institute, London, and is a Senior Lecturer in music therapy at Anglia Ruskin University, Cambridge and a Senior Music Therapist in the Cambridgeshire and Peterborough Mental Health Partnership NHS Trust, where she works with adults with learning disabilities and associated mental health problems, and supervises staff in various disciplines. She is an APMT registered supervisor. She has also trained with the Centre for Attachment-Based Psychoanalytic Psychotherapy, London, and is a psychotherapist and supervisor in private practice. She has published widely and presented numerous conference papers.

Ann Sloboda read music at Oxford University and subsequently trained in music therapy at the Guildhall School of Music and Drama, London; she qualified in 1985. After working for 7 years with adults with learning disabilities, she moved into work in adult psychiatry, specialising in treatment of patients with eating disorders. Her main specialisation since 1995 has been in forensic psychiatry. and she built up a specialist arts therapies service in the West London Mental Health Trust. She has been involved in training music therapists since 1992 and is now head of training at the Guildhall School of Music and Drama in the UK. She has published widely on music therapy in eating disorders and in forensic psychiatry. She is currently training at the Institute of Psychoanalysis, London.

Tony Wigram is Professor of Music Therapy and Head of PhD Studies in Music Therapy in the Institute for Communication and Psychology, Department of Humanities, University of Aalborg, Denmark. He is a Principal Research Fellow in the Faculty of Music, Melbourne University, and Reader in Music Therapy at Anglia Ruskin University, Cambridge. He wrote his PhD in Psychology at St George's Medical School, London University. He has written or edited 14 books on music therapy and authored more than 100 articles in peer reviewed journals and chapters in books.

Preface to the Series and to *Supervision of Music Therapy*

Supervision of Music Therapy is a title in the five-volume series *Supervision in the Arts Therapies*. The series was conceived as a result of collaboration with colleagues from the fields of art and music therapy, drama and dance movement therapy, as well as the related discipline of sandplay therapy. In particular, the idea for the series developed out of discussions with Helen Odell-Miller, over a number of years, on the links between music therapy and art therapy. This led to creative discourse regarding the roles of the various arts media in therapy and supervision. The common element in the practices explored in this series is that, in each of the arts therapies an object, sound or action (or series of objects, sounds or actions), mediates psychological processes within the context of a therapeutic relationship. The evidence is that there is a developing body of theory specific to the fields of supervision in the arts therapies but there is relatively little literature on the subject. Thus the idea of a series of books on *Supervision in the Arts Therapies* was envisaged and, with the encouragement of Joanne Forshaw, at Routledge, the series came into being.

It is a great pleasure to introduce this, the first British book on the *Supervision of Music Therapy*. Dr Odell-Miller and Eleanor Richards are leading practitioners, educators and theorists in the field of music therapy. They have assembled a group of contributors who are all highly experienced music therapists, from widely diverse international back-grounds. The result is a book that is an exciting and lively contribution to the literature in this well-established field.

Music offers the opportunity for a specific experience, which is qualitatively different from other forms of psychotherapy, and this is reflected in supervision of the practice. It is anticipated that, along with its companion volumes in the series, *Supervision of Music Therapy* will interest a wide readership: supervisors and supervisees, whether experienced practitioners or students of music therapy. However, the anticipated readership is not limited to this group; it includes practitioners of the other arts therapies, as well as analytical psychology, child and adult psychotherapy, counselling and integrative arts therapy. All who supervise music therapists, and all who are interested in understanding the role of music in professional practice, will find this book an inspiring read and an essential companion to supervision.

Joy Schaverien September 2007

Joy Schaverien PhD
Series editor
Jungian Analyst in Private Practice
Member of the International Association of Analytical Psychology
Visiting Professor in Art Psychotherapy: Northern Programme for
Art Psychotherapy, Sheffield UK

Acknowledgements

We would like to thank our colleagues, supervisors and supervisees from whom we have learned so much. We are also grateful to our families and friends, and especially to Mike, Sam, Ben and Robert.

Introduction

Helen Odell-Miller and Eleanor Richards

This book is about the supervision of music therapy work, and forms part of a series on supervision in the arts therapies and other related disciplines, such as sandplay therapy. As such, it focuses upon the unique aspects of music therapy supervision, and at the same time refers to interdisciplinary theory and practice from other professions, such as psychotherapy and psychoanalytic psychotherapy and from other health-related professions. It adds to the existing book *Music Therapy Supervision*, by Forinash (2001), published in the USA, and takes a clinical and academic focus, drawing particularly upon UK and other European practice of music therapy supervision. A major inspiration for the book was a national conference hosted by Anglia Ruskin University in Cambridge, UK, in 2003 on supervision of music therapy. Some of the thinking behind the chapters started there and many of the contributors to this book first presented their ideas at that conference.

Supervision of music therapy casework for trainees, experienced therapists and for those undertaking research and academic work, such as for PhDs, is now integral to music therapy practice and the book reflects this. Forinash's book provides a detailed overview of different approaches and theoretical thinking in music therapy supervision from around the world. In contrast, this book adds to the literature by providing a case-focused approach whereby the music therapy supervision process is described from the point of view of the context (the client group or setting). The book includes chapters about supervision of students in training, and of therapists working in a variety of settings and clinical areas, including forensic psychiatry, learning disabilities, schools, adult psychiatry, children's services, and a dedicated music therapy centre. There is also a chapter discussing supervision of music therapy research in an academic setting.

The book is aimed primarily at music therapists, both experienced clinicians and students in training, but we expect it also to be of interest to those from other related professions, such as other arts therapies, psychotherapy, psychoanalytic psychotherapy, social work, occupational therapy, medicine, nursing and teaching. This is because, at the same time as the unique aspects of working with music in music therapy are reflected upon and discussed (including the actual use of music in supervision sessions), there is a discussion throughout the book to inform the reader about good practice from psychoanalytic, humanistic, sociological and musical perspectives, which we hope will be of use to readers who are not music therapists.

The original idea for the book arose from dialogues with Joy Schaverien, editor of this series of books on supervision within the arts therapies and related disciplines. We were very pleased to be invited to contribute to the series by writing this book, particularly as there have been important links between art and music therapy supervision initiatives. Joy Schaverien had been involved in training days for music therapy supervisors, and it seemed logical to write the book as part of an arts therapies series. During the early days of formalising and developing music therapy supervision schemes in the UK, art therapists were included as advisors. (Odell-Miller, Streeter, & Mure 1988). The in-service training in universities of music therapist supervisors working in clinical placements has also included interdisciplinary training workshops from drama therapists, psychodramatists, psychotherapists and art therapists.

This book reflects dialogues with music therapists over a number of years, and covers national and international developments in music therapy supervision. We invited some of those music therapists who had been most closely involved with these developments in Europe, and others who had developed work in this area more recently, or who offered a particular perspective not yet found in the music therapy literature, to contribute chapters.

Until the last two decades, music therapists turned to members of other professions, such as psychotherapy and psychoanalysis, for supervision because music therapy clinical practice and music therapy supervision were at relatively early stages of development. In addition, the concepts of transference, countertransference, free association and other aspects of psychoanalytic theory were useful in fostering understanding of the therapeutic relationship, as well as musical understanding. Music therapy now incorporates and integrates these concepts in training and supervision and many music therapists have undertaken training in some form of psychoanalytically informed, verbally based therapy.

In this book, there are chapters discussing supervision from both clinical and conceptual perspectives. Composite examples have been created and confidentiality has been preserved, in all instances, of both clinical and supervisory material. In the opening chapter, Helen Odell-Miller looks at the history and continuing development of ideas and practice in music therapy supervision in the UK and elsewhere. Starting with a reminder that until relatively recently there was no routine acceptance amongst music therapists in the UK that they might take their work to supervision, she outlines the events in the last 20 years that have contributed to a change in thinking and have also enabled music therapists to develop their skills as supervisors.

The chapters that follow address the subject of supervision from various angles. In Chapter 2, Eleanor Richards discusses some of the issues that might be specific to the supervision of students at an early stage of training, and in particular explores the possible impact and implications for trainees of working with people with learning disabilities.

In Chapter 3, Inge Nygaard Pedersen proposes an 'integrated development model' of supervision, in which the process and intensity of supervision moves from one level to another as the therapist gains in experience and confidence. She then introduces and illustrates a model of 'integrative supervision' for use in supervision in a group context.

In Chapter 4, John Glyn identifies and describes some of the issues central to working in forensic psychiatry, attending in particular to patients' potential defences against 'triangulation'. He goes on to look at two cases and their supervision from that perspective.

In Chapter 5, David John looks more broadly at the development of the therapist, both as a student and beyond, drawing in particular upon the work of Bion as a framework for thinking about and sustaining the (largely unconscious) growth and emerging identity of the therapist.

In Chapter 6, Helen Odell-Miller and Nicolas Krueckeberg, as supervisor and supervisee, respectively, reflect on the process of supervision of a student working in a psychiatric setting in which recording was not possible; it was thus necessary to work in supervision only with the supervisee's verbal accounts of his experience with his patients.

In Chapter 7, Sandra Brown gives a reminder of the need to build each supervisory relationship afresh, rather than working in a way that is too closely tied to fixed theoretical ideas. She identifies some of the factors, both personal and organisational, that need to be actively thought about if the supervisory relationship is to flourish.

In Chapter 8, Amelia Oldfield introduces her approach to supervision and describes the development of her thinking, in particular about the supervision of clinical work with children. She draws on accounts from three of her supervisees to illustrate her approach in action.

In Chapter 9, Alison Davies and Ann Sloboda raise the important matter of boundaries and, through a range of examples, demonstrate the important function of the supervisory process in helping the clinician to maintain appropriate boundaries in several diverse areas.

Finally, in Chapter 10, Tony Wigram gives a detailed account of the key elements that must be present and sustained in a good working relationship between academic supervisor and music therapy researcher at the doctoral level.

The authors have presented their thoughts in a variety of ways. Some have written about work in specific clinical areas, and its associated implications for supervision, whereas others have explored more general issues related to the support and continuing development of the supervisee. Many have included vivid vignettes to illustrate their discussions. The final chapter is a reminder that the spirit of enquiry, which needs to be so alive in the supervision space, has its counterpart in the academic setting. We hope that this collection of writings offers some insight into the range and continuing development of ideas about this vital dimension in the working life of every practising clinician.

References

Odell-Miller, H., Streeter, E., Mure, M. (1988) *Proposal for a music therapy supervisor's training scheme*. London: Association of Professional Music Therapy.
Forinash, M. (2001) *Music therapy supervision*, Philadelphia: Barcelona.

Chapter 1

The history and background of supervision in music therapy

Helen Odell-Miller

Introduction

Discussion of clinical work in supervision is now integral to the professional life of a music therapist, and it is well recognised that engaging with another professional who can offer new insights deepens thinking and encourages clinical rigour. In 1990, the Association of Professional Music Therapists (APMT) in the UK was one of the first music therapy organisations worldwide to launch a professional supervision scheme for music therapists, and to define supervision in music therapy formally within its procedural publications, (APMT 1990). The development of this scheme will be used as a case study throughout this chapter to illustrate the professional development of supervision practice. The chapter will also include a selected literature review of writings, which illustrates different approaches and theoretical models of music therapy supervision.

The early history of the UK music therapy supervision scheme highlights essential issues for music therapists, such as the balance of musical material and words in supervision practice, the appropriate choice of professional supervisor, and model. It also illustrates the development of the music therapy profession from one supervised mainly by people outside the music therapy profession, to the establishing of music therapy expertise and an emphasis upon music therapists supervising from within the profession at trainee and post-qualification levels.

At the time of the implementation of the UK supervision scheme (APMT 1990), music therapy training was short and registration for music therapists had not become a legal requirement. There are now seven music therapy training courses in the UK, all at MA level and approved by the registration body the Health Professions Council (HPC). The European Music Therapy Committee is negotiating with the European Parliament for statutory standards of MA level for basic music therapy training. Music therapists are employed in many different settings; recent statistics show that the major employer is the National Health Service (NHS), in which music therapists often work quite autonomously with people who have severe mental health problems, learning disabilities or terminal illness.

This chapter focuses upon some of the historical developments and issues surrounding the development of music therapy supervision practice in Europe, and in particular in the UK. This discussion concludes at the present day and the recent work that is reflected in this book.

One of the earliest definitions in the literature on music therapy supervision arose from the developing clinical need for the establishment of a national music therapy supervision training and monitoring scheme for professional music therapists:

> Supervision is a process to enable music therapists to discover ways of improving their working practice through examination and exploration with the supervisor, of casework in a supportive way.
>
> (APMT 1990)

The UK scheme included the setting-up of a new register for approved supervisors in the profession who could supervise music therapists, particularly those in their early years of work. It became mandatory for music therapists to complete 32 hours of supervision with a music therapist approved by the APMT before becoming a full member of the APMT. This particular scheme ceased when the two-year, MA-level training programmes, and requirement for music therapists to register with the Health Professions Council, were established. However, the culture that arose from this earlier scheme was influential in furthering knowledge about music therapy supervision.

Meaning and supervision: Definitions of music therapy supervision

A major element in the developing process of any new professional practice is the clarification of terminology, and clarification was needed in the early days when music therapy supervision was less established. Many countries now require music therapists to be 'in supervision' as part of good working practice, for example as stated in the APMT Code of Conduct (2007) in the UK. What does this actually mean?

The APMT regarded music therapy supervision as a new concept in 1990, and it is striking that it was necessary to further clarify what was meant by the terms used in the definition quoted above. For example, it was stated that 'improving working practice' would include work with clients and issues related to interprofessional workings in the work setting. 'Examination and exploration' was clarified as being directed at increasing the supervisees' awareness of issues affecting their clinical work; and '"supportive" referred to the supervisors' respectful, non-judgemental and exploratory stance, through a relationship which promotes confidence, self-evaluation, deepening awareness and personal development . . .' (APMT 1990).

Revisiting these documents, it is clear that the practice of music therapy supervision in Europe, and elsewhere, has developed in its understanding and practice over the last two decades. The most recent statements about structures and definitions of supervision for the profession can be found in the current APMT (2007, 2008) documentation on this subject, and also in some of the Health Professions Council standards of education and practice for arts therapists (HPC 2007a, 2007b).

The setting up of the APMT supervision scheme (Bunt & Hoskyns 2002) led the way in Europe, not only to the development of a formalised scheme with standards, but also to the development of music therapy supervision as a discipline, which involved developing supervisor training curricula (Hammarlund 2001; Odell-Miller 2001a).

International collaboration

In the early 1990s, other European countries, such as Italy, Germany and Denmark, were looking at the benefits of supervision as an integral part of training and professional practice. Links between the UK and other European initiatives were particularly marked by the European supervision round-table work undertaken at the 4th European Congress of Music Therapy in Leuven, Belgium in 1998. Elaine Streeter (UK), Inge Nygaard Pedersen (Denmark), Ingrid Hammerlund (Sweden), Gianluigi di Franco (Italy), Isabelle Frohne-Hageman (Germany) and Helen Odell-Miller (UK), among others, were involved in leading the way to the development of a European focus on theoretical and practical rigour in music therapy supervision. This international collaboration resulted in the current strong tradition of supervision in music therapy found in many European countries, and included the establishment of the first training for music therapy supervisors in the Royal Swedish Academy of Music by Ingrid Hammerlund.

Before 1990, the culture of supervision in the USA and Australia tended to be part of core music therapy training, rather than part of post-qualification practice. Approaches to music therapy supervision appeared to be less dynamically reflective than in many European countries (Odell-Miller 1994). However, a significant set of presentations in a round-table discussion at the World Congress of Music Therapy in Washington, in 1999, culminated in the comprehensive book *Music Therapy Supervision* (Forinash 2001). Some of that literature will be discussed here, and this present book aims to add to that knowledge, taking a particularly European perspective.

What is unique about music therapy supervision?

A survey of music therapists about supervision practice carried out by the APMT in 1989 (Odell-Miller 1994) reflected that the most common elements in supervision were casework presentation, group discussion and discussion of work issues, such as administration. There was also an indication that some sought to include the possibility of playing music during supervision. Other issues that people wanted to be included were research and further study, personal issues and feelings encountered in the work, team interaction, observation of groups and supervision of supervision. Respondents also indicated that more dialogue with psychotherapists regarding issues such as transference and countertransference would further inform music therapy supervision practice.

The issue of whether music therapists improvise and play together as part of supervision sessions was explored in these early years by music therapists worldwide (Pavlicevic 1994; Priestley 1975; Stephens 1984); the development of this work is reflected below in the literature review. Although it is important to work through music in supervision, it might also be especially important for music therapists to explore issues both verbally *and* musically in supervision for the very reason that working only through music can merge and confuse certain processes. The following example illustrates this point, and introduces the reader to how music therapy supervision might work:

The music therapist was seeing a 33-year-old man with a diagnosis of manic depression who was an inpatient in a psychiatric setting. At first, the supervision was about helping the therapist maintain the time and confidentiality boundaries appropriately, so that the therapy did not become confused with general ward issues, or 'sabotaged' by other staff. Eventually, a relationship of trust was built up whereby the therapist was able to understand the meaning of the patient's frequent non-attendance in terms of this representing a flight from the realisation that feelings arising through the improvisations were uncomfortable. This emerged through listening to musical examples and to verbal dialogue, and, in reflecting upon these with the supervisor, discovering that this discomfort was present particularly when the therapist did not play and support his [the patient's] piano playing. The therapist was helped in supervision sessions to understand her own struggles with being drawn totally into a mother–child countertransference. She was able to use the understanding to further help the patient understand himself and his reactions by exploring his adult–child self through playing and not playing with the therapist. He began to develop a tolerance of difference in their piano playing (the work took place on two pianos) and to tolerate the shared discussions between musical improvisations, when the therapist was able to make interpretations that helped him gain further insights. The work had been rather stuck and difficult for a long time, and the supervision sessions seemed to help move the patient away from the very stuck position of merging with the therapist, which had previously seemed impossible to shift.

In this example, the supervisee was helped by listening to the music and discussing issues arising from it, with the supervisor hearing new aspects of the relationship. This material might also have been explored through improvisation in the supervision session, with supervisee and supervisor taking on different roles musically, but discussion attributing meaning to the musical interactions was also necessary to gain full insights into the case and to help sessions move forward.

Review of selected literature on music therapy supervision

Bunt and Hoskyns (2002) include a summary of music therapy supervision in the UK, whereas the comprehensive publication *Music Therapy Supervision* (Forinash 2001) provides an international collection of different approaches to supervision ranging from discussion on literature, ethics and multicultural issues, (Dileo 2001; Estrella 2001; McClain 2001), to issues in preprofessional training; Summer (2001), for example, discusses US undergraduate supervision for trainees, and Hanser (2001) discusses a systems approach to the supervision of trainees on clinical placement in the USA at undergraduate level, which is introductory and practical in nature. Peer supervision is discussed by Baratta *et al.* (2001), taking a problem-solving approach, and Austin and Dvorkin (2001) discuss a psychodynamic perspective on peer group music therapy supervision.

Specific models of music therapy supervision are described by authors who have developed their own approaches. Stephens (2001) describes the benefits of experiential music therapy groups as a method of professional supervision, and Frohne-Hagemann (2001) proposes an integrative model in which she highlights the importance of a multiperspective approach and draws attention to the different layers of construct, meaning and interaction in the supervision process. She takes a more sociological approach, drawing upon phenomenology (Pezold 1998), and emphasises the importance of interpreting meaningful human interaction from a hermeneutic perspective, as well as using a sociological approach that combines aesthetic, psychoanalytical, social psychological and social ecological ideas to make an 'integrative' approach. Alongside these theoretical concepts she emphasises the evaluative perspective and the action-orientated perspective, which are particularly relevant in music therapy, and draws attention, like Pedersen (see Chapter 3), to the different levels of approach appropriate for the supervisee, depending upon their experience.

Stige, a Norwegian music therapist, takes a European viewpoint, demonstrating the influence of narrative psychotherapy and interactive music therapy experiences using the term 'barefoot therapist' in the chapter title 'The fostering of not knowing: barefoot supervisors' (Stige 2001). Here, the supervisee and supervisor role-play together, both musically and through words, with the emphasis upon joint discovery through the telling of the story. This is in contrast to the more prescribed methods described by Summer (2001) and Hanser (2001) for trainees, which also reflect cultural differences between the USA and Europe.

Whereas Forinash (2001) includes chapters proposing different models of supervision, in this book we have taken an approach that is context based rather than driven by a particular model. The theoretical perspectives described are often rigorous, but the book aims to take the reader into various contexts and to follow the process and approach to supervision from that point of view. Hence the focus is upon the clinical, educational or academic setting, and what might be appropriate in each one. This chapter, for example, illustrates an approach designed for a particular adult mental health setting and discusses some differences that there might be in other settings such as learning disabilities, or in settings in which it is possible to obtain musical examples for use in supervision.

The place of music and psychoanalytic thinking in the supervision process

A discussion about the balance of music and words, and the impact of psychoanalytic theory and interpretation, has been prevalent in music therapy literature (John 1992, 1995; Odell-Miller 2001b, 2003). This debate is reflected in one of the few publications about supervision and music therapy in the UK by Alison Levinge, who was recently chair of the supervision committee for the APMT. In her paper 'Supervision or double vision' (Levinge 2002), she explores the complexities of discussing musical material in the supervision session and the potential for the unconscious expression or presence of primitive forces that might arise examining preverbal material, including free musical improvisation. She highlights the difficulties of listening to two dimensions at once – the musical and the verbal. Whilst basing some of her ideas on psychoanalytic thinking – for example the idea of developing the internal supervisor (Casement 1985) – she uses musical language such as 'resonance' to understand what it might be helpful for the supervisor to listen to in the supervision session. She suggests that the hidden aspects of music (which never stands still), might resonate and echo and that there might be more primitive unconscious music underlying the supervision session, which can be brought to light with the right listening approach.

Forinash (2001) also posed the question about how to include music in the supervision process, and in her book there are several examples of this (Austin & Dvorkin 2001; Jahn-Langenberg 2001; Lee 2001; Stephens 2001). This approach uses theme-based improvisation based upon Priestley's Intertherap method (Priestley 1975, 1994), which will be returned to later.

Attention to the music in music therapy supervision is essential theoretically, clinically and technically, as shown here, but so too is attention to the health setting or social context of clinical work.

Definitions of music therapy supervision in cultural contexts

Bunt and Hoskyns (2002) refer to the book *Supervision in the Helping Professions* (Hawkins & Shohet 1989), written by non-music therapists who are discussing supervision of professionals in health and social services settings. This highlights the fact that up to this point there was little existing literature on the specific issues of music therapy supervision. It is interesting here to show two similar definitions of music therapy supervision formed at the same time, one from USA (a) and one from the UK (b), in order to form the basis for a short summary of different perspectives across the world:

(a) 'Supervision in music therapy is an interactive process between a practitioner and a more experienced colleague, concentrating on musical, practical and dynamic issues. There is a mutual shared interest in the work with the central emphasis on the practitioner becoming more effective in working with clients. Through the establishment of a clear frame of meetings, the supervisor facilitates open and honest articulation of material arising from the work. The process takes place within a context that is both supportive and critically reflective' (Bunt & Hoskyns 2002 p. 262)

(b) 'The focus of the supervision relationship is to address the complexities involved in helping supervisees in their ongoing (and never-ending) development as competent and compassionate professionals. Supervision is a relationship, one in which both supervisor and supervisee actively participate and interact. It is a process of unfolding – not simply following a recipe, but engaging in a rich and dynamic relationship. Supervision then is also a journey, or odyssey of sorts, in which supervisor and supervisee learn and grow and from which both will very likely leave transformed in some way.' (Forinash 2001 p. 1)

An emphasis upon mutual collaboration rather than challenge and analytic rigour is also reflected in these definitions (Bunt & Hoskyns 2002; Forinash 2001). In a similar way, the term 'compassionate professionals' is used and emphasis is upon equality of growth and interaction between supervisee and supervisor rather than any suggestion of hierarchy. It is interesting to see these two definitions together in order to illustrate these points.

Bunt and Hoskyns, from the UK, provide a humanistic rather than a psychoanalytic perspective in their definition of music therapy supervision, which emphasises the importance of sharing. They develop the notion of music and improvisation providing an additional dimension, and see this as positive, stating 'We are fortunate as musicians in being able to explore a musical solution to a psychological or therapeutic obstacle' (Bunt & Hoskyns 2003 p. 264). They then give some useful examples of musical interactions that might happen in a supervision session, as do Nygaard Pedersen (2008), Stephens (2001) and Brown (2008). Bunt and Hoskyns include a list of different types of musical intervention in supervision (shown below), which will be useful and also familiar to music therapy practitioners, but perhaps interesting to the non-music therapy reader (Bunt & Hoskyns 2002 p. 264):

- 'the supervisee is invited to improvise around the feelings about a particular client or stage in the relationship;
- the supervisee explores what it feels like to be in the client's shoes by playing as if the client, with the supervisor taking on the role of therapist;
- using flexible exercises to allow the supervisee to shift position from the client to therapist, playing the kind of music typical within each role and gaining insight into how the roles relate from a number of perspectives;
- exploring alternative methods for handling personal dynamics or specific incidents within the therapy'

Working through musical improvisation is increasingly used as a major part of music therapy training, whereby supervisees engage with problems musically in order to reflect and understand the clinical process in more depth. It is arguable that a good understanding of countertransference would be necessary to prevent too much merge of material and boundaries between supervisee and patient, and supervisor and therapist, when using this interactive musical approach in supervision. Musical role-playing in supervision sessions is also discussed in literature from the USA (Austin & Dvorkin 2001; Stephens 2001) and was part of Priestley's Intertherap technique (Priestley 1994), developed from a psychoanalytic perspective in her training developed in the early 1970s. This is reflected strongly in the work of Jahn-Langenberg (2001), in her psychodynamic perspective approach to professional music therapy supervision. Jahn-Langenberg takes an analytic approach, and explores transference and countertransference relationships in a music therapy supervision group. The supervisor offers herself as a play partner, taking the opposite view sometimes of a theme.

Jahn-Langenberg emphasises the importance of strict boundaries between supervisee and supervisor and suggests that there should be no contact outside the supervision room; a model that seems to echo the boundaries of therapy, which are often not possible in supervisory relationships in a relatively small profession in most countries. However, her approach uses countertransference and transference musically and dynamically, revealing an analytic rigour that aims to lead to better understanding of the patient–therapist–supervisee relationship, and to an increased understanding of the patient and what is needed in the music therapy treatment to progress.

Brown (1997) started to discuss the importance of musical and other clinical meanings in music therapy, and how these are interlinked and worked within music therapy supervision. She was one of the first music therapists to include an analysis and reflection upon musical material from the sessions and to discuss the importance of such an approach for music therapists. Her chapter is reproduced in this book in an updated version (see Chapter 7).

Establishing suitable professional models and structures for music therapy supervision: A case study

The professional development of supervision in the UK will be used here as a case example of the types of issues and processes experienced in many countries and professional organisations in the attempt to establish high and appropriate professional working standards in music therapy. It is the case, although it might seem surprising, that the music therapy profession in some countries, including the UK, was at first suspicious of the campaign for formalising supervision practices. In the UK, some music therapists found the psychodynamic concepts prevalent in many supervision models difficult to integrate into a music-focused model of work. Others thought that the profession had 'arrived' and was firmly established as a profession, after a long fight in political terms; the idea that all music therapists, however experienced, should be 'supervised' was seen by some as a sign of 'infancy' and inability to work autonomously. This was before the days of 'reflective practice' now developed in other related professions, such as occupational therapy, physiotherapy and nursing, and there was a level of defensiveness about the developing discipline of supervision in some quarters. In the main, however, the introduction of supervision practice as part of a music therapist's work was welcome, and training courses were highly influenced by this movement.

Wigram, Rogers and Odell-Miller (1993) discussed the APMT's initial supervision scheme, which at first included a multidisciplinary panel in order to learn from other disciplines:

The APMT provides a list of approved supervisors; each approved supervisor has submitted an application which has been circulated to all five members of the Core Supervision Panel. This panel contains representatives from three music therapy training schools, an art therapist and a psychotherapist. The applicant is then interviewed by two members of the Core Panel, which might be an art therapist and a psychotherapist as well as a music therapist.

(Wigram *et al.* 1993 p. 597)

Music therapy training: Experiential and supervision-related issues

The training of music therapists in the UK was also discussed by Wigram *et al.* (1993), and supervision was described then as an essential part of all training and work in music therapy for the benefit of the supervisee and the supervisor. The establishing of music therapy training, since 2006, at Master's level – usually a 2-year, full-time course – has enabled a more experienced workforce to emerge AND supervision is an integral part of clinical practice.

The differences in orientation between the training courses illustrate a healthy diversity of music therapy in practice, but each course retains a strong emphasis on the quality of the musicianship of the potential therapist, the significance of the client–therapist relationship in treatment and a belief in the use of improvisation to engage a client. In addition, they all contain similar elements as part of their basic module of training. As part of the development of a more dynamic, experiential and reflective approach to training and supervision, experiential components have also increased in importance during the last 20 years. Whilst these are distinct from the more formal supervision processes and models that concern us here, the ethos of reflecting upon one's own response in relation to one's work relates to an increasing focus in music therapy practice over the last two decades upon in-depth thinking and analysis of case material, using concepts from musicology, psychoanalysis and other arts therapies.

The academic component in the training of music therapists, in addition to reflective and analytic supervision and experiential learning, is also rigorous. It is of equal importance at a theoretical level, and also at a more technical level. For example, improvisation, musicianship skills, instrumental development, composition and other clinical skills are central to music therapy training and to the continuing development of the practising therapist. It is clear that, over the last two decades, music therapists involved in training have many years of clinical experience behind them, which was not the case prior to the mid-1980s, and this in turn has influenced practice, and supervision practice in particular.

For example, all music therapy trainees in the UK, and in many other countries, will be in some type of training group: music-therapy-based, discussion-based or both. A rationale for this was described (Odell-Miller, Streeter & Mure 1988) as part of a proposal to set up a music therapy supervision training scheme. This type of group was proposed to be part of music therapy supervisors' training, as at this time many senior practising music therapists had not experienced this as part of their original training:

> Group music therapy is frequently carried out by newly qualified music therapists. The music therapist's own experience of group work is considered to be an essential element of her/his ability to contain therapeutic work with groups. In addition, there is much to be understood about the nature of musical experience, as experienced in music therapy.
>
> Music therapy group work differs greatly according to the skills and disabilities of clients. Whether a music therapist is working with learning disabled adults or preschool children, some elements of the experience remain the same, particularly in the area of improvised music. We are opening up the possibility of music therapists learning for themselves what their own music means to them within improvisational music therapy. As with other forms of training, self-experience within the therapeutic technique is the only way of understanding the music therapist's role effectively.
>
> (Odell-Miller *et al.* 1988)

This proposal was not at first accepted, as it was seen by the professional body as a whole to be too comprehensive and rigorous. However, current practice reveals many changes since 1988. In the UK and many other European countries, for example, the inclusion of some form of music therapy experience for the students themselves, usually in groups, is included on training courses. Related to this, in terms of the experiential development of the music therapists themselves, all trainee music therapists are required to undertake some form of regular personal therapy individually for themselves, similarly to the other psychotherapy professions. It seems natural that the best way to fully understand something is to experience it at some level.

The music therapy experiential training group

Music therapy experiential training groups are discussed by Davies and Greenland (2002). Such groups are convened by a music therapist and sessions take place in the same room with the same conditions each week. Instruments used can include tuned and un-tuned percussion, piano and also the students' own instruments/voice. The participants improvise and discuss the improvisations, thus acquiring insights into music therapy group processes. The group convenor may sometimes suggest appropriate improvising structures. The group also provides a support system for the student throughout the course.

Whilst different to supervision, this experiential culture, which developed in the last two decades, reflects the focus found in most music therapy trainings in Europe upon learning through experience and reflection, and added to this an analytic rigour. Musical aspects are crucial in this process and provide a different dimension to a purely verbal approach, which is reflected in the following material which discusses how current practice evolved.

Summary of a UK music therapy supervision survey

In 1989, the APMT carried out a survey to assess the supervision practice and supervision needs of the music therapy profession so that criteria and firm appropriate systems for music therapy supervision could be developed (Odell-Miller 1994). The results showed that supervision was both linked to training and arose from the workplace cultures of music therapists. Two of the three training courses at the time had set up supervision sessions that were available to ex-students of that course in their first year of work. Music therapists, both at annual general meetings and regional group meetings of the APMT, stressed their interest in, and need for, supervision, especially immediately after qualifying, although this was not normal practice or stipulated as a requirement at the time: 50% of APMT members returned the survey questionnaire and half of these were receiving supervision of some kind; those not receiving supervision indicated they would like it. Although few supervisors had been formally selected by a panel, there were by this time some music therapists supervising other qualified music therapists.

The survey also showed that, most commonly, people received supervision individually in a weekly session, but some people met in groups or a combination of both. This reflected a change from previous years, when many music therapists did not receive supervision at all.

One of the debates at that time, which still continues in many countries, was about who was eligible to supervise music therapists, and whether a person from another profession or a music therapist is preferable. The 1989 survey showed a need for more music therapy supervisors, which reflected the growth of the profession both in maturity and size. Conclusions were reached, as shown by the following excerpt from the summary of results:

> More members are supervised by a non-music therapist than by a music therapist, although some people see both. However, of those seeking supervision, the majority wanted it from a music therapist or from both a music therapist and another person. Only three people wanted supervision from a non-music therapist only. This clearly shows a need for more music therapy supervisors.

> (Odell-Miller 1994)

Profession of non-music-therapy supervisors	Percentage
Psychotherapist	42
Music therapist	20
Clinical psychologist	3
Psychoanalyst	6
Psychiatrist	6
Nurse therapist	3
Analytical psychologist	4
Probation officer	3
Occupational therapist	3
Researcher	2
Art therapist	3
Child psychologist	5

Figure 1.1 Results of APMT (1989) survey. Percentages of music therapists supervised by music therapists and non-music therapists (Odell-Miller 1994)

The professions of the non-music-therapy supervisors listed in the survey were quite varied (Figure 1.1). Although no recent figures are available, it is likely that the list would remain similar in the UK in 2008; but that a much higher percentage of music therapists are supervised by music therapists, some of whom are doubly trained as music therapists and psychotherapists. (Loth & Richards 2007). So the major change now is that it is the norm for music therapists to be supervised by music therapists, showing major developments in the field over the last two decades and the development of music therapy supervision-specific skills and expertise.

Professional and organisational issues

Before 1990, music therapists were more commonly supervised by professionals outside the profession, such as psychotherapists and psychologists, (Odell-Miller 1994), and the APMT scheme was an attempt to consolidate and build up knowledge gained and to encourage music therapists to become skilled supervisors. Currently, in 2008, with the move to 2-year MA-level music therapy training, and in the climate of increased legislation and standard setting by the government, the APMT no longer stipulates that the original requirements of the scheme for newly qualified therapists must be met, but music therapy supervision is an expected part of practice for all music therapists and music therapy trainees. One of the cornerstones of the APMT scheme was the setting of criteria for those eligible to apply to the scheme to become approved supervisors. These original criteria did not include a focus on musical components of the supervision sessions (APMT 1990), and the more recent criteria, outlined below, illustrate the addition of music-based criteria and of requirements for the supervisor to participate in continuous professional development (CPD). The scheme ran for over a decade and was later led by Pauline Etkin and Ann Sloboda (Darnley-Smith & Patey 2003). Although the scheme is under review at the time of writing (2008), the guidelines are reproduced here and are useful for any organisation wishing to produce standards of practice for supervisors, or to set up similar schemes.

Criteria for application to become a registered music therapy supervisor for the APMT (2007 pp. A10–A10a)

Professional requirements

i)   The applicant must have been qualified for five years with a minimum, clinical practice of 1500 hours (which would normally represent two working days per week).
ii) The applicant will need to demonstrate that they have participated in CPD activities in line with APMT requirements.
iii) The applicant must be in receipt of not less than monthly supervision during the two years. The supervisor must demonstrate a degree of awareness of his/her own limitations.
iv) The applicant must be a full member of the APMT. They must adhere to the Code of Ethics of the APMT and any recommendations made by the APMT concerning supervision.

Clinical criteria

i)   The applicant must be able to discuss in detail examples of supervision received and given, and discuss what benefits have been perceived.
ii) The applicant is expected to demonstrate a depth of understanding regarding the clinical material, both musical and non-musical, brought to supervision and of the supervisory relationship.
iii) The applicant should be able to demonstrate an ability to assist the supervisee with clinical musical skills.
iv) The applicant must be able to demonstrate an ability to a supervise with a respectful understanding of the supervisee's theoretical approach.

v)   The applicant must be able to demonstrate an ability to enable the supervisee to focus on the client/therapist relationship.

vi)   The applicant must be able to demonstrate an insight into his/her competencies and limitations as a music therapy supervisor.

vii)   The applicant must demonstrate an awareness of issues pertaining to practising as a newly qualified therapist.

viii)   The applicant must demonstrate an awareness of the professional role of the music therapy supervisor including:

- maintaining appropriate time boundaries
- setting and charging appropriate fees
- maintaining confidentiality regarding both the supervisee and clinical material brought to supervision.

The application included written evidence of casework of supervision given and received in addition to an interview with a panel composed, in more recent years, of experienced music therapy supervisors.

Early history and development of a music therapy supervision scheme in the UK

The scheme summarised above followed earlier work started in the mid-1980s and culminated in the aforementioned first proposal to the APMT of a music therapy supervision scheme (Odell-Miller et al. 1988), which suggested the development of more formal structures. Aspects of this early history are interesting to note as the influence of developing experiential work can be seen in parallel with developing reflective supervision practice. The early proposal included experiential work, which is now at the heart all music therapy training in the UK, as discussed above; but at that time most music therapists who had trained before 1990 had not participated in such reflective experiential approaches during their training. Experiential music therapy group work and supervision were seen as essential for the proposed supervisors' training for experienced music therapists.

The first proposal was not accepted owing to financial considerations for therapists, but there was also some resistance to the idea of reflective, in-depth supervision for experienced therapists, as if it undermined their capabilities and skill rather than embraced the intended possibilities of in-depth discussion about experiential musical components of music therapy within an analytical approach.

The early proposals were a response to the short length of training in the UK at that time, and also aimed to develop a more reflective approach to supervision, taking some existing models of psychoanalytic and psycho-therapeutic practice, to parallel clinical developments. A shorter scheme was proposed and accepted by the APMT and ran for 12 years, leading to increased knowledge in the field arising from cross-training approaches and dialogue between supervisees and supervisors; and also through the interview process itself. As part of the interview process for becoming approved, a case as supervisor and a case as supervisee was written and discussed (Bunt & Hoskyns 2002), and this remained part of the process throughout the life of the scheme.

As can be seen from these examples from historical accounts of professional development of music therapy supervision practice, and from the examples from the literature, music therapy supervision is now a central element of professional practice in many countries. Approaches are diverse and culturally bound in order to fit music therapy clinical trends and professional requirements. The major unique and significant contribution to knowledge in the field and to the literature in general across the psychotherapies, from music therapy authors and practitioners, is the integration of musical and non-musical dimensions, so crucial in music therapy practice.

References

APMT (1990) *APMT Supervision criteria*. London: Association of Professional Music Therapists.

APMT (2007) *Code of conduct*. London: Association of Professional Music Therapists.

APMT (2008) *Clinical Supervision: information and guidance document*. London: Association of Professional Music Therapists.

Austin, D., Dvorkin, J. (2001) 'Peer supervision in music therapy' in M. Forinash (ed.), *Music therapy supervision*, Philadelphia: Barcelona.

Barratta, E., Bertolami, M., Hubbard, A., Macdonald, M., Spragg, D. (2001) 'Peer supervision in the development of the new music and expressive therapist' in M. Forinash (ed.), *Music therapy supervision*, Philadelphia, Barcelona.

Brown, S. (1997) 'Supervision in context: a balancing act'. *British Journal of Music Therapy*, 11(1), 4–12.

Brown, S. (2008) 'Supervision in context: a balancing act' (revised version) in H. Odell-Miller and E. Richards (eds), *Supervision of music therapy: a theoretical and practical handbook*, London: Routledge.

Bunt, L., Hoskyns, S. (2002) *The handbook of music therapy*, London: Brunner Routledge.

Casement, P. (1985) *On learning from the patient*, Hove, UK: Brunner-Routledge.

Darnley-Smith, R., Patey, H. (2003) *Music therapy*. London: Sage.

Davies, A., Greenland, S. (2002) 'A group analytic look at experiential training groups: how can music earn its keep?' in A. Davies and E. Richards (eds), *Music therapy and group work*. London: Jessica Kingsley.

Dileo, C. (2001) 'Ethical issues in supervision' in M. Forinash (ed.), *Music therapy supervision*, Philadelphia: Barcelona.

Estrella, K. (2001) 'Multicultural approaches to music therapy supervision' in M. Forinash (ed.), *Music therapy supervision*, Philadelphia: Barcelona.

Forinash, M. (2001) *Music therapy supervision*, Philadelphia: Barcelona.

Frohne-Hagemann, I. (2001) 'Integrative techniques in professional music therapy group supervision' in M. Forinash (ed.), *Music therapy supervision*, Philadelphia: Barcelona.

Hammarlund, I. (2001) *A Music therapy supervision training for supervisors* (verbal contribution to round-table discussion). Naples: European Congress of Music Therapy.

Hanser, S. (2001) 'A systems analysis approach to music therapy practice' in M. Forinash (ed.), *Music therapy supervision*, Philadelphia: Barcelona.

Hawkins, P., Shohet, R. (1989) *Supervision in the helping professions*, Buckingham, UK: Open University Press.

HPC (2007a) Standards of proficiency for arts therapists. Online. Available: http://www.hpc-uk.org/aboutregistration/standards/standardsofproficiency/ [accessed 15 September 2007].

HPC (2007b) Standards of education and training for arts therapists. Online. Available: http://www.hpc-uk.org/aboutregistration/standards/sets/ [accessed 15 September 2007].

Jahn-Langenberg, M. (2001) 'Psychodynamic perspectives in professional supervision' in M. Forinash (ed.), *Music therapy supervision*, Philadelphia: Barcelona.

John, D. (1992) 'Towards music psychotherapy'. *British Journal of Music Therapy*, 6(1), 10–12.

John, D. (1995) 'The therapeutic relationship in music therapy as a tool in the treatment of psychosis' in T. Wigram, B. Saperston and R. West (eds), *The art and science of music therapy: a handbook* (pp. 157–166). Chur, Switzerland: Harwood Academic.

Lee, C. (2001) 'The supervision of clinical improvisation in aesthetic music therapy: a music-centred approach' in M. Forinash (ed.), *Music therapy supervision*, Philadelphia: Barcelona.

Levinge, A. (2002) 'Supervision or double vision: an exploration of the task of music therapy supervision'. *British Journal of Music Therapy*, 16(2), 83–90.

Loth, H., Richards, E. (2007) *Is music therapy sometimes not enough? A preliminary study of music therapists who pursue further training in verbal therapies*. Paper delivered at the 7th European Music Therapy Congress: Eindhoven, the Netherlands. Unpublished; available from Anglia Ruskin University, Cambridge.

McClain, J. (2001) 'Music therapy supervision: a review of literature' in M. Forinash (ed.), *Music therapy supervision*, Philadelphia: Barcelona.

Odell-Miller, H. (1994) *Supervision of music therapy in the UK*. Paper delivered at Australian Annual Music Therapy Congress: Brisbane, Queensland University.

Odell-Miller, H. (2001a) *Music therapy supervisor's MA training course curriculum planning*. Paper delivered at European Congress of Music Therapy: Naples, Italy. Unpublished; available from Anglia Ruskin University, Cambridge.

Odell-Miller, H. (2001b) 'Music therapy and its relationship to psychoanalysis' in Y. Searle and I. Streng (eds), *Where analysis meets the arts* (pp. 127–152). London: Karnac Books.

Odell-Miller, H. (2003) 'Are words enough? Music therapy as an influence in psychoanalytic psychotherapy' in L. King and R. Randall (eds), *The future of psychoanalytic psychotherapy*. London: Whurr.

Odell-Miller, H., Streeter, E., Mure, M. (1988) *Proposal for a music therapy supervisor's training scheme*. London: Association of Professional Music Therapy.

Pavlicevic, M. (1994) 'Supervision (Stretto)'. *Journal of British Music Therapy*, 8(1).

Pedersen, I.N. (2008) 'Music therapy supervision with students and professionals: the use of music and analysis of counter transference experiences in the triadic field' in H. Odell-Miller and E. Richards (eds), *Supervision of music therapy: a theoretical and practical handbook*. London: Routledge.

Pezold, H.G. (1998) *Integrative supervision, meta-counselling and organisatiosentwicklung*, Junfermann, Germany: Paderborn.

Priestley, M. (1975) *Music therapy in action*. London: Constable.

Priestley, M. (1994) *Essays on analytical music therapy*. Philadelphia: Barcelona.

Stephens, G. (1984) 'Group supervision in music therapy'. *Music Therapy*, 4, 29–38.

Stephens, G. (2001) 'Experiential music therapy group as a method of professional supervision' in M. Forinash (ed.), *Music therapy supervision*, Philadelphia: Barcelona.

Stige, B. (2001) 'The fostering of not-knowing: barefoot supervisors' in M. Forinash (ed.), *Music therapy supervision*, Philadelphia: Barcelona.

Summer, L. (2001) 'Group supervision in first-time music therapy practicum' in M. Forinash (ed.), *Music therapy supervision*, Philadelphia: Barcelona.

Wigram, T., Odell-Miller, H., Rogers, P. (1993) 'Music therapy in the United Kingdom' in C. Maranto (ed.), *Music therapy: international perspectives*, Pennsylvania: Jeffrey Books.

Chapter 2

Whose handicap? Issues arising in the supervision of trainee music therapists in their first experience of working with adults with learning disabilities

Eleanor Richards

In this chapter, I discuss some aspects of supervision of music therapy trainees undertaking clinical work for the first time with adults with learning disabilities. I attend to the backgrounds, musical and professional, from which students have come, their expectations of themselves and their work, and their initial assumptions and aspirations about music therapy with this client group. I also consider the anxieties aroused by both the overall training experience and by the experience of embarking for the first time upon clinical work. I suggest that clinical work with this population brings its own particular anxieties and associated defences, which must be addressed in supervision if the work is to move forward.

The background

This chapter emerges from my experience as a teacher and supervisor on the MA in music therapy at Anglia Ruskin University in Cambridge; this postgraduate training has been in existence since 1994. It is established as a 2-year, full-time training, on successful completion of which students gain an MA and are deemed fit to practise music therapy in the UK and eligible for registration with the Health Professions Council, the regulatory body for the profession.

The intake of students is diverse in terms of both age and background, ranging from those recently emerged from university or other higher education to those in their thirties, forties and beyond who have had well-established careers in other areas of music. We also have occasional students who are musicians of the required standard and whose professional background has been elsewhere (nursing, social work, etc.). From the start, this training has placed strong emphasis on active and extended clinical experience. Like many other trainings, we try to achieve an appropriate balance of emphasis in three areas: theoretical studies, musical/improvisational skills and clinical practice. Students are required to be in individual personal therapy during their training and there is a weekly group experiential session, run by a music therapist working along analytic lines.

The course is one that might be described as 'eclectic'; it promotes no single theoretical position or way of working, but provides students with a grounding in several approaches, encouraging them to use appropriate models of work according to need and context. I think the experience of our students would be that the course is psychoanalytic in emphasis; within the central teaching team both psychoanalytic and developmental models of working are strongly represented. Our visiting lecturers represent a broad range of perspectives. So we place value on students finding their own way of working within a secure theoretical framework. Our hope is that we will be able to foster a culture in which students do not feel that they have to emerge as copies of their tutors, but will rather feel free to develop their own thinking and personal styles of working with confidence. Theoretical preferences and styles of practice, if they are to be articulated with integrity (perhaps rather like religious beliefs or political convictions), must come ultimately from the therapist's sense of herself (together with a grounding in knowledge and experience), not from a search to imitate or to satisfy someone else, however much admired. This is not always an easy thought for the student in the early stages of training, who may simply want to ask 'What works?' and 'What should I do?'

The experience of training is one that might necessarily involve infantil-isation and regression. People who have been confident and successful professionals or students can find themselves in circumstances in which some deeply internalized elements of upbringing and education might be very readily reawakened. The training takes place in a university, a setting that might be easily associated with earlier experiences of education and with the competitive struggle for survival. There are written assignments to complete, which are judged and marked, and which the student will pass or fail. There are deadlines to be met. There is theoretical material to be read, understood and discussed. There are new technical skills to acquire. There is implicit pressure to show results and to make progress, and underlying all that might be the fear of being the one who does not fit in, or fails, or might even be advised to leave. I emphasise this not only because it forms part of the climate in which students take their first steps towards becoming clini-cians, but also because they will meet, in their learning disabled patients, people who are defined precisely by their deficits in areas such as these, and whose sense of being the outsider, or the one who is not good enough, might be very strong.

Therapy training can be a time of great excitement and fulfilment, but it also brings disturbance. For instance, students generally arrive with a secure sense of competence and achievement as musicians. This might have been conferred by the endorsement of other organizations (through the awarding of diplomas, for instance) or by appreciative audiences. Some students come from careers as teachers, in which they have been able to follow the progress and success of their pupils. Whatever form it takes, the communication will have been reciprocal; audiences will have applauded and pupils will have been grateful. The trainee's own deep personal pleasure in music might have associations of warm relationship – of mutual appreciation, of satisfying the demands of a parent or teacher or of exciting and moving an audience and fellow players. There might also be associations of distinctiveness: music makes a difference and musicians can make their mark in the world. There might be associations to the healthy, functioning, competent aspects of the self: something that can be depended upon and that feels alive. It is also an area of specialness: not everyone can be a musician.

For many, their training in music might have had much to do with ideas about accuracy or loyalty to a text. Playing or singing in tune, sustaining rhythmic consistency, or simply 'getting the notes right' are all fundamental necessities for performing musicians, especially those from within the 'classical' tradition. Beyond that, the demands of technique are great: many musicians will have spent long hours working on the purely physical aspects of their relationship with their instrument or voice, so that they can feel a certain 'mastery' over the music, however demanding it might be. All these might be factors contributing to the student's feeling of adequacy and assurance as a musician.

So students will arrive carrying a range of powerful inner musical associations, conscious and unconscious. At one end of the spectrum might be something connected to a non-verbal, passionate world of expression, exchange and unspoken understanding, but at the other end might be associations with performance, technique, judgement and competition.

In the course of music therapy training, students can find that some of those aspects of their musicianship that had been so valued by the world receive less acknowledgement. Technique for its own sake receives less emphasis, and the ability to present a 'performance' in the traditional sense seems to be low on the list. Instead, the capacity for spontaneous, creative attunement in the moment to the emotional state of another in improvisation is emphasized and, furthermore, might be evaluated. Students find that their musical expertise is not, of itself, enough. Instead, they are being asked to investigate and develop the therapist in themselves that lies behind the music, and to turn their music to its service. So those aspects of musicianship that have not only contributed to the student's sense of self and entitlement to a place in the world, but have also fulfilled a healthy defensive function against self-uncertainty, must be let go of to allow of something much more unknown. This can be a time of disorientation and deep uncertainty, calling for 'a reorganisation in the sense of self' (Jacobs, David & Meyer 1995 p. 33).

Among the risks here is that, in the search for a defence against such feelings of helplessness, students might seek to apply to the content of the training some of the criteria that have helped them through other, earlier experiences of musical learning. They might become assiduous in studying 'techniques' and approaches to therapy, and they might become well informed about theory and produce well-ordered written assignments. They might go into clinical sessions ready to 'apply' a technique that they hope will bring about some discernible change, or that seemed to work for another therapist. They might also go into sessions and become something of their old performing selves, losing sight of the patient in the interest of a way of playing in which they themselves can feel secure.

The risk at this stage is that the student adopts a rigid, fixed position in terms of theory and approach because the alternative – to engage with a culture that seeks to investigate the unconscious and the unknown – is too daunting. Main (1967) points out that theories or ideas themselves can become internal mental objects and can thus form part of the student's wider scheme of object relations (something she might already have played out in her relationship with music). Thus theoretical or technical material might be granted the position of a stern and demanding superego with its fixed values. This defensive ordering of ideas can result in learning and knowledge being used to avoid speculation or feeling and their accompanying anxieties. It offers a refuge from unease and uncertainty, and from the struggle of having to discover and trust in one's own way of working in relation to theory. Instead, one depends upon existing precedents, and secondhand rationales for action are deployed. Ideas become beliefs, handicapping thought, and the possibility of enquiry is lost. It takes time for theory to find a more mature place within the therapist, leaving room for a more immediate response:

> Much of our hard-won theory and conceptualising [and our relationship with music?] becomes gradually metabolised into our own being so that eventually we hardly know, when we think, decide and speak, from whence it comes. There is nothing wrong with this – indeed, I see it as an aim for young therapists still earnestly acquiring the wherewithal of their trade.
>
> (Coltart 1992 p. 188)

In their first semester, before clinical work begins, students undertake a brief mother–infant observation. This takes place in the context of seminars and lectures about differing theories of infant development, and it is striking that the areas to which students often feel most drawn are to do with attachment and containment. This is a stage in training at which students often feel very anxious as they approach the start of their own clinical work. Much thought is given to the implications of the observation and seminars for the student clinician. There is discussion of the therapy space as a 'secure base', in attachment terms, from which the patient can begin to explore his experience or try new ways of relating. There is discussion of the space as a 'container' or 'holding environment' in which the patient can feel confident enough to encounter new aspects of himself and new experiences of relationship and activity.

Starting work

So this is the background against which students embark, in their second semester, upon their first clinical work. Here are some memories from recent students of first clinical encounters:

- I worried about the 'surface' things: what was to be done with someone who had very little physical movement, had poor vision, did not seem to understand language, and whose capacity to engage with me in any way was difficult to discern? When I first met Phil, my heart sank. He was slumped in his wheelchair with his eyes half closed. I could see that he was breathing, but my first momentary thought was actually that he was dead. I wanted to go away quickly. I couldn't imagine how music could do anything.

- She was sitting on the floor and rocking slowly. She seemed quiet and contented and when I said hello she didn't look up. Instead, she rocked more. I felt that she didn't need me at all and that I could easily do her harm.

- The first time I was supposed to see my client my train was cancelled and I was an hour late. I arrived feeling bad about it, but then the staff said that he had been asleep for most of the time anyway and had probably forgotten I was coming. I had been worried about letting him down, but I felt better when they told me he probably hadn't noticed, and I thought that to greet him now might be confusing for him.

In each of these instances, the student experienced powerful countertransference reactions; each seems to interpret the experience as telling her that she is powerless, dangerous or just redundant; she is left questioning the value of the work.

It is a simple truism to say that people with learning disabilities present us with some of the things we most fear: helplessness, dependency, 'stupidity', no sense of growth or of a future, being 'different' or 'unwanted' and being part of a group in which others might question our value. This can have immediate parallels with some of the experiences of the trainee music therapist. Within the training group itself there may be fears of inadequacy, not fitting in or falling behind. The student might be very afraid, in the face of teaching that places such value upon not only academic but also intuitive understanding, that she has insufficient capacity for either.

People with learning disabilities might turn to compliance as a means to try and find a greater sense of secure inclusion. For many, the fear of losing any attachment that there is, or of having to take the consequences of the full extent of handicap being experienced, has led to the development of an elaborate 'false self', which seeks to present a more acceptable face to the world at the cost of the person's real life and originality. This might have started early on, at the point at which the child saw something of the shock and disappointment in his mother's face, and set about becoming whatever was needed to be sure of some kind of continuing acceptance and love, whatever compromise might be involved. Similarly, the student might feel the need to be at all costs the 'therapist' that she believes is expected of her, both by the professional group around her and by her own demanding superego. This might extend into the supervision space, when the supervisor might be identified as the parent who cannot patiently bear her child's limitations and has no faith in her originality or distinctiveness.

It is interesting to see the defences that can arise in the face of this. Symington (1992) suggests that many therapists who work with people with learning disabilities do, in fact, on some level, feel contempt for their patients. He points out the many subtle ways in which we might treat learning disabled patients differently, and the assumptions we might make about their limitations. (All this is generally done by therapists who are outwardly passionate about the needs and entitlements of people with learning disabilities and who often believe themselves to be doing very special work.) He suggests that this contempt arises in response to the power of the learning disabled person to put us in touch with some unbearable, handicapped aspect of ourselves. As our dislike and fear of that experience arises in contemptuous feelings, we might also feel guilty and so overcompensate by behaviours that appear considerate or concerned, but are actually limiting. This brings the risk of therapist and patient getting stuck in a place that is familiar, but without hope of change. For change to be possible, both must be able to face the reality of disability and of difference.

Therapy with people with learning disabilities

Specialisation in the psychiatric treatment of people with learning disabilities has only been established since the 1920s and remains a small professional area, even in the Western world (Hollins 2000). Therapy conducted on psychodynamic lines with people with learning disabilities is a development much more recent still, and had its beginnings in the UK. For many years, treatment of learning disabled people was limited to the enhancement of skills, pharmacological intervention and, when needed, the management of behaviour. Just as earlier psychiatrists were at first inclined to see changes in behaviour or mood as no more than new manifestations of existing disability, rather than as potential indicators of mental illness, so it has taken a long time for people with learning disabilities to have people around them seeking to understand and find meaning in their behaviour and ways of relating, rather than ascribing everything to a central, unalterable organic cause. It was not until the late 1970s that psychodynamically informed work with learning disabled people began to be explored, initially by Neville Symington and subsequently by Valerie Sinason and a group of colleagues at the Tavistock Clinic. Their work did an enormous amount to bring to recognition the capacity of people with learning disabilities, like anyone else, to engage in and benefit from therapeutic approaches that place emphasis on the power of the internal world and the playing out in the transference of existing patterns of relating. Above all they demonstrated that people with learning disabilities are as open as anyone else to the possibility of profound personal change in the context of a containing therapeutic relationship. But for change to become possible there must be recognition and mourning of past traumas and of those aspects of past experience and current circumstance that cannot be altered. For many people in the learning disabled population, their condition has been a source of such trauma to those around them that they have not had the opportunity to address their own sense of themselves and have had to develop sophisticated defences against seeing and feeling the reality of their circumstances.

Valerie Sinason and Jon Stokes propose the concept of 'secondary' or 'opportunist' handicap (Stokes & Sinason 1992). They suggest that patients might present with two handicaps, one that is organic, and another ('secondary') that exaggerates the features of the existing handicap and forms part of a complex unconscious strategy for emotional survival. I will return to this later. Sinason and her colleagues did not confine themselves to working with people with some command or understanding of language; they sought to work with people whose level of disability was such that ordinary verbal exchange was not available. Not surprisingly, their work has been of great interest to arts therapists.

When I asked some former students to recall what they had felt when they learned that their first clinical work was to be with learning disabled people, I encountered some strongly felt answers of two apparently different kinds. One group seemed apprehensive:

- I thought that the six months would be long and dispiriting for both of us;
- I was afraid he wouldn't respond and that I would feel stuck;
- I was afraid that I might be embarrassed by some of his behaviour;
- I worried that I might feel completely out of my depth;
- I thought that I would not be able to do anything for him and I would feel stupid.

It is notable that these reactions came from students who had spent the first semester of their training studying theoretical and diagnostic aspects of learning disability in some depth, and had seen examples of casework by experienced clinicians; none the less, faced with prospect of an immediate meeting with the patient, some much more primitive assumptions and anxieties emerged.

Neville Symington (in the language of his day) says of the dangers of such feelings:

> . . . unwanted despair on the part of those helping mental defectives is a far greater handicap than the organic defects. Neurological growth can be stimulated and is not static. What remains static is people's expectations that change can occur.
>
> (Symington, 1981 p. 199)

Another (smaller) group of students, however, remembered feeling greater apparent optimism:

- They told me she'd not had music therapy before and that she always liked something new;
- They said he was a cheerful person; I thought that sounded promising;
- I looked forward to helping her express herself.

Both of these positions imply a rather fixed view, at one end of the spectrum or the other, of what life with the patient will be like. They also reflect, at another level, something of the often unintegrated extremes that we may meet in people with learning disabilities themselves: on the one hand there is an apparently static, unchanging state whereas on the other there is the ordinary impulse towards life, expression and inner movement which can emerge in a creative relationship.

Supervision

At the start of supervisory work with a student I say something, hoping not to be over-prescriptive, about what supervision might entail. It might be along these lines:

> As we discuss the work you are doing with your patient, we will think about your relationship with him, and about what your experience of being with him, musically and in other ways, might mean. We will think about what your patient brings to the session, and it is sometimes very helpful to think, too, about what you may be bringing. We will consider carefully how deeply to go into your feelings and responses, and especially what aspects of them are more appropriately taken to your personal therapy, but some attention to them is a necessary part of supervision. We will also take some time to look at our own pattern of working, since it may be that things take place in our exchanges which are useful pointers to what may be happening with your patient.

I hope that we can develop this as a place where discussion can be as free as possible. I will also sometimes give you advice, both to do with your clinical work and with handling the circumstances surrounding it, and I may take the opportunity to remind you of theoretical ideas, and suggest things you might read. Supervision is not intended to be a place where your work is going to be judged or criticised, but rather somewhere that offers the opportunity to find ways to think together about your work that may help it to move forward.

I also ask the student to say something, even if she has little experience so far of supervision, about what she hopes for from the sessions. Both participants will have some goals in mind, both conscious and unconscious, and if these are not acknowledged as far as possible, the process itself may be hampered.

In spite of my last introductory sentence, both participants need to be aware that there is what Frawley O'Dea and Sarnatt (2001) have called an 'asymmetry' in the situation. The supervisory relationship is one that depends upon the supervisee's readiness to disclose the workings of her mind and the state of her feelings. In a therapeutic relationship, the patient may legitimately hope for a non-judging response; in supervision, by contrast, the student supervisee is aware that part of the supervisor's role is to evaluate her and her work, and that to an extent her progress on the training will be subject to that evaluation. The supervisory setting is characterised by this central conflict.

Supervision is a place in which emotions as intense as anything experienced in therapy can arise. For the student therapist whose clinical work is not there just to be supervised, but also in some way to be evaluated, this can be an especially alarming prospect. It is a familiar enough phenomenon in therapy trainings of many kinds that, although there is much talk of encouraging one's patients to be emotionally open, the atmosphere of evaluation and rivalry that training inevitably engenders may lead some students to feel extremely wary of revealing their uncertainties or showing how powerfully they are moved or disturbed by their work. Edwards and Daveson (2004) have examined some of the resistances that may arise in student supervision at a later stage of training; here I want to consider some defensive strategies that might arise early on in supervision in an attempt to keep things steady and, above all, remain at a distance from emotional experiences that may feel shameful or simply overwhelming.

David

One possibility is to take refuge in intellectual or theoretical discourse. David, a student working with a man with unpredictable and sometimes risky behaviour, spent much time in supervision asking me about different theories of learning disability and about where he might find more research information about Fragile X syndrome. By drawing the conversation away from the particular patient and his relationship with him and into something more general, but apparently full of appropriate studious enquiry, he hoped to be able to skirt round his feelings of intense nervousness with his chaotic patient and feel himself to be someone more mentally organised and in command. At first it was difficult in supervision to find a means, in words, to stay with his anxiety; eventually I asked him if he could create a musical portrait of his patient. He responded with an improvisation on the cello that started carefully enough but became furiously loud and dissonant. Afterwards he was able to say that it reflected not only something of his patient but also of his own fear and frustration in the work. It also emerged that he had been spending a good deal of time in sessions trying to talk with his patient (in other words, to try and stay with his familiar territory of coherent language). In subsequent sessions he found more faith in the possibilities of co-improvised music, however chaotic, and in supervision he was more readily able to consider his countertransference experience.

Jane

Another potential defence, perhaps paradoxically, is the expression of shame. Jane came to supervision repeatedly saying that she was no good: she had not organised her group well enough, she could not make sense of what was going on in sessions, her music was not versatile enough and so on. In other words, she wanted to present a sort of 'secondary handicap' in which she placed emphasis only on her supposed shortcomings, in the hope that I might assume that all this was true and there was no further clinical progress to be made, or that I might get caught up in a repeated but futile pattern of offering her encouragement. Jane was a student whose progress in the academic and musical aspects of her training was going well; why did she need to express such doubt about her clinical work? We talked about 'secondary handicap' in relation to one of Jane's group members, a very shy man who could function well on his own, but became paralysed when in a group of people who might respond to him or question him. He managed his fear by appearing helpless in the group, apologetically saying that he could not play instruments or understand what others were saying. Jane knew something of his traumatic personal history, which had resonances with some events in her own life, and she acknowledged that she found him and his elective isolation painful to experience. In supervision she found herself echoing something of his behaviour to spare herself the struggle of thinking about him and about the group process.

Hugh

Hugh, by contrast, came to his supervision sessions with detailed notes and carefully edited video clips. In his presentations he seemed to want to sum up everything about the sessions and leave nothing open to question. I felt that he had no wish for any sort of working relationship between us, but rather wanted his supervision to be an occasion to which he could simply bring a report on work well done. If I asked him anything, especially in relation to his own experience, he had a fluent reply; if I voiced thoughts of my own, he acknowledged them politely but showed little sign, either in the discussion or in his subsequent work, of having taken them in or considered them. He often said that he thought that his patient, Chris, was 'doing well'. Chris was a young man with mild learning disabilities who seemed in many ways verbally adept and practically competent, but whose outer appearance skilfully disguised some areas of real difficulty in understanding and remembering. He cultivated a rather aloof air in relation to professionals and to personal friendships; he complained that the tasks he was given at his place of work were 'silly', and he rejected overtures of friendship from others who lived in his group home, saying they were 'too stupid'. In the sessions he took no risks, and confined himself to playing simple repetitive music on instruments that were easy to manage, whilst verbally denigrating the whole idea and telling Hugh that playing music was 'for kids'. In supervision, it was in discussion of the music that Hugh was ultimately able to express his frustration at the state of things. I asked him to show me by playing himself, rather than through a recording, something of the feel of Chris's music; in due course he broke off and said 'This is what I can't stand; why can't he see that we could do much more than this?' That made for the start of a discussion in which we could look at Chris's rather lofty, dismissive style as a very basic defence against his misery and shame at all the ways in which he was disabled. We were also able to think about the spirit of our sessions thus far, and to recognise how difficult it had been for us, too, to explore at any depth.

Emma

In the conventional sense Emma was a good student. She managed academic and practical tasks efficiently and she approached her training with often-voiced enthu-siasm. Her first piece of clinical work was with Amy, a middle-aged woman with significant learning disabilities. Amy played the instruments that Emma offered her, often copying Emma, but took no initiatives of her own; the sessions were often punctuated by long silences. In supervision Emma was anxious for advice, took a lot of notes and seemed to regard our meeting as one in which she would simply receive comments and instructions about how to approach the next session. She found it hard to locate her own thoughts and feelings about her relationship with Amy, other than to say that she often worried about whether she was doing things right, and that she found Amy's careful imitation of her oppressive.

What is striking about these four examples is that they represent patterns of defence that are very often turned to by people with learning disabilities themselves. In each case they indicate an attempt to set oneself apart from emotional realities and to avoid the possibility of thought or of making connections. They also seek to put the other person (here, the supervisor) in some sort of fixed role so that there can be no unexpected developments or demands.

Bion (1962) proposed that the capacity for thought develops through the mother's reverie and her receptiveness to her infant's unformed, unprocessed feelings and sensations; through that receptiveness she helps to give meaning to the infant's experience. Without maternal receptiveness the infant is unable to tolerate its anxiety and resorts to the projection of feelings and a closing down of any capacity for thought. While such measures can bring some short-term relief from unbearable inner experience, they may engender rejection by others and so compromise the person's capacity to make secure, trusting relationships.

Lee and Nashat (2004) comment on what may happen when the infant has a disability: Although some mothers are able to grieve and overcome the loss of their 'normal' infant and bond with their baby, there are also many who are unable to do so. In these cases the mother is unable to identify with her infant and therefore cannot transform the infant's anxieties into thoughts. Additionally, those infants with learning disabilities often have a greater intolerance for frustration. Both these factors contribute to making more likely the experience of 'nameless dread' and similar states of mind. (Lee & Nashat 2004 p. 116).

Our need to experience containment by another continues throughout our lives, especially at times of anxiety and distress. That containment is part of the function of supervision; without it, the supervisee might continue to feel unable to encounter new and sometimes difficult feelings, or to make those emotional connections that can allow her clinical work to be alive. Sinason describes succinctly the potential of response of clinicians overcome by the extent of the pain they were meeting:

> Perhaps the biggest shock was that we had all managed *not* to see something; we had gone 'stupid', knocked silly by the grief we were witnessing. From this I learned how stupidity could be a defence against the trauma of knowing too much of a painful kind.
>
> (Sinason 1992 p. 7)

There has been much written about what might be the impact, conscious and unconscious, upon professionals of working with people with learning disabilities (De Groef & Heinemann 1999; Simpson & Miller 2004; Sinason 1992). An aspect of this, which needs particular consideration in this context, is the place of the therapist's musical self and how it might be affected by these experiences. Schwartz (2007) has called this 'the music therapist's music world'. Each of us carries within us a complex musical history; that history is as emotionally charged as, and is wholly enmeshed with, our history of human relationships. So it is vital for the music therapist to attend to integrating and acknowledging her musical self, including those areas associated with shame, failure or humiliation, as much as with intense pleasure or delight, if she is to be as emotionally available as possible through music to her patients. She needs to have access to as wide a range of authentic musical expressivity as possible. Musical fluency, like verbal fluency or theoretical expertise, can easily become a defence against painful countertransference feelings, or against the difficulty of responding to subtle and complex moments of interaction. The more the therapist can feel in honest contact with her musical self – including the recognition of the part played by her current musical tastes and assumptions – and with the associations that the music arising in sessions might bring, the more she will be able to improvise freely in response to the events of the moment. I turn now to some more detailed examples of the supervisory process:

Example 1

A student therapist, Sarah, was about to undertake the first piece of individual clinical work of her training. Her patient was Tom, a man in his 30s who was a client at a day-centre for people with learning disabilities in a large city. Sarah's home was in the same city, and she had had a successful professional career there as a prominent flautist, performing with both classical and folk groups. She had many friends in the area who were musicians. On the training course she was hard working and efficient.

Sarah brought this work to a supervision group, in which discussions about her work with Tom began whilst preliminary practical plans were being made. These involved Sarah in having to liaise with his carers about the time and place of sessions, transport arrangements for Tom (the sessions were to take place in another day-centre a few miles away) and the availability of instruments. Sarah busied herself to a great extent with these practicalities, making frequent phone calls to the day-centre. She reported with some irritation that they did not seem well organised and that it was difficult to get clear confirmation of arrangements with the speed and clarity that she would have liked. She made an appointment to visit the centre in person to check that all the plans were complete; that was also the occasion on which she was to have had a first informal meeting with Tom and his key-worker. In the event, Tom was delayed returning from another activity and, although she was assured that he would not be long, Sarah chose to leave the day-centre without meeting him. She recounted these events in supervision and her rather critical emphasis was upon the unsatisfactory disorganisation of the centre and its staff team. The tone of her account suggested that she was inviting me and the group to share her annoyance.

I invited members of the group to reflect on these events and to investigate whatever came to mind. Interestingly, group members responded from a variety of angles. One person was warm in her support of Sarah and sympathetic towards her. Two people were concerned about Tom and about the fact that he had not had the opportunity to meet Sarah as arranged (in other words, already beginning to think about the relationship). A fourth person suggested to Sarah that perhaps her irritation with the apparent confusion of the staff team was telling us something about her own state: was it to do with a possibility that she herself was anxious and uncertain about the prospect of this work and that her anxiety was exacerbated by these confusions? (An initial invitation to Sarah to look inwards and consider the meaning of her own responses.) Sarah quickly dismissed this last suggestion and reiterated that she just wanted to work somewhere with 'good professional standards'.

Tom was a man without any verbal language who seemed very preoccupied with himself and gave no obvious indications of any impulse to engage with Sarah, musically or otherwise. He showed little curiosity about her or the instruments, and would sometimes suddenly leave the room. His key-worker, who waited for him outside, would bring him back and things would continue in the same way. Musically, Sarah tried to engage Tom in various activities, which he would sometimes attempt for a few moments and then abandon.

For some weeks both the clinical work and the supervision process felt very stuck. Nothing changed much, and I was aware of feeling that I was somehow missing something, or that I should be saying something that would magically transform the situation. I also realised that I did not particularly look forward to hearing Sarah present the latest session. Meanwhile, Sarah talked about Tom in a rather detached, descriptive way and found it very difficult to say anything directly about her own experience in the room. She often spoke with an unchanging bright smile on her face, which had little resonance with the rather dreary atmosphere she was describing. I noticed that in the work Sarah was using her flute very little. Instead, she used various percussion instruments, which she then offered to Tom; he would use each one briefly and then drop it onto the floor. When I asked Sarah why she did not use her flute, she said she was afraid that Tom would grab it and damage it. At that point she lost her usual fluent flow of talk and there was a long silence. She broke it by saying that after the sessions she often went home and played the flute on her own, usually improvising. (She also spoke about her experience of playing the flute professionally elsewhere, when she could feel confident of her place in the music and sure of the appreciation of others.) In the following weeks we began to explore why that improvised flute music needed to happen *outside* the sessions; Sarah said that when she was with Tom she could see how uneasy he was, and that she wondered whether he did not use the instruments much because he was afraid of trying things out and risking them going wrong. That was the first time she had voiced any thought about what might be the meaning of Tom's behaviour. She felt the same about her own clinical practice: she wanted to be a 'proper therapist', but felt paralysed and uneasy. It was not that she thought that what she was doing in the sessions was necessarily 'properly therapeutic', but rather that she was so anxious that she found it impossible to be musically imaginative, and the possibility of bringing her expressive, flute-playing self into the session did not come to mind. We discussed whether Tom's intense anxiety about the risks of exposing his supposed limitations might have some echoes for Sarah. In subsequent sessions Sarah began to use her flute. She spent less time seeking to bring Tom into a conventional musical dialogue, and simply tried to attend to him and to play in response to her sense of him in the room. Tom began to be more settled and to watch her as she played. A relationship began to emerge in which she felt more emotionally connected with, and acknowledged by Tom, and in which he gradually started to make to vocal contributions of his own. At the same time, the group began to listen with more curiosity and subtlety to the tapes Sarah brought to supervision. The quality of our discussions in supervision shifted; Sarah described the work with increasing flexibility and emotional variety, and I felt more alive in my own thinking.

An important part of the function of supervision in this process was to bring other minds – the group members' and my own – to think about the potential meaning of events, and to observe some parallels. Just as Tom might have felt afraid to play because of the risk of 'failure' and exposure of his disability, so Sarah was afraid at first to bring to supervision her own uncertainties, instead choosing to speak fluently and with a smile. It was when we could begin to see her experience of these events as important clinical material, rather than just as examples of success or failure, that Sarah felt freer to bring her deeply felt and expressive flute playing into the work. Supervision also offered some containment for the power of countertransference feeling about Tom that improvising on the flute brought to consciousness for her. Above all, it enabled her to engage more completely with her musical self, and so to bring into the work a new dimension of warmth and responsiveness.

> If knowing and seeing involve knowing and seeing terrible things, it is not surprising that not-knowing, becoming stupid, becomes a defence. However, it is a mad defence as it takes away the possibility of communication and gaining help or understanding.
>
> (Stokes & Sinason 1992)

This thought is useful in two ways in relation to Sarah and Tom. First, it offers one means of articulating something about the experience of being and working with people with learning disabilities that student music therapists often report such difficulty with. They describe a sense of the impossibility of change and of their own despondency in the face of it. At best it might lead to a succession of sessions in which little takes place except perhaps some rather repetitive, lifeless music making; at worst, it might bring out in the student a hostility to the patient that is in danger of being acted out in more damaging ways. Is this also a manifestation of the student's own 'secondary handicap'? Is it easier to say that clinical work is going well, if repetitively, or to say that the patient is too handicapped to work with, than it is to recognize that real engagement with the patient might bring the therapist face to face with disturbing levels of trauma and despair? Second, 'secondary handicap' can be seen as one manifestation of what Sedlak calls 'anti-developmental forces' (others might call it the 'death instinct'): those elements in the patient – and therapist – most resistant (not just for defensive purposes but rooted in some much more profound place) to life, relationship and change.

Students at this stage in their training will be in their own therapy but this might not have been the case for very long. Sedlak (1997) writes usefully about the possibilities and limitations of psychoanalytically informed supervision of therapists who are, in his terms, 'untrained' or at an early stage of training. He points out very directly the limitations that can arise in any therapy, but which might be especially present when the therapist herself has had little opportunity for self-development.

> . . . a therapist's work will deteriorate at the moment at which he is unable to deal with the transference in a professional, psychoanalytic manner. More specifically, it is when a negative countertransference is being experienced and cannot be managed that problems most frequently arise. This can be a greater handicap to the therapist and pose a greater risk to the therapeutic endeavour than the therapist's lack of knowledge of the finer points of the theory of psychoanalysis.
>
> (Sedlak 1997 p. 25)

At the stage at which they begin their clinical work, music therapy students at Anglia Ruskin University will have had not less than 3 months of weekly personal therapy, and they will have had the beginnings of some study of psychoanalytic ideas. A common feature of all trainings that have any significant psychoanalytic element is the understanding that training is not just to do with matters of technique or application of theory, but above all with acknowledging and accommodating the profound underlying emotional (and largely unconscious) impact of therapeutic work. If the therapist's own emotional experience – in other words, her countertransference – cannot be engaged with appropriately, much is at risk. Speaking of the need to identify and relate internal emotional experience to the events of the therapeutic relationship, Sedlak goes on:

Such emotional and cognitive work on the part of the therapist allows a psychoanalytic activity – that is, the translation of emotional forces into meaningful words [or music] – to continue. A failure to do such synthesizing will lead to acting in, acting out and failures of understanding and therapeutic endeavour.

(Sedlak 1997 p. 25)

Although the discussion quoted here is related primarily to work in verbal therapy, its central proposition is clear: both personal therapy and supervision are of great importance in enabling the therapist to manage her own experience in the service of the therapy and so of the patient. Through personal therapy, the student can become more able to accommodate both outer and inner realities, and in turn have less need of a grandiose or omnipotent view of the world; she will also be more able to perceive and handle projections. She might also become freer of the stern superego that might otherwise prevent her from being open to the range of her feelings, thoughts and uncertainties (Sedlak 1997 p. 27). Only then will she be able to allow more room to let herself 'not know' what is going on, and become freer of the assumption that competence implies consistent knowledge and understanding. She might also be able to feel more free of the sense of pressure for results – a common enough experience in university life and, in one sense, the very thing that has brought her into training – in favour of the capacity to wait and to let the therapy take its course.

Example 2

Linda's life before training had involved teaching jazz piano and playing in bands. She was also a composer. Her first referral was to work with Peggy, a young woman in her 20s with profound physical and intellectual disabilities, who lived on a large ward in a long-stay hospital and had no contact with her family. Linda brought this work to individual supervision with me.

She described openly how shocked she had felt on first meeting Peggy on the ward. Peggy was very thin and small for her age, sitting in a wheel chair. Her body was distorted so that she seemed to be looking to one side and sometimes almost over her shoulder. Her eyes were half closed and she made no attempt to look towards Linda or, indeed, to acknowledge her in any way. She was without speech, had no flexibility of facial expression, and could apparently make very little purposeful movement. She could not use or even hold an instrument. Linda said that she felt a 'moment of sympathy' for Peggy but, much more, had felt repelled by her appearance, and overcome by a sense of disappointment. All her fantasies of a satisfyingly creative, growing relationship, expressed through improvised music, were replaced by a feeling of despair. She felt very conscious of the silence in the room. She admitted that she had found herself wishing that Peggy could be replaced by someone 'more alive'. She added that the care-worker who introduced her to Peggy had said 'You won't get much out of her'. She had felt shocked, and yet had understood, and then felt ashamed of the understanding.

At this stage in supervision it seemed important to acknowledge Linda's own feelings, and to recognise that she was very aware of and able to express to me her strong reactions. We thought about Linda's own musical history and the fact that her activities as a jazz musician had been a great source of life and energy to her. She described how exciting she had found it performing and improvising with other musicians, and how she often felt deflated and low when the concert was over. We agreed that the place and function of music in her own life was something to explore in her own therapy, but that Peggy's silence and apparent inertia had confronted her with something she found difficult to tolerate. At that stage I did not offer Linda any advice about how she might approach the work other than suggesting that she might attend to Peggy as closely as she could (we thought here about her experience of infant observation) and use music in whatever way came to mind.

Linda reported that in the first session she had found it very difficult to focus upon Peggy. She had found Peggy's apparent unresponsiveness and inactivity oppressive, and although several times she had begun to improvise gently and slowly, she had lost the focus of her attention towards Peggy and 'wandered off' into music of her own that gave her greater satisfaction and comfort; after a few minutes she would realise uncomfortably what she had done. She recalled how often she had checked the clock, longing for the session to end.

In the course of describing all this she broke off and said to me 'I feel sorry for you; you've got to sit and listen to me rambling on like this'. That led us into a speculative discussion of what might have been Peggy's experience of her parents' response to her disability. Had Linda, in that meeting and first session, simply found herself in the position of Peggy's mother, perhaps horrified and repelled by her daughter's disability, unable to find in herself any impulse to make contact with her, and yet ashamed of her feelings? She no longer had any contact with her daughter; had she, as Linda had in her own music, found other activities that were more enlivening and yet remained conscious of having abandoned Peggy? We considered Linda's remark to me; was she assuming that I, in turn, would be frustrated by her 'handicap' as a therapist and be longing for the supervision to end? We ended by thinking about the importance of countertransference experience as a source of vital emotional and thus clinical information.

Linda found this discussion painful, but started to speak with more curiosity about Peggy's experience and to think about what that might mean for her sense of relationship now. In other words, supervision had begun to open a space for thought and imagination, and for containment of the strong and conflicted feelings which Linda had had on meeting Peggy.

In subsequent sessions Linda began to work with music in two ways. First, she developed a capacity to improvise to and for Peggy. Linda's most familiar musical idiom was a fast-moving, harmonically complex, flamboyant jazz piano style; she recognised that she needed to find some other 'voice' in her relationship with Peggy and felt daunted at the prospect. It became clear that this capacity for exciting, technically dazzling playing was a central part of Linda's sense of her musical self; to do without it left her feeling vulnerable. She also began to recognise that her difficulty in knowing how to 'speak' to Peggy musically was an articulation of her feeling of fearfulness and bafflement at Peggy's state. In supervision we tried to attend to this by simply talking about Peggy; I would ask Linda to describe a few moments of being with Peggy, rather in the manner of an infant observation, and gradually it began to emerge that Peggy was not as frozen as Linda had first supposed. As Linda began to be able to see beyond the broad manifestations of handicap to the many subtle changes in Peggy's behaviour – in movement, small vocal sounds, changes in her breathing – so she found a more open, simple style in her improvised music. It remained often full and resonant, however, and sometimes left little space for Peggy to be heard.

Peggy had a repertoire of sounds and gestures, including tapping her foot against her wheelchair, grinding her teeth, and making repeated jerking movements with one arm. Although Linda could at first see no 'structure' in what Peggy was doing, we decided that she would watch and listen, and try to experience Linda's activity in terms of its potential as part of a piece of music. The following week Linda brought a tape of the session, which included a few minutes of Peggy's fragmentary, inter-mittent sounds. We listened to it twice, partly to try to foster the steady focus upon Peggy that Linda found so difficult and that she could so easily replace with busy piano playing. I suggested that she should think of Peggy as an improvising partner and in fact as the leader in the improvisation. We recalled that Linda was a composer, and thought about the challenges of bringing that inventive aspect of herself into this new arena. I suggested that she should listen to some piano music (by Schoenberg, Webern and Cage) that sought for expressiveness through minimal resources. In the succeeding weeks Linda became more confident in allowing for spaces in the music, and in responding distinctively but minimally to Peggy's sounds and movements. A new idiom began to develop in which the silences began to take their places as pauses in some broader musical structure, and in which Linda's need for time to be measured through the energetic rhythmic playing she could do so well was replaced by a more spacious and slow-moving overall musical pace. The music also began to have discernible mutual rises and falls in emotional intensity, as the two partners became more intuitively aware of one another.

I think the function of supervision here was to sustain Linda, often by talking primarily in musical terms, in becoming more attentive to Peggy and more able to explore a musical approach very far from what she was familiar with. As she began to have greater faith in herself as a more versatile but less 'driven' improviser and listener, she found the experience of being with Peggy more immediate, and she became more aware of how much Peggy was making active choices in her participation. That, in turn, allowed Peggy to take her place as an equal partner in an emerging musical relationship.

In supervision of therapy with this client group it is often most useful to work at first in this world of sound, gesture, music and feeling. This has nothing necessarily to do with the idiom of the therapist's music, or with how much the session is planned in terms of structure. Whatever the therapist's approach in those respects, it remains that at the centre of the work is relationship, and the task of supervision is to enable the therapist to feel alive and flexible within it.

In the earliest stages of life mothers and their infants develop a complex preverbal vocal, visual and gestural repertoire that is the vehicle for profound feeling and intuitive understanding. The development of such a repertoire is itself a place for excitement and lively curiosity, as each partner hears or sees the other do something new, which carries meaning, invites recognition and duly becomes part of their shared language. For a comparable process to be possible in clinical work, the student therapist must find the courage to shed her acquired assumptions about music, in terms of what is acceptable, or of what is familiar and safe, or of what certain sounds mean or imply, in favour of a more open and curious stance. That means finding what Meyer (1956) calls the 'aesthetic attitude':

> . . . a stimulus or gesture which does not point to or arouse expectations of a subsequent musical event is meaningless. Because expectation is largely a product of stylistic experience, music in a style with which we are totally unfamiliar is meaningless. However, once the *aesthetic attitude* is brought into play, very few gestures actually appear to be meaningless.
>
> (Meyer 1956 p. 37)

Similarly, John Cage writes of

> . . . a continuity which is free of individual taste and memory and also of the literature and 'traditions'. The sounds enter the time-space centred within themselves unimpeded by any service to abstraction, their 360 degrees of circumference free for an infinite play of interpenetration.
>
> (Cage 1951 p. 2)

That aesthetic dimension, as Bergstroem-Nielsen (2006) points out, is fundamental. We can only allow new links – musically and psychically –

when we can be open to the prospect that anything is possible, and find pleasure in the unexpected. Can the student let go of her security in the familiar, both in music and beyond, and move from a technical (or perhaps even thinkingly musical) response to what she hears to something more wholly affective?

> To some minds the disembodied feeling of affective experience is uncanny and unpleasant, and a process of rationalisation is undertaken in which the musical processes are objectified as conscious meaning . . . Thus while the trained musician consciously waits for the expected resolution of a dominant seventh chord, the untrained, but practised, listener feels the delay as *affect*.
>
> (Meyer 1956 p. 40)

That 'delay' or 'disembodied feeling of affective experience' – the moment charged with feeling from which things might move in any direction – is at the heart of therapy. As Rance puts it:

> This is not simply an emotional or intellectual process, but an intuitive interaction between subject and object that is simply aesthetic.
>
> (Rance 1992 p. 47)

Adam Phillips suggests that therapy:

> . . . aims to restore the artist in the patient, the part of the person that makes interest despite, or whatever, the early environment. For the artist of her own life, it is not so much a question of what she has been given as of what she can make of what she has been given . . . setting the dreamer and the child off on the work of transformation.
>
> (Phillips 1998 p. 12)

The business of supervision, in turn, is to restore and sustain the artist in the *therapist*, so that she can bring her imagination and originality to the encounter and become fully engaged in the mutual process of change.

References

Bergstroem-Nielsen, C. (2006) 'The importance of aesthetics as a dimension in music therapy activity'. *Voices: A World Forum for Music Therapy*. http://www.voices.no/mainissues/mi40006000202.html (accessed 18 June 2008).

Bion, W. (1962) 'A theory of thinking'. *International Journal of Psychoanalysis*, 43, 306–310.

Cage, J. (1951) Commentary on *Music of Changes*, quoted in sleeve notes to recording by Joseph Kubera (piano) in 1998. LCD 2053.

Coltart, N. (1992) *Slouching towards Bethlehem*. New York: Guilford Press.

De Groef, J., Heinemann, E. (eds) (1999) *Psychoanalysis and mental handicap*. London: Free Association Books.

Edwards, J., Daveson, B. (2004) 'Music therapy student supervision: considering aspects of resistance and parallel processes in the supervisory relationship with students in final clinical placement'. *The Arts in Psychotherapy*, 31(2), 67–76.

Frawley O'Dea, M., Sarnat, J. (2001) *The supervisory relationship: a contemporary psychodynamic approach*. London & New York: Guilford Press.

Hollins, S. (2000) 'Developmental psychiatry – insights from learning disability'. *British Journal of Psychiatry*, 177, 201–206.

Jacobs, D., David, P., Meyer, D.J. (1995) *The Supervisory Encounter: a Guide for Teachers of Psychodynamic Psychotherapy and Psychoanalysis*. New Haven: Yale University Press.

Lee, P., Nashat, S. (2004) 'The question of a third space in psychotherapy with adults with learning disabilities' in D. Simpson and L. Miller (eds), *Unexpected gains: psychotherapy with people with learning disabilities*, London: Karnac.

Main, T. (1967) 'Knowledge, learning and freedom from thought'. *Psychoanalytic Psychotherapy*, 5, 49–78.

Meyer, L (1956) *Emotion and meaning in music*. Chicago: University of Chicago Press.

Phillips, A. (1998) *The Beast in the Nursery*. London: Faber & Faber.

Rance, C. (1992) 'The aesthetics of group analysis'. *Group Analysis*, 25(2), 171–181.

Schwartz, D. (2007) *The music therapist's music world'. Unpublished paper delivered at the European Music Therapy Congress: The Netherlands*.

Sedlak, V. (1997) 'Psychoanalytic supervision of untrained therapists' in B. Martindale *et al.* (eds), *Supervision and its Vicissitudes*, London: Karnac.

Simpson, D., Miller, L. (eds) (2004) *Unexpected gains: psychotherapy with people with learning disabilities*. London: Karnac.

Sinason, V. (1992) *Mental handicap and the human condition*. London: Free Association Books.

Stokes, J., Sinason, V. (1992) 'Secondary mental handicap as a defence' in A. Waitman and S. Conboy-Hill (eds), *Psychotherapy and mental handicap*. London: Sage.

Symington, N. (1981) 'The psychotherapy of a subnormal patient'. *British Journal of Medical Psychology*, 54, 187–199.

Symington, N. (1992) 'Countertransference with mentally handicapped clients' in A. Waitman and S. Conboy-Hill (eds), *Psychotherapy and mental handicap*. London: Sage.

Chapter 3

Music therapy supervision with students and professionals

The use of music and analysis of counter-transference experiences in the triadic field

Inge Nygaard Pedersen

Introduction

In 1998, an international supervisors' peer group was established of five experienced music therapists from Denmark, Sweden, the UK, Germany and Italy. We met regularly over 3 years to discuss the content of a proposed postgraduate supervision training for professional music therapists.

We worked experientially to try out methods in which music and the analysis of transference and countertransference in the triadic field of supervision were included. In this chapter I elaborate on the inspiration gained and lessons learnt from this group work, and offer an understanding of supervision from different models and perspectives of structuring. I illustrate the theoretical elements by analysing two cases from my own work as a supervisor. I have been a supervisor of music therapy students for 23 years and, for the last 5 years, I have been a regular supervisor for both newly qualified and experienced music therapists working in hospital-based and social psychiatry.

Definitions

The word 'supervision' literally means to 'oversee' or 'survey'. In the clinical context, I understand 'supervision' in a much broader sense as a mixture of meta-sight, insight and intuition. The main task of the supervisor is to listen empathically and from this position to form a general view of the area of problems the supervisee presents, as well as to point out directions the supervisee might choose to follow. This involves sorting out these problems through the supervisory relationship, in which the supervisor is an interactive partner in the supervisor/supervisee relationship. Altogether this means that the supervisor is covering a continuum that calls on the one hand for a subjective involvement in the process and on the other hand for objective 'expert' knowledge. The supervisor is the outside-observer, an intermediary, as well as a resonator both to the therapist/client relationship and in the supervisor/supervisee relationship. From movements within this continuum the supervisor has to find and refind a way of representing a constructive 'meta-sight', which the supervisee is not expected to have.

How might one frame a brief definition of clinical supervision? I know from participation in round-table discussions that there is general agreement internationally among music therapists that *the goal of supervision is to develop the music therapist's identity and professional competencies.*

There is also general agreement that a supervisor is not simultaneously a personal therapist for the supervisee, and agreement on the importance of defined boundaries between the supervisor and the supervisee. In most cases, a written contract is needed. This contract is a statement of the purpose, the conditions and the framework of the supervision, and it ensures that the work is focused on the process of clarifying professional areas of difficulty.

As my background as a professional music therapist and a music therapy supervisor is analytically orientated, I must add to this general goal of supervision that my understanding of the therapist's 'identity' and 'professional competencies' includes openness to considering the entire field of unconscious realities involving the complex triad of patient–therapist/supervisee–supervisor.

When supervisors limit their understanding of the supervision process and omit the issue of countertransference, or restrict this to the supervisee's countertransference towards patients, this might be called a 'treat' approach, which Rosbrow (1993) distinguishes from a 'train' approach. In supervision research and practice I see this 'treat or train' approach as a false dichotomy. I think understanding of supervision can be expanded by triadic influences using an 'inter-subjective matrix', as defined by Brown and Miller (2002), including the entire field of both conscious and unconscious realities involving the complex triad of patient–supervisee–supervisor. It is not a question of implementing either a treat or a train approach in the supervision process, but of including both. I find it important to include the mutual transference experiences at a triadic level in supervision; this may have considerable impact on the supervisee's development of therapeutic skills and techniques.

It is important to clarify that supervision is neither teaching nor psychotherapy. Supervision is a learning process, in which the supervisee learns about his/her needs and boundaries. The need for extra teaching or personal therapy for the supervisee might be identified in the supervision, but must be taken care of elsewhere.

The supervision process as a continuum approach

In my own practice I have supervised both students and experienced music therapists, all of whom have a psychoanalytically orientated training background that includes self-experience as an element of the professional training. It is my experience that this background invites students to be open to and to learn from the triadic field of supervision when they are still in training.

According to the 'treat and train' approach mentioned above, the supervision of music therapists can be viewed as a continuum between A and B, where A is an 'instruction-oriented' approach with no use of triadic influences and B is a 'matter-of-fact' approach that includes the process of identifying role ambiguity in the supervision process. In my work I want to include a third dimension that allows for a continuum with a more instruction-oriented approach together with identification of the role ambiguity approach at the one end (mostly with students still in training), and a 'mutual learning process' at the other (mostly with experienced music therapists). In the mutual learning process there is room for 'not knowing' and for working with joint associations. In this continuum approach I often use music as a 'third' helping tool for inquiry, which can deepen associative and emotional exploration all the way along this continuum.

So my professional background as an analytical orientated music therapist is a platform for my understanding of the supervision process. However, in my professional supervision work I also seek to go beyond my training background and be open to what is needed and what is possible in the supervision process of developing the music therapist's identity and professional competencies.

In this respect, supervision for music therapists can be described as a tool to maintain and strengthen the work of an individual or a team, or the work of anyone engaged in any kind of consultation, leadership, teaching, care or therapy, and therefore there are many factors to be taken into account in any supervision process. These include: the stage of development of the therapist (student, newly qualified, experienced therapist), the level of experience of the supervisor (newly qualified or experienced) and the phase and context of the supervision process. I will consider these factors as part of the structure of the supervision within the continuum approach.

In my continuum approach to supervision there are four essential elements: the client, the therapist, the supervisee and the supervisor. I distinguish between therapist and supervisee as each role implies a rather different learning process. As a therapist, the supervisee is an expert, whereas in the role of a supervisee s/he is a learner learning from another expert, the supervisor. Learning from being identified in this dual role should be an assimilating process where something can be taken in and integrated with what is already known. It is not an accommodative learning process where something has to replace what is already there. In music therapy there is an additional fifth element – the music – which can be applied as 'a tool in the therapeutic process' as well as a 'therapeutic medium in itself'. As a therapeutic medium, the music might take over the process and bring it to another level of understanding. The active use of music in the supervisory process can lead to new learning and deeper experiences of the work.

I have also been inspired by another model – an Integrated Developmental Model – which is based on descriptions of the different stages of professional development of the supervisee (Stoltenberg, McNeill & Delworth 1998).

An Integrated Developmental Model

The American psychologists Stoltenberg, McNeill and Delworth (1998) present a model of supervision called the Integrated Developmental Model (IDM). They describe different supervision models that vary according to the professional level of the supervisee. Based on three levels of professionalism [level one (novice), level two and level three] it is possible to inquire into the development of the supervisee from three overall categories:

1. awareness of oneself and the other
2. motivation
3. autonomy.

Level one

In the theory of IDM, the supervisees on level one (the novice level) of the three levels of professionalism are those occupied with acquiring techniques. The supervisees use much of their cognitive capacity to consider rules and guidelines for a concrete practice. Their self-concept is dependent upon how far they succeed in applying a technique; they are very concerned about themselves. This concern about their own performance often gets in the way of awareness of the patient and his material. Novices are mostly not aware of their own reactions to the patients. This can be reinforced by anxiety about being in the new role of therapist, by insecurity, and by negative evaluation of their own performance. Finally, supervisees at the novice level can be very preoccupied with thoughts about approval or disapproval from both patients and the supervisor. Their *motivation* here is very much based on a wish to be able to cope quickly with the situation of being a therapist and so reduce the anxiety. Sometimes at this novice level, a reduction in motivation can occur when some interventions succeed. Greater motivation mostly returns when the therapist realises that her luck was based on a quite simple understanding about what psychotherapy (or in this case, music therapy) is about. The therapist at this level is rather dependent on the supervisor. The supervisee expects the supervisor to be a person who can give advice and transfer knowledge, and provide the supervisee with adequate information and techniques. The supervisee expects the supervisor to be responsible for the structure of the supervision and may model her working style on that of the supervisor. At this stage awareness of transference/countertransference issues (Pedersen 2000) and parallel processes (Haugaard-Jacobsen 2000) most often have to be held as implicit knowledge by the supervisor.

Level two

When supervising therapists at level two, the supervisor may encounter supervisees, as newly qualified music therapists, who at one level are very professional whereas at another level they are still novices. Stoltenberg *et al.* (1998) describe the 'puberty' of the supervisee fluctuating between autonomy and dependency, which once again influences motivation. Supervisees have more trust in their work and their focus has moved from concern with the application of techniques to a focus on the patient, which allows for deeper empathic understanding of the clinical situation. There is a risk of overidentification with the client, followed by very strong countertransference reactions. The focus on the client might reduce the therapist's ability to be aware of herself and her own reactions towards the client. Often, the therapist is seeking a personal therapeutic style and a relevant theory to accompany it, and might not want too much 'interference' from the supervisor. It is very important for a supervisor to be aware of such mechanisms and to remain supportive and flexible. When giving advice it is important to give alternatives and to support the supervisee in finding the most meaningful way forward. It is essential to help the supervisee to formulate her own ideas about interventions and understandings, of her own sense of the relationship with the patient, as well as with the supervisor. It is possible here to begin carefully to clarify transference/countertransference patterns and parallel processes in the triadic field.

Level three

This level is mostly first achieved after several years of clinical practice, when the supervisee has developed a consciousness of her own reactions, a varied understanding of the therapeutic process and a well-developed capacity for empathy and understanding. Countertransference mechanisms are much more conscious, and the supervision is much more of a mutual interplay where both partners can reflect at an equal level. It is to be expected that any confrontation will be met at an analytic reflective level and seen as the basis for further investigation.

I recognise these definitions of levels clearly from my own work as a clinical supervisor. I have noticed that music therapy students with an analytically informed theoretical background, together with long-term comprehensive self-experience in music therapy, develop openness to inquiries within the triadic field in supervision. By the time of their long-term clinical placement in their ninth semester they often work in supervision at level two – or even at level three while they are still in training

– before they become newly qualified or experienced music therapists. Here confrontations are met at an analytic, reflective level at the same time as this level of supervision with advanced students is still coloured by acquiring techniques and advice from level one.

The influence of the training level and background of the supervisor and the supervisee

It is very important that the supervisor is informed about the training background of the supervisee. In the field of music therapy today, most music therapists who offer supervision identify with a training approach, such as analytical music therapy (AMT), the Bonny method of guided imagery in music (GIM), or Nordoff–Robbins (N-R) music therapy. This development seems natural, as there are very few existing supervision training courses for music therapists. Supervision of qualified music therapists can be carried out by psychologists, psychoanalysts or psychiatrists, or by qualified music therapists with many years of clinical experience, who identify with a music therapy approach and a certain area of client population.

In the book *Music therapy supervision* (Forinash 2001) there are comprehensive chapters on supervision from a perspective of three different music therapy approaches: AMT (Scheiby 2001), GIM (Ventre 2001) and N-R (Turry 2001). These descriptions are very important steps towards the understanding of differences and similarities in supervision practice within different approaches.

All three models emphasise the need for supervision of qualified music therapists, and also emphasise respect for the supervisee's own identity, style and clinical understanding. All of them work within the following six points of foci: client, relationship, therapist, music, institution and/or professional focus. The differences, as far as I see them, are mostly related to ideology, theoretical orientation, methodology and techniques. Understanding and application of transference and countertransference experiences in the triadic field are not always included in supervision in the different approaches. They might be included in relation to the patient/ therapist relationship but not to the supervisor/supervisee relationship.

It would be an interesting and creative process for professional music therapists to develop future supervision training programmes in which integrative models could be objectives for the training and in which a consciousness of how different ideologies influence on methodologies and techniques could be part of the supervision training, whatever the trainees' educational and theoretical background.

I think supervision within a single music therapy approach is needed on music therapy training programmes and in institutes that undertake supervision of students and newly qualified music therapists. However, I believe that for more professionally advanced music therapists there might be a need to have supervision with a supervisor advocating another approach. I do not think we should build too many rigid boundaries of approaches at this more advanced level, which might avoid the rich experience and influence of different approaches. I hope future supervision training programmes will provide knowledge and basic skills to enable trainees to be able to supervise music therapists from different training backgrounds.

Integrative supervision for music therapists

I now want to introduce a short description of one attempt in the field of music therapy to build a model for group supervision at a meta-level. I have been very inspired by the model developed by Frohne-Hagemann (1999, 2001). This model is valuable and applicable for music therapists from different training backgrounds, as she offers comprehensive descriptions of applying musical techniques.

Frohne-Hagemann has created this model based on her hermeneutic heuristic background. It suggests a continuing spiral movement in the progression of supervision, moving through the following four phases (Figure 3.1).

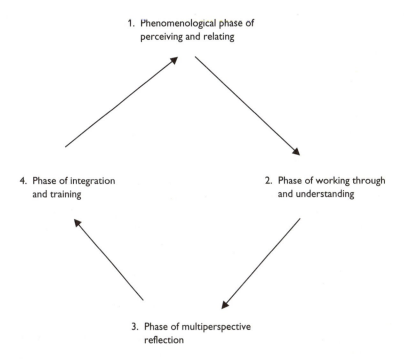

1. Phenomenological phase of perceiving and relating

4. Phase of integration and training

2. Phase of working through and understanding

3. Phase of multiperspective reflection

Figure 3.1 Model of group supervision (based on Frohne-Hagemann 1999, 2001)

1. The phase of perceiving and relating

In this phase, the themes of group supervision might be inquiries about:

- What is the topic?
- What is happening now?
- What is the key element of the therapeutic process?
- The therapeutic relationship
- Psychodynamic aspects
- What do we perceive, and how?
- How does it affect us?
- How does the supervisor/group resonate to that?

To work with these themes, different improvisation techniques might be used. An example is a 'feedback technique' used in a group setting. Here, the supervisee presents his/her problem with a client, after which the members of the group express their immediate countertransference experiences to the story in a musical improvisation. This might help the supervisee to gain new insight about her client and her relationship with the client.

Another technique is the 'spontaneous amplifying group improvisation' (so called by Eckhard Weymann 1996 p. 175). This is used immediately after the verbal introduction given by the supervisee to the group members. It can be very helpful when the verbal introduction only touches the surface of the problem or if the group members are tired and a change of perspective is needed. This technique leaves space for working with feelings of countertransference as well as personal resonance.

2. The phase of working through and understanding

In this second phase, the themes of the group supervision might be:

- What is the real narrative?
- Does the therapist/supervisee recognise this issue from other situations?
- What is the underlying emotional material which generates transference/ countertransference experiences?
- What are the resistances in both client and therapist?
- What parallel processes may be occurring in the course of the supervision?

Useful improvisations in this phase might be 'the musical portrait' or 'musical therapeutic identification'.

In the 'musical portrait' the therapist/supervisee will be asked to choose appropriate instruments and to paint (play) a musical portrait of his client. This portrait is treated as a mirror of the relation the therapist feels towards the client and the relation the client feels towards the therapist in the therapist's opinions. Thus the portrait reveals the therapist's own projections. The focus here is 'on the problems the therapist has with the client, and the group members look at therapeutic situations as intermediate encounters' (Frohne-Hagemann 1999 p. 264). Another improvisation technique is 'music therapeutic identification' where psychodrama and Gestalt therapeutic approaches are applied with a systemic and social constructivist perspective:

> This technique in supervision is applied as a musical portrait from the projected client's view. The supervisee identifies with his client and directs a musical reconstruction of the client's situation. . . . This very consciously directed improvisation focuses upon the client's point of view and how the therapist assumes the client is experiencing him.
>
> (Frohne-Hagemann 1999 pp. 264–265)

3. The phase of multiperspective reflection

In this third phase, the theme is the understanding of the experience from different perspectives including at least the following four dimensions:

1. The political dimension
2. The theoretical dimension
3. The practical dimension
4. The respective ethical position.

These four dimensions are described by Frohne-Hagemann (1999 p. 266).

4. The phase of integration and training

In this fourth phase, the themes of the group supervision include:

> What are the consequences for the clients?
> How could the problems be solved by the supervisee?
> How can we prove our therapeutic skills?
>
> (Frohne-Hagemann 1999 p. 267)

It is mentioned here that, for this phase, useful improvisations should be experimental:

> . . . in order to find and test out more efficient musical approaches to, and musical interventions for, the client. Useful techniques could be music therapy experiments with Intertherap (Priestley 1997), role playing and verbal approaches, etc.
>
> (Frohne-Hagemann 1999 p. 267)

The model of 'Intertherap' in peer supervision groups

This model was originally developed by the English music therapist Mary Priestley (1975) and proposes a group of three professionals working together in a music therapy setting. In the supervision process they take turns in being client, therapist and supervisor on a peer basis. This setting gives professionals the possibility of examining problems from clinical practice in a context with colleagues where the aim of being in the client role is to develop clinical skills. It also gives professionals a chance to keep sensitively alive in their perception of clinical work when many years of repeated clinical practice might have established too many habitual routines.

Verbal training

Verbal communication is part of the 'Intertherap' model and here it is important to continuously examine how the supervisee communicates: how he/she enters a dialogue, brings a subject to the point, deepens the process verbally, and works through the process after having improvised or listened together with the client. How does he/she lead the client into a phase of reflection and integration, which kind of words does he/she use, and how does his/her theoretical background influence the use of words?

In this fourth phase, the focus is very much on utilization of experiences and insights. The end of the spiral is (according to Frohne-Hagemann) always the beginning of a new one. There is no end to the integration of the different worlds we are living in, and there will never be an end to learning from our colleagues, supervisees and clients. All clinicians need to be kept alive in a spiral process such as that presented here.

Supervision case study extract: The novice level

I now want to analyse an individual supervision from the perspective of Frohne-Hagemann's Integrative model and the IDM model. The first example is an extract from a supervision session with me as the supervisor working with a female student in the training programme at Aalborg University. The student is in her nine-semester half-year clinical placement at a home for severely emotionally disturbed children who have been taken away from their family home. The student has undertaken 3 years of 'experiential training in music therapy' (ETMT) and is at a novice level.

The student (supervisee) presented her problems with a teenage female client, who was very negative towards all the activities taking place at the children's home. The client mostly answered with only one word (mostly 'no') and had the attitude that everyone and everything is rather stupid or childish. According to the supervisee, staff members had expressed the opinion that they did not really believe that the girl would turn up for music therapy. However, the client agreed to attend music therapy. She turned up, but only wanted to play the flute. She had learned to play classical flute, and she was constantly concerned about playing 'right' or 'wrong'. Additionally, she wanted to sing a few well-known songs. She found suggestions about improvisation or other activities absolutely stupid.

In the following vignette, I describe the co-operation between me and the supervisee based on the four stages in the integrative model.

Phase of perceiving and relating

The supervisee wanted: (1) to follow the wishes of the client; as well as (2) to try to enlarge the range of activities taking place in the music therapy sessions. She presented her problem in supervision and was overwhelmed by insecurity. She did not feel 'good enough' when facing the client's rejections, and felt as if she was invading the client when she suggested other activities. In summary, she felt rather stuck.

I felt an impulse as a supervisor – as in a parallel process – to: (1) meet the overwhelming emotions of the supervisee empathically; and (2) guide her by suggesting certain techniques (to enlarge her range of activities). The supervisee told me that she did not know which words to use or how to cope with demands or suggestions when she was together with the client. I realised in the situation that I felt stupid as well, and at the same time I felt a need to rescue the student. I felt insecure while at the same time I wanted to take over and offer her a role model.

I was aware that I was supervising a nine-semester student who needed to be supported and to be 'met'. However, she also needed my meta-sight observation and some modelling from me in her process of building up her music therapist's identity. I am aware that from an analytical point of view I could be identified as a rescuer who wants to save her from having these painful feelings, but I considered it not meaningful to disclose my experience of the dynamics of the therapist/client relationship at this initial stage, so I chose a more didactic style of supervision at this point.

I began asking her questions like:

- Which musical activities have you tried out with your client?
- What happens to you in the situation?
- Which roles/moods do you find yourself in?
- How do you feel yourself if someone suggests to you something you normally don't do?
- What happens to you when you tell me that your client is totally rejecting of your relationship?
- What do you imagine would happen if you questioned the client in the way you tell me you don't dare to question her?

- Could you imagine that when you question her the client might feel other things than being invaded?

By posing these questions I offered a space for inquiry into the student's emotions, roles, efforts and further associations to the presented problem. I experienced countertransference feelings of being uncertain and doubtful about whether I could help this student, but I kept these feelings to myself.

Phase of working through and understanding

After having explored the problems and put them into words, I suggested to the supervisee that we try a role-play. We set up a musical activity where she played the client and I played the music therapist. The focus of the role-play was: 'the transition from a verbal exchange: how to come to musical improvisation.'

Role-play of supervisor/supervisee: Verbal dialogue before the improvisation

The supervisor role-played the therapist (Th), the supervisee role-played the client (Cl):

Th: Okay R. We will be together here for a while in music therapy, and it is not primarily because you are going to learn to play music – it is more a way of being together in the music, and I would like to play with you in such a way that both of us play only on the black keys at the piano.

Cl: Hm.

Th: And now we try out that first you play some keys, then I play some keys and then you come in again and so we go on, and we only use the black keys, not the white ones.

Cl: Actually I have never tried to play the piano before.

Th: No, I thought so and . . .

Cl: And I don't think I am able to do it.

Th: No, I thought that was what you would tell me, and this is OK, but I think now, that when we play on the black keys, we can't play wrong – it never sounds wrong – and therefore I thought, we could start there quite simple.

Cl: I don't feel like playing such stupid things.

Th: No, I understand you, and I follow what you are saying. I am thinking right now that maybe we should make up a rule saying, that if any of us feel it is stupid during playing we just stop immediately – a rule for both you and me.

Cl: Hm.
Th: So this is our rule: that if one of us – also if I get to feel that what I
      am doing is stupid – then I stop and the same to you.
Cl: Hm.
Th: How does that sound for you?
Cl: Well – hm – we can try.
Th: Should we try then?
Cl: Hm.
Th: So you can choose one of the chairs at the piano, and choose if you
      want to sit to the left or to the right.
Cl: I want to sit there (pointing to the right side – top part of the piano)
      (both sit down).
Th: Yes – I feel like playing with closed eyes because then I listen better.
      When I have my eyes open I come to look at the instrument and at
      my own hands or something, and then I can get confused – so this is
      what I want to do – I wonder what you want?
Cl: Hm – if I play with closed eyes then I can't see anything.
Th: No, but if you imagine that you can feel the keys – the black ones
      because they stick out from the others – then you can easily feel which
      keys are the black ones.
Cl: Hm – (she starts feeling the black keys).

Music improvisation (therapist and client play on one piano)

The client played unintentionally on the black keys and gradually this
started an improvisation. The therapist accompanied her and added a
rhythmic flow and energy to the fragmented music of the client. It seemed
as if the client almost did not notice that the music had started until she was
in the middle of it. She responded clearly in certain parts of the music and
step by step let herself be 'seduced' by the flow of the music.

Verbal dialogue after the music

Th: (looking inquiringly at the client)
Cl: Hm.
Th: OK, I didn't feel stupid at any moment, I kept on playing.
Cl: Hm. I didn't think it was totally stupid either – actually it was also a
      bit funny.
Th: Yes?
Cl: Hm.
Th: OK, R, then I will suggest we play like this some of the time each
      session, and that we play the flute and sing well-known songs, so we
      have a variety of things to do.

Cl: Hm.
Th: How does that sound to you?
Cl: Hm – maybe – Hm. Maybe we could do so – hm at least we can try.
Th: You sound hesitating – is it overwhelming for you?
Cl: No, but it is rather different from what I am normally doing.
Th: Hm.
Cl: I don't think I am good at it, but still we can try.
Th: May I ask you something?
Cl: Yes.
Th: When you played with closed eyes, did you think about if you were
      good enough?
Cl: Actually I didn't play with my eyes closed.
Th: OK, it is just me who is stupid – because I had my eyes closed, I
      thought of you also having your eyes closed.
Cl: OK – no it was strange, I didn't really think about if I was good
      enough.
Th: Hm.
Cl: So.
Th: Do you want to hear my experience of our joint improvisation?
Cl: Yes.
Th: I thought it was fun, and I enjoyed very much to play with you.
Cl: Hm.
Th: Also, I thought it was nice to feel the energy in the music – almost like
      playing other games with a ball or so.
Cl: Hm – yes.

The role-play seen from the level of the multiperspective reflection

In the phase of multiperspective reflection we talked about the fact that, in
the institution, this client had serious difficulties co-operating and negotiating with others, and that the staff accepted and wished the music therapist might offer the client another frame that would allow ways of coming
to terms with this more authoritarian institutional tradition within which
the girl is told what to do. What are the consequences if she does not do
what she is told?

The supervisee was convinced that this was the way she wanted to work
with the client, but simultaneously inner voices rejected this way of working
and found it childish and stupid. We further explored this, and the supervisee said that she herself normally easily feels an impulse in the clinical
situation either to follow the client's mood and mirror the negative energy,
or to take the role of an authority figure who gives orders. She recognised
this reflection as a real learning process for herself. She recognised the
problems from her own teenage years, when she was very negative towards
suggestions from adults and did not want to share, which made her isolate

herself. This led us to discuss the fact that the supervisee on one hand really expected me to tell her what to do (to rescue her) and on the other hand knew that she would resist me if I became too authoritarian.

My experience was that puberty patterns at level two were 'in play' between us. In our role-play the supervisee realised the effect of being given the responsibility of feeling stupid herself as very strong. She accordingly realised that it is possible to learn from an 'expert' (here the supervisor), without feeling humiliated. As the supervisor I applied a technique with a focus on countertransference mechanisms. I was sensing and using my countertransference feelings when I suggested a mutual rule about being stupid between the client and the therapist.

The role-play seen from the level of integration and reflection: Identifying the learning issues

In the next supervision sessions, we talked about our different roles, and her developing openness and consciousness in the first session, relating to the parallels in her own life story. This made it easier to move forwards and for me to offer her my knowledge of myself as one who (for biographical reasons that I did not share with her) easily wants to rescue others who feel insecure and overwhelmed. Insecurity became an overall issue of our supervision co-operation – insecurity of the client, of the therapist and of the supervisor. I gradually moved along the continuum away from a pure instruction-oriented approach where I was a role model, towards a more 'matter of fact' approach where ambiguity of the therapist was allowed and even towards a 'mutual learning process'. Musically, this was acted out in another role-play in which the supervisee role-played being the therapist and I role-played being the difficult client. This caused situations of real insecurity for her but also a lot of humour and reflection. She succeeded in gradually trusting her own life experience and in integrating this experience as an inner supervisor for her to draw upon in the here-and-now situation with the client. Insecurity was allowed to be there for all three parties as a sensitive guide towards new solutions.

In this phase of integration and reflection, we talked about what could be done in practice. It was important for me as a supervisor to point out to the supervisee that my way of handling this situation in the role-play was one of 'role model', but that she could feel free to find the way that feels most natural to her in practice. I summarised guidelines for her from our role-play which in this case included:

- Going with the resistance of the client.
- Showing the client that you can follow her and understand her also when she is negative.

- Integrating negotiation to be part of a common playing rule (the therapist is also allowed to feel stupid and to stop the music. It is a general human right to feel stupid).
- Being aware of how to accompany the client, so that the therapist takes the responsibility for the flow in the music at the beginning as a way of drawing in the client to be involved in the interplay.
- Checking with the client what she feels about the activity and again accept her answers (it is 'hers').
- Listening openly to the patient's 'rigid ideas' of only playing something if you are perfect – it is also a natural wish for someone of her age.
- Trying to put your own (the therapist's) wishes into the relationship to balance hers – to be visible for her as a person.
- Encouraging her by telling how you felt about the joint improvisation and about feeling stupid.

In this supervision process, music was used as a tool for building up dialogues where there was resistance – it was brought out at a simple level (playing only on the black keys of the piano) but the supervisee experienced how a state of 'feeling stupid in playing music' was transformed into 'actually it was also fun to play music'.

The knowledge that arose from analysing the triadic field was primarily an implicit knowledge by the supervisor, but it was brought into the interplay through the 'joint topic of insecurity', which moved from being 'an enemy' to being 'a sensitive partner' in the situation. Overall, we were examining how the supervisee could imagine finding a way of better handling the countertransference and her insecurity so that she could permit herself to put suggestions forward without feeling authoritarian or feeling that she was invading the client.

Supervision case study excerpt with a professional music therapist in psychiatry

In this second case example, I was the supervisor leading a group supervision session with three experienced music therapists working in adult psychiatry. The presentation includes the members' retrospectively written reports of their experience of playing music as part of phase two in integrative supervision – the working through and understanding phase.

Phase 1: Perceiving and relating

The supervisee presented a problem concerning being a team member in a forensic ward with a tradition of a therapeutic community. There was a difficult mixture of roles on the ward, as the music therapist functioned as an individual primary therapist for some of the patients at the same time as being part of the therapeutic community setting.[1] The supervisee was clear about accepting this double role and tried to cope with it. Fundamentally, she found the role meaningful when dealing with often very difficult and traumatized patients. In the supervision she presented a picture of herself as often identifying too much with the patients in relation to the team, and thus in her eyes being too demanding or too dominating in meetings. She often found herself expressing her ideas without really feeling grounded in the situation. In coping with reactions from the team, she realised that she might quickly change from being 'up-front' to being too withdrawn if she gave up when it came to negotiations or confrontations. She said that the team was basically accommodating the fact that she had another form of contact with, and role for, the patients.

She presented the problem as if she could not come to a constructive transformation of her 'inner raised energy' and sometimes 'rage' towards the 'destructive' treatment of the patients. Sometimes she felt as if she was isolating herself unnecessarily, although she seemed highly valued by other treatment colleagues (e.g. psychiatrists and psychologists) who encouraged her to continue being that engaged and enthusiastic about her work.

I listened to her and felt immediately as if I was meeting with very strong energy, which I understood as a metaphor of male energy, and at the same time with a weaker energy, which I understood by the metaphor of a 'little girl' energy. These two kinds of energy were not able to remain in dialogue.

Phase 2: Working through and understanding

I suggested we play an improvisation and asked the supervisee to decide which roles she wanted the three of us to play. The creative energy she showed in telling a story was not audible in this initial part of the improvisation. She decided to choose a djembe and to sit on the floor. She asked us to play what we felt like after having listened to her.

One group member chose another djembe and placed herself behind the supervisee, another group member chose the grand piano and I chose the electric marimba. We played for about 10 minutes and I tried to challenge the male energy she had brought forward in the verbal part. I played in a provoking and dominant way and invited her to a kind of musical dramatised fight. The supervisee kept a stable rhythm at the djembe throughout the improvisation, and she only slightly changed tempo and dynamic.

Before presenting her reflections in the verbal part after the music I want to present three short narratives written by the three supervision group members. I asked them, retrospectively, to write down a description of their

---

1 In the original Danish language this was written as 'environmental milieu', but the nearest translation close to this model is 'therapeutic community' in English.

experience of being in the music in that specific situation. Some days went by before I had the idea of asking them to do this, so it is a picture of an experience reflected upon in retrospect. I found these narratives extremely important in understanding what went on between us in the group improvisation.

Supervisee X was sitting on the floor at a djembe:

> It was very important for me that I could hear my own music all the way through this improvisation – that I could hear my own music as more important than if others could hear me. I felt safe and had at no time the experience of being lonesome. In between I was tempted to play with the others – to go into a musical fight game. Simultaneously I realized that it is not necessary for me to play that loud to join the game. At one point I was also tempted to lie down on the floor and become invisible. Through the whole improvisation I was very convinced that my task was to keep the same tempo no matter what happened around me.

Group member A, playing the djembe and sitting behind the supervisee:

> I chose to play on the same instrument as the supervisee. I was sitting at the instrument behind her so I was invisible – almost as a shadow. I suppose this would have been the most provocative position for X. My expression was loose, without tension, quiet and seeking. X did not let herself be moved – she was playing steadily. The group members B and C were loud and whirling. I changed the character in my playing – took more space – made the sound deep and authoritarian. I listened to the others and enjoyed the interplay. It was nice to listen to the professional intimacy. I knew they were there. My thoughts moved to X – what made her so persistent and engaged, insisting in her treatment work. I thought of her patients – their faith. One of my own patients came to mind. I decided to take her to my own supervision. My playing changed again – it became very distinct. I sensed the drum skin very clearly, felt the hair. I seized the drum – a picture arose – a person was hanging out from a cliff projection – the pain of the patients!! It felt safe to know that three colleagues were there. The loneliness! I played very loudly – my playing was distinct (with syncopations and in triple time). I let the sounds lead me – felt the pain, as if I was crying; it hurts . . . A picture from a dream I had after a therapy session with my patient arose. 'The sounds flow'. My awareness moved outward again towards the room 'I am in with the others'. The music calmed down.

Group member B, playing the grand piano:

The task I gave myself was to give a 'counter play' to X. I chose the grand piano and tried through this dominant instrument to represent the team which X felt provoked her. I continued dominating the playing, and in contrast to the music of X. I stayed at a dynamic level which could be heard all the way through – short repeated minor melodies. I made small breaks to go against her steady rhythms at the djembe. I felt in between as if I should take care of her – that she had disappeared – suddenly I could not hear her any more. So although I really tried empathically to stay in my role as the provocative team member, I kept getting the feeling that I should take care of her as if her quiet stable rhythmical playing in between appealed for care.

Just after the improvisation we tried to verbalise our understanding and reflect on the joint experience. It became clear that the three of us had intuitively taken different roles from the intradynamic (the 'male energy' and the energy of the 'little girl') and interdynamic field (the team being in opposition to her) that the supervisee had presented. I identified with and played her male energy and invited her to fight and to stay with it also whilst being in opposition. Group member A identified with the little girl that the supervisee was conscious of using as part of her being very empathic to the patients. Group member B played the part that was in opposition to X but changed her way of playing when she realised that the supervisee was very stable in her playing. This opened a space where the group members listened to the energy of the 'little girl' inside the supervisee who also needed to be taken care of.

The supervisee expressed how clearly she realised how to cope with the presented problem in playing music in a safe place in the supervision. She was able to keep a stable rhythm where she could hear her own expression, take care of her own needs and still be audible and steady towards the surroundings.

Phase 3: Multiperspective reflection

This music therapist supervisee was very conscious of her own strength and weaknesses and she was able to use the situation and the music to find a realistic solution for her with us as peer role players. If we analyse her problem within the triadic field this becomes very complicated. The supervisee identified with the patients and therefore was sometimes against the team feeling isolated and insecure. Together with the patients she was an expert, and she wanted to be their rescuer in the therapeutic community, while another part of her identified so much with the patients' vulnerability that she became invisible and gave up on negotiations and fights with the team. At the same time, she was encouraged by her team colleagues to continue being that engaged even when this might go against the treatment tradition of the team.

In the supervision process the supervisee presented her problem in a very engaged way, but when she wanted the group to be her partners she became 'invisible' and did not tell others which roles she needed them to play. I understood this as a parallel process to her everyday life where she becomes confused over her different roles in her surroundings. She cannot control and at the same time suffer in her identification with what she experienced as negative relationship patterns. Sometimes her solution to this was to be unnecessarily isolated and invisible.

Phase 4: Integration and training

I invited the supervisee to control her surroundings in the supervision situation by letting her tell us which roles she needed us to play. Instead of controlling, she passed this task back to us. I realised that I might also need to control her role confusion by asking this question. I therefore accepted her choice (making myself invisible) and trusted the group members to be able to give relevant support to the supervisee in the improvisation through their professional empathy. This gave the supervisee the possibility of diving into the feeling of being 'almost invisible' and of finding a third solution other than controlling her surroundings. In the musical improvisation, the supervisee kept her own stable rhythm whether we played in opposition to her or empathically with her music. She took the responsibility to be able to hear her own voice all the way through the improvisation and here she realised that this was what she could do in order to cope better with the confused role situation. In the last part of the written report she wrote:

> The following days and weeks the word discipline came up as a mantra very often after this supervision – this word gave me peace and helped me to stay centred and keep my focus better when being in similar situations again.

Conclusion

In the first example, the novice supervisee showed me, being her supervisor, that she wanted to fight against her insecurity. This phase of supervision might have similarities to personal therapy, but with the clear purpose of becoming a better therapist in the professional work. The supervisee showed her readiness to move in and out of role-playing and consciously to reflect on her own personality problems and possibilities in her clinical work. She also let herself be seduced by the music and experienced at a conscious level the effect of verbal and musical interventions. She moved through a spiral in this one session just to be ready to enter a new spiral in her process of developing her identity as a professional music therapist.

In the second example, the supervisee at level three was clear about her expertise with the patients. Her focus was the team and role confusions. She allowed herself to show both her strength and vulnerability, and the group of professionals was there to create a working frame for the supervisee to help her and the group members to provide more clarity. This is a clear example of a level three supervision, in which the work is at a peer level even if there is an identified supervisor present.

Whereas the application of music in the first example is a catalyst for breaking a resistance and starting a musical dialogue, the application of music in the second example is much more a symbolic tool that makes it possible to contact the unconscious countertransference experiences, make these conscious and find solutions.

Both cases together show the continuum approach and how IDM and the hermeneutic spiral of integrative supervision can be applied in supervision of music therapy work that is based on an analytically oriented training and how the supervisor can structure the supervision by having different foci in the work.

The two cases illustrate the theories that describe how the supervisor has to move through a continuum from having a more instruction-oriented approach to a more matter-of-fact-oriented approach to a mutual learning process approach dependent on the level of experience of the supervisee. Awareness of the triadic field is in both cases a valuable tool to deepen the process and the understanding in supervision. The movement on the continuum here is about when the supervisor moves from keeping this awareness of the triadic field as an implicit knowledge at the novice level to a more explicit joint knowledge and negotiation at level two and three.

It is my hope that more models and training courses in music therapy supervision will be developed in the future and that they will be developed for supervisee trainees across multi-training and institutional backgrounds.

References

Brown, L., Miller, M. (2002) 'The triadic inter-subjective matrix in supervision'. *International Journal of Psycho-Analysis*, 81, 273–290.

Forinash, M. (2001) *Music therapy supervision*. Philadelphia: Barcelona.

Frohne-Hagemann, I. (1999) 'Integrative supervision for music therapists' in T. Wigram and J. De Backer (eds), *Clinical applications of music therapy in developmental disability, paediatrics and neurology*. London: Jessica Kingsley.

Frohne-Hagemann, I. (2001) 'Integrative techniques in professional music therapy group supervision' in M. Forinash (ed.) *Music therapy supervision*. Philadelphia: Barcelona.

Haugaard-Jacobsen, C. (2000) Parallelprocesser i psykoterapi og supervision.

[Parallel processes in psychotherapy and supervision]. *Psyke and Logos*, 21(2), 600–630.

Pedersen, I.N. (2000) 'Inde-fra eller ude-fra – orientering i terapeutens tilstedeværelse og nærvær'. [From in-side or from out-side – the therapist's orientation in therapeutic presence and attentiveness] In: *Årsskrift 2, 2000. Musikterapi i Psykiatrien*. Musikterapiklinikken. Aalborg Universitetet/Aalborg Psykiatriske Sygehus.

Priestley, M. (1975) *Music therapy in action*. London: MMB Music Inc.

Rosbrow, T. (1993) 'Significance of the unconscious plan for psychoanalytic theory'. *Psychoanalytic Psychology*, 10(4), 515–532.

Scheiby, B. (2001) 'Forming an identity as a music psychotherapist through analytical music therapy supervision' in M. Forinash (ed.), *Music Therapy Supervision*. Philadelphia: Barcelona.

Stoltenberg, C.D., McNeill, B.W., Delworth, U. (1998) *IDM supervision: an integrated developmental model for supervisors, counsellors and therapists*. San Francisco, CA: Jossey-Bass.

Turry, A. (2001) 'Supervision in Nordoff–Robbins music therapy training programme' in M. Forinash (ed.), *Music therapy supervision*. Philadelphia: Barcelona.

Ventre, M. (2001) 'Supervision in the Bonny method of guided imagery and music' in M. Forinash (ed.), *Music therapy supervision*. Philadelphia: Barcelona.

Weymann, E. (1996) 'Supervision in der musiktherapie'. *Musiktherapeutische Umschau, 17, Heft 3/4*, 170–182.

Chapter 4

Two's company, three's a crowd

Hatred of triangulation in music therapy, and its supervision in a forensic setting

John Glyn

Introduction

This chapter looks at aspects of music therapy supervision in forensic psychiatry. I begin with some general thoughts about forensic patients and their impact on clinicians. Whilst emphasising the necessity of supervision for all those working with such patients, I also try to point to more specific difficulties that music therapists often experience and need help with. I then give two case examples of music therapy supervision to illustrate the issues raised.

The word 'forensic' means different things according to the context in which it is used; it carries powerful associations, whilst often being mis-understood. In terms of this chapter, it refers both to a category of patient and to a type of institution. Forensic patients have generally committed dangerous and violent offences, and at the same time are diagnosed as being mentally disordered, with severe mental illnesses such as paranoid schizophrenia. The forensic institutions described are secure psychiatric hospitals, 'secure' meaning that patients' freedom is highly curtailed under the most restrictive sections of the Mental Health Act, which require them to be detained in hospital until they are granted a discharge as authorised by the Home Office. Patients are under the care of a consultant forensic psychiatrist who heads a multidisciplinary team (MDT) consisting of a number of professionals from different disciplines, often including arts therapists. The task of the MDT is to monitor and assess risk and to undertake the patient's treatment; and patients are highly unlikely to be discharged without the recommendation of the consultant and MDT. Whilst music therapists may be employed in other forensic settings such as prisons or young offenders' institutions, it is in secure hospitals over the last decade or so that they have had an increasing presence.

The starting point and focus of this chapter is forensic patients, but there is much attention to how the psychopathology of patients affects pro-fessionals and the dynamics between them, in ways the professionals themselves often cannot know about. For therapists working in forensic psychiatry, the combination of mental illness, violent offending, the legal system and the custodial setting constantly impacts on clinical work. Although the ostensible task of the clinical supervisor is to think about the encounter between patient and therapist, the institution makes itself felt in every aspect of the clinical relationship. The task for the supervisor therefore involves thinking about 'how the constant dynamic interchange between patient and therapist is influenced by the presence or lack of a secure setting . . .' (Cox 1996 p. 202).

One issue that I have struggled with is the need to be aware of the tendency to relate to forensic patients as if they are much less ill than they actually are. This is partly due to the intellectual and imaginative leap required to grasp the nature and quality of psychotic modes of thinking. It is very difficult to be mindful of this when patients may superficially present as relatively undisturbed. This normalising can also be a defensive response, protecting professionals from the destructive aspects of the patients and the demoralising experience of being unable to bring about positive change. I will also argue, however, that there is something about the internal states of these patients, which in the title I describe as a 'hatred of triangulation', which affects clinicians and the institution as a whole, making it enormously difficult to operate with an alert and independent mind. An insistence on a two person view of the world and hostility to the existence of three way relationships characterises the emotional world of these very ill patients, and their unconscious aim is to do away with any evidence of the three person world.

The task of any clinical supervision is self-evidently to provide a third, outside, view of the clinical situation. However, I will look at supervision in this setting from a starting point that opposition to triangulation in these patients, and the knock-on effect this has on professionals, is a key issue that supervision needs to address. In the theoretical material and two case examples of music therapy supervision that follow, I will attempt to illustrate this.

Forensic patients: Some initial thoughts

First, a vignette from my own clinical work. A male patient had expressed an interest in doing individual music therapy. He had spent many years in a secure hospital having committed a horrific multiple manslaughter, as a young man, of people very close to him, whilst in a highly psychotic state. He had been a musician. An articulate and intelligent man, he had mostly been co-operative and pleasant during his long period in hospital. However, he showed a complete lack of remorse for what he had done, and any regret he expressed was centred on how badly these events had affected his own life. He was highly taken up with world events, particularly disasters and wars, and took in a vast amount of information every day from the news media. In our first meeting he told me the kinds of music that had been important to him, many of which corresponded to my own likes, and then started to guess about my musical interests. He did so with uncanny and unnerving accuracy. Although I did not tell him so, he gleaned that he had been right and then said triumphantly and delightedly, 'It's amazing, we're exactly the same!'

What I want to draw attention to is that when the patient said, 'we're exactly the same', he was expressing more than just a common surprise or pleasure at possible similarities between us. He believed what he said, that we were 'exactly the same'. My experience on this occasion, and often subsequently, was of being told that we *had* to be the same and that I was not permitted to possess any separate identity whatsoever. Rosenfeld (1983) referred to a symbiotic or parasitic type of relationship in which the subject appears to live inside his object. An omnipotent narcissistic phantasy held by the subject is that the object welcomes such a relationship, which then becomes idealized, and so the destructive nature of this degree of projective identification is denied.

The unconscious purpose of drawing both of us together in this way was to prevent either of us from gaining a view of his terrible offences, his massive internal devastation and his external losses. Any cleavage between us would bring him into contact with these realities, the underlying fear being that this would bring about further psychotic breakdown and the loss of his meticulously constructed normality. His interest in world events had a similar function. His discussion of these situations had a super-real quality as if he had actually witnessed these events first hand. To me it was clear that when he talked about a war, a famine or a terrorist act, he was actually describing his own ruined internal state. He projected himself so totally into these situations, however, that he was prevented from recognising these parallels. When I made any move to suggest them he would be nonplussed or irritably dismissive.

This indicated an inability, but also a defensive refusal, to operate any kind of triangulation. Britton (1989) talks about triangulation, or the 'third position', in relation to the oedipal situation. The pre-oedipal infant believes that all its needs can be magically summoned via its fantasy of omnipotently owning and controlling the mother. To develop beyond this position involves relinquishing this belief and accepting that there are creative relationships, prototypically that between the parental couple, from which the child is excluded. Once this reality is accepted, different forms of relating become possible, involving: (1) separate links to each parent; (2) being able to observe a third (i.e. parental) relationship; and (3) being observed and thought about by that couple. However, to achieve this involves the painful loss of his earlier belief that the mother is his sole possession.

The adult psychotic patient seems to relate to the world in ways that are rooted in a pre-oedipal state that defends strongly against more mature triangulation. As Morgan (2001) says, 'Accepting this link, that couples get together to make babies, is difficult: it excludes and exclusion can only be managed by attacking and destroying any representation of the parental couple, or, as in schizophrenia, by attacking all links so that nothing gets together to make anything else.' Forensic patients form a particular sub-group in that they have broken the law, usually violently, as a result of their mental illnesses. Their violent acts can be seen either as a response to an intolerable experience of something intruding into an infantile dyadic universe or as an attempt to break into an excluding couple, the law standing for a prohibiting paternal authority. Whatever has driven them to act violently, a lack of triangulation is highly evident in the types of relationships they form, including those with therapists.

Patients' avoidance of these fundamental aspects of reality can be seen in the way that clinicians are made to feel that the facts of the immediate relationship (that it aims to provide therapy, that the therapist is part of a team of professionals, and that he or she has a life in the outside world) are too hard for the patient to bear. But it is not just the therapist's external relationships that are felt to be intolerable. As with Britton's (1989) patient who shouted 'stop that fucking thinking' at her analyst, the experience of one's therapist having a separate relationship with his own mind, and so of being forced to experience a triangular relationship rather than a dyad, can feel unbearably excluding and envy-producing. The therapist is made to feel that the patient should be protected from any experience of the therapist getting together with his own thoughts.

The following vignette from my own work illustrates other characteristics of these types of patients.

A middle-aged male patient had been extremely violent in the early part of his life, but over many years in a secure hospital became an institutionalised, shuffling figure who would seemingly never hurt a fly. His psychotic belief that he was going to become a billionaire diamond merchant indicated a grandiosity far removed from the humble patient most people saw. He spent part of his individual music therapy sessions pounding heavily and monotonously on a timpani drum whilst wearing a gratified expression. At other times he could join with me in a simpler, gentler musical interaction. The drumming, however, had a vicious and punishing quality. I spent many sessions trying to think about this behaviour, sometimes managing to connect more with him but primarily aware of feeling puzzled. I was very struck one day when I asked the patient what he was thinking about when he played like this. He said:

'I am on a slave ship, full of slaves being beaten by the slave driver.'

'And which are you?' I asked.

The patient looked at me as if this was a ridiculous question. 'I'm the slave driver', he said.

In my view when the patient said 'I am the slave driver', he did not mean 'I imagine myself as the slave driver but know that I am not'. That level of symbolisation was not available to him. He meant more concretely that at such times he *became* the slave driver. This had been the source of my puzzlement, and he had had no problem in answering my question once I got round to asking it.

My patient was operating at the level of what Segal (1957) termed 'symbolic equation'. Segal highlighted the schizophrenic's drastically reduced capacity to distinguish between an original experience or person, and a substitute or symbolic representation which can stand in for the original object. Segal contrasted normal forms of symbol formation with symbolic equation, a primitive level of thinking in which '. . . the symbol *becomes* the original, and attracts the same conflicts and inhibitions as the original because of the fusion of the self and the object that comes about with pathological projective identification' (Hinshelwood 1989 p. 453). The offences committed by forensic patients nearly always demonstrate the absence of a capacity for symbolic thinking. McAlister (2002) describes these phenomena as they arise in drama therapy work with forensic patients.

With my patient there *was* a substitution, in that he was hitting the skin of a drum and not of a person, but the symbolisation was rudimentary. It would have been more sophisticated if I had felt more personally affected, because in that case the symbolisation would have served to express and communicate violent feelings towards a separate me in an alternative non-dangerous way. But in this case there was not that degree of mental separation. Instead he was caught up in an enactment in which a helpless and cowering slave part of himself had been projected into the drum and was being hit again and again by a cruel and tyrannical bully part of himself. His words, 'I am the slave driver', and 'I am on a slave ship . . .' contained no suggestion of him being *like* the slave driver or the drum being *like* a slave.

Forensic patients, music therapy and supervision

Therapists who work with patients who have acted violently, and whose concrete thinking means they have little capacity to look objectively at what they have done, expose themselves to unprocessed and highly disturbing projections. The therapist has to remain open to these projections in order to provide some kind of container for the disturbance that the patient cannot consciously experience. However, the task of disentangling the transference and countertransference dynamics from such a close-up position requires the help of a third party. From this it is clear that supervision is a '. . . *sine qua non* of all forensic therapeutic undertakings' (Cox 1996 p. 199), i.e. an absolute necessity.

As I try to point out throughout this chapter, professionals of all types who work with violent mentally ill offenders need to be aware that the index offence is in some way going to be relived in their interactions with the patient. This is a terrifying prospect, and it is worrying when professionals appear to be unconcerned about it. Both patients' and therapists' defences against this experience are understandable and indeed necessary. The therapist, in offering him- or herself as a good containing object, is in effect doing something highly provocative for a patient who cannot experience triangulation. What is opened up is the patient's inability to grapple with a three-person world, which he is confronted with by a therapist who goes away and expresses his separateness in countless ways. It is when the good object is discovered to be part of another couple that the violence erupts.

The music therapist's active participation in simultaneous improvisation with patients, in many ways a unique and helpful tool, can also lead to the patient believing that a perfect world is being offered. Just as the intrusion of reality has been the trigger for their earlier violent acts, an impingement on the sensuous experience of the music and of the therapist following closely can cause patients to feel their perfect dyad has been ripped away, which can feel intolerable. Alongside healthy instances in which patients are helped to emerge from states of deadly torpor, music therapists can also feel they are being drugged into a mind-numbing sleep by a patient's endlessly repetitive music. Similarly, for every patient who begins to show some real liveliness and creativity, there are others for whom what is awakened has a more murderous and killing-off quality. These phenomena are very frequent and have been described in a number of music therapy papers (Glyn 2002, 2003; Loth 1994; Sloboda 1996; Sloboda & Bolton 2002; Stewart 1996). Such are the types of difficulty presented through patients using the musical medium. More verbal patients sometimes refuse to use the sessions for playing music and the therapist can be made to feel that his or her couple relationship with her musical and therapeutic expertise is being attacked by a patient who cannot bear to feel left out of such a partnership.

It is naïve to put someone in a room, whether experienced or not, without thinking about what is likely to happen. If you offer an unstructured setting to such patients it can be no surprise that the index offence will be enacted in some way. Therefore, at the beginning of any such piece of work it is the task of the supervisor and therapist to think about how the index offence is likely to emerge, and what implications this has in terms of how to work and the stance that needs to be taken.

In both the cases I now present, the music therapists found themselves struggling with patients who, in very different ways, attempted to turn the therapy into a dyadic enclave in which the therapist's real therapeutic task was blocked so as to defend the patient from experiencing the presence of any kind of third position, or triangulation. As we will see, as soon as triangulation did make itself felt, there were extreme reactions in the patients. One task of supervision was to help the therapists to mentally separate themselves from clinical relationships in which they felt their thinking and observing capacities to be severely reduced as a result of the patient's need to prevent triangulation.

Supervision example 1: The perfect fit

A music therapy trainee had come on placement to a medium secure unit, and began once-weekly work with a male patient. The therapy was to cover a period of 12 weeks. The patient, Mr A, was a young man in his late twenties with a history of serious wounding with intent, and a diagnosis of paranoid schizophrenia. The onset of his mental illness had been in his mid-teens and his violence had escalated from that time onwards. His index offence involved a dangerous attack with a knife on a shoe-shop assistant who was serving him. He had delusional ideas about the man wanting to sell him the wrong pair of shoes, and a voice had told him to attack him. The patient had been withdrawn since being admitted 18 months previously, and although amenable and co-operative, had engaged very little with the treatment programme and the staff generally. People felt they did not know him, and his MDT had been unable to form a clear view of his mental state. However, staff were confident that he did not present an immediate risk of violent behaviour in the hospital. He played recorded music in his room, and was referred to music therapy in the hope that his liking of music could enable a therapeutic relationship to develop. Mr A himself had said that of all the therapies on offer, music therapy was the only one he was prepared to try.

The trainee had begun his placement enthusiastically and the setting stimulated a lot of thoughts and ideas. He tended to question the ethics of the forensic mental health system and felt that many of the patients were wrongly diagnosed and unjustly detained. Early on his supervisor found him lively and engaging, but felt the supervision sessions to be rather vague and discursive.

The trainee described his first few sessions with Mr A extremely positively; it seemed that Mr A had engaged surprisingly quickly and easily. He had shown an intuitive ability to use the instruments and to play with his therapist, which suggested a capacity to listen and to relate non-verbally. This was in contrast to the withdrawn and encapsulated presentation seen elsewhere.

It was a requirement of the training that music in the sessions should be recorded for analysis and discussion. The trainee was anxious about how Mr A would feel about this, particularly given that his supervisor had said it was the practice of the department to not let patients take recordings for their own use on the ward. The reasons for this were discussed in supervision, and the trainee seemed to have come round to the view that it was not helpful for patients to have copies.

The supervisor, on listening to the recordings, was aware of experiencing the music as empty and mechanical, with the therapist providing a keyboard backing over which Mr A superimposed repeating melodic phrases, rather as in dance tracks. The pieces were long and repetitive and had a sedating effect on the supervisor, making it difficult to gather her thoughts about the interaction. She was aware of a disparity between her response and that of her supervisee, who was enthusiastic about the music and his interaction with Mr A.

Parallel to the developing clinical relationship, the trainee became disaffected with the MDT and ward rounds. He felt that the patient was misunderstood and did not suffer from a mental illness so much as from the effects of social disadvantage, and that the hospital was, if anything, compounding his problems. He found reasons not to attend ward rounds for a number of weeks. Meanwhile, he felt that the therapy and music had the potential to turn Mr A's life around and for some weeks his commitment to Mr A became almost evangelical.

About mid-way through the placement the supervisor became aware of changes in her supervisee's view of the therapy. In one session he spoke about being uncomfortable that he had agreed to let Mr A take recordings of the music away with him, despite their earlier discussions. The supervisor had not known about this and it was presented as a guilty disclosure. He also began to talk about feeling stifled and restricted within the musical interaction. He had avoided mentioning anything about the approaching ending to Mr A despite the importance of this having been emphasised in supervision.

Alongside these changes in the trainee, the supervisor felt that her own ideas about the treatment were becoming clearer. So far she had felt herself to be a rather unwelcome presence in relation to a thriving couple, a redundant and excluded third party. Her attempts to think with her supervisee about boundary issues had made her feel like a tiresome authority figure with nothing to offer. This had the effect of preventing her from saying anything that she feared might deflate the trainee, and of undermining her conviction in herself as a helpful external figure. By recognising these as countertransference phenomena, however, she was able to get closer to a fundamental dynamic within the clinical relationship, namely a need in Mr A to pull his therapist into an exclusive type of relationship and away from his wider role. She was then able to translate this to the trainee in a way that helped him to understand the situation and approach it differently.

The trainee began to recognise that his patient had been exerting considerable pressure on him to 'renounce' his separateness and external ties. This applied to the music itself, in which he had increasingly felt he could not function independently, but had to fit in exactly with what Mr A demanded. He began to experiment with degrees of closeness within the music they played. He described how, when he attempted to be more musically separate, he experienced something bordering on panic, and quickly sought to restore the status quo. As this was now better understood by him and his supervisor, he could persevere in trying to move towards more musical separation without making Mr A feel completely lost. There were two sessions in which the trainee felt a different and more genuine contact had been made.

After seeing these things more clearly the trainee returned to the ward round and made concerted efforts to convey the work and his thoughts about it to the MDT. The team found his feedback useful and it was felt important that Mr A should be given the opportunity to pursue music therapy after this piece of clinical work had ended.

In the third-to-last scheduled session the trainee brought up with Mr A that the therapy would be ending. He felt his attempts to think about this with his patient were completely blanked and was not even sure whether the information was taken in. Strikingly, Mr A did not come for his last two sessions, on both occasions choosing to go on ground leave just before the sessions were due to start. When his therapist visited him on the ward, first encouraging him to attend his final session, and again to say goodbye, his presence was scarcely acknowledged and he was treated as if he was a stranger. The trainee was shocked and upset about this but in his last supervision was able to understand his feelings as largely the result of a massive projection into him by his patient of a devastating feeling of abandonment giving rise to a violent wiping out of any trace of him.

Discussion of example 1

The trainee would have arrived at the placement full of anxieties about the nature of the placement itself, with all its connotations of violence and madness, alongside general anxieties about his training. The situation is usually very unsettling for students, who need much containment, and supervisors often find themselves carrying a lot of anxiety on behalf of students. Having once found a patient to work with, there is then worry as to whether the patient will engage. In this instance there was a good fit between the trainee and the patient, in that the trainee could connect with Mr A through being able to understand and work with the kind of music he liked. However, there were other ways in which this superficially good fit obscured more disturbed aspects of the patient and his enactment with the therapist.

It is interesting to think about Mr A's offence in relation to what took place in the therapeutic relationship. The patient experienced somebody providing a service to him (the shoe seller) as forcing him into something that didn't fit properly. This produced murderous and catastrophic feelings, and he attacked the man. It suggests an idea and a demand for a perfect fit, standing for a perfect symbiotic coupling. This idealised relationship defended him against an opposite set of feelings, that his object could do something terrible to him, leaving him helpless and abandoned. It brings to mind the story of Cinderella: on the one hand the perfectly fitting shoe symbolises a union of everlasting fulfilment, on the other the lack of fit leads to the narcissistic rage of the unwanted ugly sisters. The shoe fitter is either a perfectly attentive partner or a dangerous object of paranoia.

The clinical relationship between Mr A and the trainee reproduced these elements. We can see how powerfully Mr A's need for an idealised perfect fit, expressed in the musical relationship by controlling his object and making him follow very closely, was projected into his therapist. When his therapist did something that signalled his separateness, Mr A reacted in a way that brings to mind Britton's (1989) outraged patient who shouted 'stop that fucking thinking', and my patient who exclaimed, 'we're exactly the same!'.

Although the trainee started off with a predisposition to question authority, this was greatly intensified through his contact with Mr A. He found himself identifying strongly with a withdrawn patient who was suspicious and hostile towards the existing structures, and he quickly began to see the team and the institution as unsympathetic, non-understanding and persecutory. His healthy questioning of the system became susceptible to a more extreme and destructive type of splitting in which all the bad qualities were thought to reside in the institution and the benign ones in the patient. This was modified with the help of a thoughtful and experienced supervisor, but the pattern is a familiar one in trainees and professionals encountering the setting for the first time, and when it persists can be highly damaging to team working.

Similarly, the issue of the recordings highlights how powerfully these patients can project their paranoid anxieties into inexperienced staff. For the trainee to record the music for his own training purposes implied a relationship with an 'other', whether another person (tutor, colleague, supervisor, etc.) or with his own thinking mind. Before even introducing the idea, he was afraid that this would provoke unbearable feelings in his patient. Any kind of observing couple is felt to be hostile and the therapist was made to feel that Mr A should not have to tolerate this kind of triangular relationship. To manage his guilt he then found himself colluding with Mr A's unrealistic alternative model of their work, that it was geared to turning him into a record producer. For a period the therapist himself spoke optimistically of this scenario in supervision.

One can see exactly why the therapist has been anxious about taking up the ending by seeing what happens when he finally does. Mr A not only appears to kill off the communication itself, but he then symbolically kills off his object by behaving as if he never existed in the first place. Upsetting as this was for the trainee, he then became able to connect with what he had previously been only half able to hear, namely the paramount importance in time-limited work of helping the patient with the ending as soon as the clinical work gets under way.

The supervisor was able to help the trainee through her awareness of parallel processes taking place within the therapeutic relationship and the supervision relationship. Essentially the same transferences were being enacted in both. In the earlier part of the work she was uncomfortably affected and to a degree controlled by these. However, as she became more aware of this she was able to use these experiences creatively and develop the trainee's understanding and his ability to work with Mr A.

Example 2: 'Completely nuts'

A patient in his early forties, Mr B, had been in secure care for many years and had a diagnosis of paranoid schizophrenia. He had a number of fixed delusions, such as being under surveillance, being a top lawyer and being fabulously wealthy. His offence had been to assault a delivery boy who was riding his bicycle, in the belief that he was observing Mr B in a threatening way. Mr B was something of a loner, superficially easy-going and friendly but also aloof and argumentative. In ward rounds he seemed to 'hold court', engaging in incomprehensible disagreements with his consultant with an air that implied that he thought everyone except him was mad. He insisted that nothing was wrong with him and that he should be discharged. He caused unease amongst his care team, particularly in relation to predatory approaches made to women he encountered in the grounds. Despite periods of engagement with the arts therapies, psychology and group psychotherapy, there had been little progress, and Mr B presented as a chronic patient, resistant to medical and psychological treatments.

During one of the frequent 'bargaining' discussions, Mr B told his consultant that he would be prepared to try individual music therapy and would like to try to compose some songs, saying that he used to be a good singer. As in many such situations, the MDT was eager to grasp any possible move towards therapeutic engagement, and although aware that this could be another false start, was keen that the music therapist attached to the team should take up the referral. She was an experienced music therapist who had been working for a number of years in this setting. Knowing a little about Mr B, she had some misgivings about the referral and the pressure she found herself under to take on the patient. The MDT did consider her reservations and thought about the risks connected to Mr B working with a female therapist. However, these were not seen to absolutely rule out the work, and they were keen to give music therapy a try. After discussing it in supervision, the therapist agreed to give Mr B an assessment. Somewhat to her dismay, he expressed enthusiasm about the assessment, and told a number of members of the treatment team how much he wanted to do music therapy. After further discussions in supervision, it was agreed that a trial period of therapy should be offered.

Mr B mainly talked in the sessions, and although he once tried to play percussion instruments, he said that he found this demeaning and childish. The music therapist tried to take forward his ideas about singing and writing words to songs, but this seemed to make him feel painfully inadequate. He did share some important memories of his childhood in a distant country, which gave a picture of an impoverished early life with traumatic losses and separations. However, the music therapist felt she was not allowed to offer any thoughts about what he said and that she was being enlisted solely as a sympathetic listener. This made her call into question whether her patient could make use of the therapy. At a conscious level Mr B came to place great importance on his sessions, spoke about them to nurses, and was always ready and waiting when the time came.

He was keen that the therapy should continue and this was seen by his team as evidence that a therapeutic engagement had been made. His therapist found it impossible to impress upon the team a very uncomfortable transference in which she felt increasingly controlled and powerless. It was discussed in supervision that her experience of team meetings, in which she felt trapped and unable to separate and think, was very similar to her experience in the sessions with Mr B.

A holiday break approached and when the therapist told Mr B that she would be taking time off he became highly inquisitive as to what she might be doing and who she would be going with, and pressed her to tell him whether she had a partner. Things became increasingly difficult, culminating in him coming for a session with a large bulging plastic bag, which he eagerly handed over to the therapist. She looked inside and saw that it was full of an assortment of nuts. He explained that it was a gift. The therapist, feeling intensely anxious, said she could not accept it and gave it back, whereupon Mr A became offended and angry. He then refused to come to sessions, but any relief was offset by his predatory and threatening behaviour outside the sessions, with the therapist noticing him virtually stalking her in the grounds and intercepting her at surprising moments.

The MDT now became aware of how the situation had developed, and concerned about the potential danger Mr B posed to the therapist. In supervision it was agreed it would be helpful for the supervisor to speak to the consultant and a meeting then took place. This led to the consultant meeting separately with the therapist and her line manager. The issues then began to be discussed more thoughtfully in ward rounds. Careful consideration was given as to how risks could be minimised and to the need to bring the work to an end in a way which felt tolerable for Mr A. Although he was deeply affronted when any of the underlying issues were raised, it was made possible for him to 'leave' the therapy. However, many weeks passed during which the therapist felt unsafe and very shaken by the entire episode. Her clinical supervision sessions throughout this period were dominated by the issue, and I will now discuss the role of clinical supervision within the overall case.

Discussion of example 2

It might seem surprising that a potentially dangerous situation such as this could occur in an institution that places so much emphasis on containment and risk reduction. But I think the case illustrates how unconscious processes can affect everyone's capacity to think clearly.

Mr B's index offence involved an attack on a young boy doing his deliveries, who was felt to be looking at him in a threatening way. But what is it that is bad about the act of 'looking' for Mr B? You could say that the problem for him originates with a positive transference. He is extremely pleased to have found someone whom he can be with, talk to and be listened to by, but the longing and need this arouses brings with it unbearable feelings. Inextricably linked with this good listening object comes the idea of a couple, and a couple from which he is excluded. In his mind the explicit couple is one involving an external sexual partner, but in fact the therapist's professional couple relationship, both with her professional identity as a music therapist and with the team, are felt to be equally intolerable. He deals with his enormous levels of envy by intrusively 'looking', placing himself in fantasy inside or between his objects in an omnipotent attempt to reverse the feelings of envy and need. Thus in the ward round he 'becomes' the consultant, surveying the other professionals from a position of superiority. This defends him against the reality of his relationship to the MDT, in which discussions about him need to take place privately. In relation to his therapist he peers into her external relationships and tries to place himself between her and any possible partner. This turns the positive transference into one full of concealed hostility, in which his object is suspected to be cheating behind his back. Unconsciously he knows that his 'looking' is aggressively intrusive, aimed at controlling and restricting his object from having any outside relationships. His index offence could then be seen as a response to a paranoid projection of his own 'dangerous' looking.

Mr B's attack on the couple is enormously disturbing and disabling for his therapist, as well as for the team. What is in effect being attacked is her internal couple (Morgan 2001) and any doubts or ambivalences she may carry become seized upon and exploited. Her difficulty in communicating with the team and getting adequate support from it are partly due to failures in the team. But it is also the result of Mr B's powerful projection into her. The intense pressure to abandon the couple relationship, centrally that between herself and the MDT, is illustrated when she is given the bag of nuts. To accept the gift would mean entering into a nutty omnipotent universe in which Mr B's need is reversed, he becomes the abundant provider for his therapist's dependency, and the fantasy ideal couple replaces the existing partnerships she belongs to. Crucially, she is able to hold on to her mind and hand back the nuts, but not without her confidence in these relationships being severely undermined and her feeling that she has done something to compromise her links to the team.

It is impossible to know what actual danger Mr B posed to the therapist, although it might have been quite substantial. But we can say that a split occurred between her and the team, and that any such split is dangerous. In my view the split involved different and opposed parts of the patient being projected into the therapist and the team respectively. The hated and unwanted parts went into her, and she was left feeling humiliated and powerless, with no voice that could be heard. The team took into itself the more defended, manic and avoiding parts. This meant that the potential of the team to provide a triangular thinking function for the clinical pair broke down.

Mr B's refusal to use the musical medium raises the need to distinguish between a patient who is showing genuine difficulties and can possibly be helped to adapt to the medium, and one who is more destructively trying to prevent the work taking place. His anxieties about feeling inadequate were such that to participate in a more ordinary way was felt to be submitting to a cruel control by the therapist. This experience of being controlled was then projected into the therapist, leaving her feeling helpless and lacking resources. It seemed that he was more actively preventing the core musical task from taking place, giving a poor indication in terms of music therapy engagement.

In supervision sessions, the therapist's feelings were communicated very powerfully to the supervisor. In such circumstances there is strong pressure to view the situation through the experience of the supervisee, and for the supervisor to be drawn into the split already described. There clearly were failures in the team to think about Mr B and all the issues arising from this episode. However, such failures are inevitable when working with patients who operate at this level of primitive projective identification, and it is impossible for anyone, supervisors included, to stand back and see things with a clear eye.

A parallel with the wider situation can easily develop within the supervision relationship, with the supervisor feeling that she ought to be able to manage the entire situation herself. This response is at least in part due to the splitting I have been describing, and the supervisor can become infected by the same kind of omnipotence seen in the patient. The assumption that the supervisor 'knows' whereas others do not leads to the type of enclave that Mr B was trying to establish with the therapist. This misconstruing of the role of clinical supervision is all the more likely in a setting in which the patients' illnesses and mental states are in reality so unknowable. At an institutional level, different treatment and theoretical models can then come into unhealthy competition through professionals defending against the shared experience of not being able to understand.

In this case, the main task was to think with the therapist about the dynamics that she was at the centre of. However, the supervisor felt that some kind of triangulation was required between the therapist and the team in order to arrive at an appropriate risk-management strategy. This meant that the core reflective and supportive functions needed to be supplemented by some ordinary and boundaried communications with relevant professionals. This thinking prompted the approach to the consultant, leading to the more effective interventions by the team. The risk factor needs to be emphasised here: if there had been no risk, the lack of triangulation would have been ordinarily unsatisfactory and frustrating. With the additional element of risk, triangulation became essential.

Implications and conclusion

Both the case examples illustrate problems that music therapists in forensic settings often encounter, and which clinical supervisors are required to help with. A problem shared by all professionals involves being in touch with the nature and extent of these patients' disturbances and how these are being enacted in their relationships with the professionals working with them. The same underlying disturbances were expressed in the offences they committed, and there are invariably correlations between what was acted out in the offence and what is enacted in the clinical relationship. These relationships are characterised by an absence of triangulation, which these patients actively defend against.

The task of anticipating how patients' offences are likely to re-emerge in the course of therapy is a particularly crucial part of music therapy supervision. It can then be possible to think about appropriate and helpful ways to work with the patient. The medium has much to offer in this setting, but its particular qualities, such as unstructured improvisation, can also be taken by patients as an invitation into an exclusive form of relating, reproducing the very things the patients need help to overcome. In the first example, it is the trainee who needs help from the supervisor to see that he has been drawn into a symbiotic dyad with a patient. In the second example, the supervisor helps to provide triangulation for a split, originating within the patient, which has developed between the music therapist and the MDT.

Acknowledgement

I would like to thank Claire Miller for her kind and invaluable help with this chapter.

References

Britton, R. (1989) 'The missing link: parental sexuality in the Oedipus complex' in R. Britton, M. Feldman and E. O'Shaughnessy (eds), *The Oedipus complex today*, London: Karnac Books.

Cox, M. (1996) 'A supervisor's view' in M. Cox and C. Cordess (eds), *Forensic psychotherapy: crime, psychodynamics and the offender patient*, London: Jessica Kingsley.

Glyn, J. (2002) 'Drummed out of mind' in A. Davies and E. Richards (eds), *Sound company: music therapy and group work*, London: Jessica Kingsley.

Glyn, J. (2003) 'New York mining disaster'. *British Journal of Music Therapy*, 17(2), 97–103.

Hinshelwood, R. (1989) *A dictionary of Kleinian thought*. London: Free Association Books.

Loth, H. (1994) 'Music therapy and forensic psychiatry: choice, denial and the law'. *Journal of British Music Therapy*, 8(2), 10—18.

McAlister, M. (2002) 'Dramatherapy and psychosis: symbol formation and dramatic distance'. *Free Associations*, 9(3), 353–370.

Morgan, D. (2001) 'The internal couple and the Oedipus complex in the development of sexual identity and sexual perversion' in C. Harding (ed.), *Sexuality: psychoanalytic perspectives*, London: Brunner-Routledge.

Rosenfeld, H. (1983) 'Primitive object relations and mechanisms'. *International Journal of Psychoanalysis*, 64, 261–267.

Segal, H. (1957) 'Notes on symbol formation'. *International Journal of Psychoanalysis*, 38, 391–397.

Sloboda, A. (1996) 'Music therapy and psychotic violence' in E. Welldon and C. van Velson (eds), *A practical guide to forensic psychotherapy*, London: Jessica Kingsley.

Sloboda, A., Bolton, R. (2002) 'Music therapy in forensic psychiatry: a case study with musical commentary' in L. Bunt and S. Hoskyns (eds), *The Handbook of Music Therapy*, London: Routledge.

Stewart, D. (1996) 'Chaos, noise and a wall of silence: working with primitive affects in psychodynamic music therapy'. *British Journal of Music Therapy*, 10(2), 21–33.

Chapter 5

Getting better: some thoughts on the growth of the therapist

David John

Introduction

Bion remarked that '. . . there is a great deal to be said for being an analyst – provided of course that one can learn how to be a better one' (Bion 1994 p. 58). From a vantage point of working for over 20 years in a psychiatric facility in the NHS and as a psychotherapist in private practice, it seems to me that there is a clearly observable developmental process in one's students and junior colleagues as they seem to get stronger and more confident in their work. There is, too, although perhaps less objectively experienced, a noticeable enhancement of something in oneself as one's relationship with the work deepens. My conjecture is that it is possible for a therapist to continue 'getting better' throughout their working life, and to work more effectively as a result. Although externally we might observe more confidence in the practitioner and an enhanced sense of personal integrity generally in relation to the work, it is strikingly difficult to define the development. This, I feel, stems from the fact that the development is largely unconscious.

In this chapter I want to focus on the development of the therapist as a feature of the therapeutic worker's personality. I acknowledge that this is very closely allied to the development of the personality in general; but it is not simply the development of a person that is involved in the development of the therapist; there is also something else. My concern here is with formulating a way of saying something about what the therapist's development actually is. Because much of the therapist's development seems to be unconscious, I find that a theory that considers the relationship between unconscious and conscious contents and processes is appropriate for any exploration of it; furthermore, as one's best subject for enquiry into the private regions of a therapist's development is indeed oneself, a degree of self-reflection is a required tool. In essence, one might say that the therapist's growth is a facet of the enhancement of his or her sanity or, in other terms, an improved interface between conscious and unconscious parts of their mind. Although 'the sanity interface' receives much less attention than pathology in psychological work, a theory that embraces and thinks about the healthy rather than the problematical functioning of the mind is needed to explore it.

I am going to use the container/contained model provided by Bion to explore aspects of the therapist's development and will outline 'alpha' function as a special feature of container/contained. I will also touch on how the model might be relevant to our understanding of the work of supervision. In addition, I will briefly comment on the capacity to create the therapeutic setting of participant observer as a provision related to Winnicott's concept of holding, and relate this to elements of the container/contained (Bion 1962; Winnicott 1960). Because these capacities of personality become illuminated in the specific context of a therapy, I will start by considering the beginning of their application by looking at the importance of acquiring the identity of therapist.

My focus, although broad and hopefully generally applicable, stems from an immersion in psychoanalytic practice as both a psychoanalytic psychotherapist and music therapist. I see music therapists as therapists first and foremost. By focusing on the development of the 'therapist' part of the title (apart from being an interesting thing to consider in itself), I hope to contribute something to the thinking about training and about supervision.

The identity of the therapist

I am assuming that if all goes well the learning to be a 'better' therapist is something that can continue until retirement or until we find jobs as something else. I am talking about a function within the personality and it becomes quite a challenge to isolate this function. I would say that the function exists as a feature of an ordinary developing personality but becomes applied and shaped specifically when allied to the individual's *identity* of being and working as a therapist. In selecting candidates for training there must be some scanning for this ordinary function, which, when boiled down, is probably a capacity for receptivity and emotional empathy allied to a good degree of natural warmth and intelligence. The assessors also need to see a quality of self-awareness; in fact, self-awareness is often felt to be the most reassuring aspect of a candidate's personality when meeting someone who may be impressive musically or intellectually.

Basic training in music therapy is often the first opportunity for a trainee to begin to embody the term 'therapist' and form it as part of their work identity. I feel strongly that a therapist's identity is quite a personal matter and that it can develop only if she has worked as a therapist in a way that has really *made sense to her*. In the beginning, therefore, supervised placements have a central role in the development of the therapist. It is the clinical setting that affords the opportunity for students to have the necessary experiences for the term 'therapist' to start to become meaningful for them; for each of them to start to make a relationship with the therapist function of their personalities. This process often involves a shift in identity; in music therapy it is often the case that to someone's identity as a musician a new identity of therapist is added (Richards 2008).

Music therapy students come to training with music usually as a very meaningful and rich aspect of their lives. Their identity and skills as musicians can lend a lot of confidence to their sense of having something to contribute in a clinical setting. A facility with music is such a visible skill that it places the music therapy trainee on placement in an institution in a position of having a practical, observable 'something' to contribute to patients' lives. Other staff might well respond positively to these active musicians based on their own appreciation of the value of music. Sometimes I feel students of other disciplines, even other arts therapies students who come on placement, do not have such an easily imagined 'something' to give, to apply and to use. Interestingly, as a result of not having it, issues around their identity as therapists can become all the more urgent to them. This may be one of the reasons why the terms 'art psychotherapist' and now 'movement psychotherapist' are more established in the vocabulary than 'music psychotherapist'. Is it that the visible skill of music making interferes with or is seen as a suitable alternative to the development of the therapist function? Do music therapists put the music before the therapist in their identities? And if they do what are they not developing in themselves?

It might be that the musical skills and identity of musician are a safe haven of identity – a shelter from the more exposed and challenging landscape of learning to enhance the therapist function in the self. We know in our bones that a music therapist cannot develop by simply enhancing their interactive musical skills or by learning about patients' problems in isolation; the therapist function of the self is more than sensitive musical responsiveness allied to some understanding of psychopathology. So to become a music therapist, the therapist's identity and function have to evolve together.

In most psychological therapies, a therapist is someone who functions psychologically *on behalf* of someone else. This functioning, if effective, can maximise the conditions for an aspect of psychological growth to take place in the inner world of the patient. This is similar to a mother who can only function as a mother in relation to a baby: one can only function as a therapist when one is working in an emotionally alive relation to a patient. So a therapist has to *function* as a therapist. 'Therapist' is not a name for a person, it is a term used to describe a function which that person performs on behalf of someone else. To be a therapist, one has to function as a therapist for at least some and hopefully for all our cases; and if not all the time, then hopefully some of the time, or at least enough of the time to make it worthwhile for all concerned.

If the training institution is suitably confident in the student's identity and functioning as a therapist, the term 'therapist' is conferred on the student by the training. The gathering-in of meaning to the term 'therapist' over our working lives and over time is likely to be unique to the individual, but there might well be common themes. Bion elegantly says 'Development is not in itself an object that can be "desired"' (Bion 1970 p. 79). We have not developed as therapists simply out of a desire to develop as a therapist. We accept in our students that the wish to be a therapist is a reasonable wish but we are suspicious of someone who really, really wants to be one. We all recognise that we cannot become a therapist overnight; we have to grow into one and, hopefully, if all is going well we continue to develop. It is this sense of the development of the therapist over time that makes us suspicious if there is too much desire for it. We might, however anxiously, seize the identity of therapist and here I think lies the first pitfall in development, which is the assumption of the identity before the function of therapist is effective. Everyone knows that to parody a therapist all we have to do is incline our heads and say in a slow concerned way 'and how does that make you feel?' This parody, although humorous, is actually saying something important about how it feels to be on the receiving end of someone whose identity of therapist is overriding their function of therapist. The position of therapist is adopted but without the functioning to go with it. In essence it is a therapist's false self that is experienced by the patient as either something to comply with or get away from.

Developing as a real therapist therefore involves many processes, most of which are to do with finding and mobilising personality functions that have been there anyway, shaping personality elements for use as therapeutic tools. The crucial aspect of Bion's statement is 'learning to be a better one'; this implies learning from one's experiences, which crucially means being constantly open to new information, whilst at the same time not being too overwhelmed or confused. I believe that the development of the mental functions that are applied when working as a therapist is fundamentally connected to an individual's capacity to learn from his or her emotional experience in (and out of) the consulting room. This is especially noticeable in psychoanalytically orientated work because the psychoanalytic space is one that seeks to create maximum conditions for reflective contemplation, together with the experiencing of feelings and associated ideas provoked by the transference relationship.

In psychoanalytic work, because of the focus on relationship as transference, the psychoanalytically oriented music therapist is presented in particular with the challenge of using personality experiences as material for observation and therapeutic use. The musical interaction adds a high degree of intersubjective experiencing, which puts extra pressure on the therapist's interpersonal interpretative skills. The concept of countertransference becomes relevant to the interpretation of subjectively experienced emotional states as part of interpsychic relating. In general, psychoanalytic music therapy differs from any music therapy work where transference interpretation is not considered to be the mutative component of the task and where countertransference may have no relevance.

The therapist's functions

One of the fundamental and most important abilities of a therapist is the capacity to provide a setting that the patient can use. As part of the setting, the personality of the therapist is also offered for use, in specific application to the patient's needs. Therapists have to have a working model of how they work and of how the patient can be helped to use the work. Therapists must also be able to create a usable space where this work can happen and where participation and observation are both possible. They need to be able to create an atmosphere that promotes work, whilst keeping levels of anxiety bearable. I describe this important thing as 'creating the stance' – this is the appropriate position (physically and psychically) for therapists in relation to their patients. The concept of 'stance' is allied to the capacity to create and maintain a therapeutic environment over time. The stance is crucial – it is the emotional position we inhabit when we do the work of being a therapist, and it is closely related in my mind to Winnicott's idea of holding – holding the self, the mood, the illusions, the state of the patient, as well as holding the patient's need for relating through various means (Winnicott 1960). As emphasised by Winnicott, time is a central component of holding – we hold patients in a process that, hopefully, allows for an unfreezing of their growth potential.

The stance, then, is the provision of a setting that allows for participation, observation and psychological work. Through establishing the stance, therapists must also be able to psychologically experience their patients and allow mental freedom to exist. They must also have faith in the process and possess the courage of their convictions. In essence, therapists must allow themselves to become a working psychological space for the patients to come into and use. This other function, which is an important element of 'the stance' is what Bion terms the container/contained. The theory of containment places the emotional relationship between the therapy participants at the centre of the work. Bion's work developed Klein's idea of projective identification, but rather than focus on the defensive use of projective identification, Bion emphasised containment as a function that transforms projected experience into coherent thought and which is a normal part of maternal function (Bion 1962; Klein 1952). His particular emphasis was based on the idea of an innate expectation of a container in the human condition – an inborn *a priori* notion of an organising principle. Projective mechanisms can thus be seen as forms of primitive communication and it is essential that the mechanism of communicative projective identification is available to the infant.

The helpful part for my purposes here is the question of the nature of the container. This is the way we think, not only *what* we think but the *way* we think and process experience. What kind of experience does the individual have when it meets its object's container function? Is it, for example, a receptive container capable of reverie and transformation or is it a claustrophobic container afraid of ingress, or a kind of string bag where things go in but dribble away without much digestion? Is it a dogmatic container stuffed with presuppositions, or perhaps an intuitive receptive container but without courage? The quality of the container and the nature of what goes into it are related directly to notions around what occurs psychically when we are both able and unable to do psychological work with our experience, and thus has great relevance to the functioning on behalf of someone else that therapists provide. Important questions are: how successfully do we think when we work? What creates discovery, growth and a sense of change? What creates blocks, impasse or false understanding and a sense of what may be termed 'stuck knowing'?

The British independent analyst Nina Coltart helpfully quotes Kant, who said 'Concept without intuition is empty, intuition without concept is blind' (Coltart 1992 p. 5; Kant 1781). Her view (and Bion's) is that there must be an optimal arrangement in the therapist's thinking where thoughts are capable of holding both concepts and facts of experience gathered from intuition. Concept could be seen as our theoretical underpinning – whether it be psychoanalytic theory or a theory of creativity, gestalt, developmental theory, Nordoff–Robbins rating scales, philosophical ideas or a combination of any one or several of these, in addition to many other theoretical constructions. The conceptualisation of what is going on in theoretical terms is very closely related to our conscious processes. It evokes the idea of one's first thoughts rather than second thoughts. Concept is what comes to mind when our intelligence is given free rein to comment. It is present in what we say to colleagues when we have to describe our work and when we think about and make lists of therapeutic aims. It is the mental function we use when we need to publish our thoughts for others to understand; this includes making our interpretations to our patients. Concept is essential and involves finding a set of conceptual tools, some of which might be highly abstract, which help us to think and express in words our understanding of the therapeutic processes. This is also especially important in our communication with ourselves. For the psychoanalytic practitioner, the psychoanalytic theories that are understood and used are many and varied, and find their application differently with different patients. Such theories, once understood, can be represented in shorthand, for example, merger, separateness, denial, projection, destructive narcissism, healthy narcissism, separation anxiety, annihilation anxiety, oedipal issues, regression, etc. To me, the value of psychoanalytic theories is their breadth and depth; I would say they are broader and deeper than any other set of therapeutic theories.

Intuition is a different matter. In *Attention and Interpretation*, Bion (1970) compares psychoanalysis with medicine and suggests that intuiting is as a good a word as any to parallel the physician's use of his senses. Stitzman (2004), in a recent paper, described intuition as '. . . the sensory function destined to register the emotional transformations that another mind accomplishes' and suggests it is 'unconscious and involuntary'. Emotional transformations can be couched in various forms, art-making being a principal example, and therefore intuition is applicable to any means of communicating. Music therapists will intuit their patients' affects in and out of the music; it is the sense that is used to hear the music behind the words and the emotions behind the music. We also importantly intuit the non-expressed, or more accurately that which is not felt but defended against; we may sense that something is there but is not forming part of the patient's outward expression. We may intuit that the emotional state evoked in ourselves has something to do with the patient's projective use of us. We intuit the patient's need for us to be a certain way – responsive, waiting, challenging, for example – and we use intuition to decide whether it is a need or a desire. I think intuition forms an essential part of the container/ contained because it involves the idea of real receptivity – an emotional state that is open to the other with a capacity to take in without too much anxiety and without saturation as a defence (i.e. without filling the experience with instant 'off the peg' understanding).

I feel that theory should be understood on a deep emotional level but not applied to a patient directly; it should be allowed to dance around one's mind freely. The more the theory is understood, the more freely it can dance. There are certain conditions that, according to Bion, promote the functioning of intuition and its hopefully dance-like relationship with concept. He advocates a certain negative capability, which is expressed in his famous maxim in which he suggests the ideal state of mind for a therapist is to be 'without memory or desire or understanding.' (Bion 1970 p. 41) The idea of negative capability comes from Keats, who commented on Shakespeare as 'a man of achievement' in a letter to his brother (Bion 1970 p. 125). To Keats, Shakespeare was able to induce a condition of mind where one can '. . . remain in doubt uncertain without an irritating reaching after certainty or fact' (Bion 1970 p. 125). This negative capability, this state of tolerating doubt and being receptive to intersubjective experience with our patients, is a vitally important function of the therapist's mind. However, it must be wedded to the function of conceptualising, otherwise it remains blind. Concept must not fill the open space needed for intuiting the psychological state of the patient in such a way as to saturate that space with conceptualisations. Bion referred to an unsaturated preconception waiting to mate with a realization – a kind of mental space which is both receptive and not full but which has some shape. T.S. Eliot, in *Little Gidding* (Eliot 1943), seems to be referring to such a thing when he describes 'an empty husk of meaning from which the purpose will break if it breaks at all'. This is not a concept looking for a bit of a patient to fill it, as in a diagnostic medical interview or in the mind of the therapist who finds patients to fit her theories; this a receptive space with form, which will be able to make some sense of the emotions and ideas that come into it.

However, this openness is likely to take one into the area with the patient where emotional turbulence is greatest, and the open, intuitive functions of the therapist mean that the therapist's conjectures are often based on minimal sensory experience and can therefore feel unjustifiable. It is for these reasons that courage and faith become important parts of the therapist's armoury; these aspects in particular are only likely to develop after a lot of experience in trusting thoughts that might seem wild or unbidden.

In parallel with concept and intuition, the container and contained can be seen as distinct personality factors that reflect the separation between thoughts and thinking. The container (conscious and unconscious thinking) is the mental function that works on thoughts and feelings so as to digest them like a mental digestive tract. It is a continuous process related to dreaming and a capacity for reverie, and negative capability is central to its healthy working. The contained (preconscious, conscious and unconscious) is also not static but is, in health, expanding and changing. Essentially, it is the thoughts and feelings that are continuously being derived from lived experience that are formed and given meaning by the functions of the container.

We could say in a nutshell that psychoanalytically oriented therapy aims for an expansion in both container and contained for the patient – the patient's thoughts and feelings are encompassed and the encompassing processes that deal with them are enhanced. This expansion is in relation to the therapist's provision of the appropriate setting and their personal capacity for relationship. The therapist uses their own conceptual and intuitive functions to engage and understand the patient and share this understanding with them.

Example

A music therapy student on placement was working with an elderly patient in her 90s in the later stages of Alzheimer's disease. The student's musical playing was sensitive and empathic. Her manner was fine and appropriate as she seemed to know just how close to be to her patient without overwhelming her. Unfortunately, she was thrown into an encounter with a visiting senior manager in the coffee room who asked her how music therapy worked. She was struck dumb and mumbled something about communication, leaving the manager troubled by her lack of understanding of what she was doing. Her empathic meeting of the patient was great and hugely valuable but it was not linked to a theory of why she was doing what she was doing. She also, in an important way, lacked the courage of her convictions.

Example

Some of these thoughts about the therapist's relationship to theory can be illustrated in this traditional Zen story. A professor of philosophy decided one day to learn about Zen. He went off to a local Zen master and introduced himself: 'I am a professor of philosophy who has made a study of world religions and I want to learn about Zen, what can you tell me?' The Zen master smiled and said, 'Have some tea'. He then proceeded to pour the tea and kept pouring – the tea overflowed and went everywhere. The professor exclaimed 'Look, it's full, can't you see it's full?!' The Zen master smiled and said 'I can get no more tea in – first you must empty the cup.'

Supervision as container

The container/contained model puts the focus on the intersubjective field of play between the therapist and patient. It seems that some experiences in and out of the consulting room activate and contribute to the therapist inside us, whereas others interfere with or disrupt the working of the therapist inside. Put another way, we might say that some experiences enhance our capacity to contain our thoughts and feelings about some aspect of our work – we feel there's flow, and we develop our conceptual or intuitive skills or both – and some experiences put our containers under severe overload so our intuition suffers and conceptually we cannot think. This latter state of affairs occurs frequently in sessions with more disturbed patients or where the projective use of the therapist is very strong. We do, under normal conditions, accept the discomfort of difficulty with thinking as part of the work. In fact, interference in our feeling of flow and understanding is always part of any development of new understanding, but sometimes the interference can be a real problem, resulting in states of painful and chronic mental indigestion that are often defended against.

I find Bion's theory of alpha function and beta elements helpful conceptually when thinking about these phenomena. They are only concepts about real things, not real things themselves, but nevertheless are sufficiently abstract to afford a high degree of mental mobility; this I believe was one of Bion's design features (Bion 1962). Alpha function is Bion's term for the mental function involved in making sense of what we take in through our senses – including an intuitive sense. It is sponsored and enhanced by the containing function of an external object. Essentially, if therapists are able to contain their emotional experiences and, through reflective understanding, 'alpha-ise' them into something meaningful for the patient, then over time the patient's alpha function will be sponsored. A capacity for reverie is necessary to maximise alpha function, and the hallmark of reverie is receptivity. In therapy there needs to be a willingness to take in the patient's communications, whether in the formed arena of meaningful sentences, organised patterns of sound, and visual images or in the less formed projective arena of disorganised speech, noises, gestures, disorganised patterns of sound, marks on paper, and so on.

Alpha function generates alpha elements, which are pieces of mental stuff that can be thought about. Bion terms the pieces of mental stuff that cannot be thought about 'beta' elements, because they cannot be processed (alpha-ised). These are fit only for evacuation out of the mind in unconscious projective phantasies. Here Bion is suggesting that an emotional experience has to be processed before it can be used. If a series of visual elements occur in a dream, for example, it is likely that they could lend themselves through association to a realization of something about one's emotional state of mind. In other words, they can be used for further alpha function during self-reflection. The visual element is an alpha element and is some piece of our experience that has been subject to alpha function, hence its appearance in the dream. Let us say instead that the dreamer wakes and goes to the toilet, or has indigestion, or gets a headache while asleep. It might be that alpha function has failed and the undreamt stuff (beta elements) has to be evacuated in urine, or into the head or stomach.

The indigestion here is a graphic portrayal of a failure to mentally digest something through dreaming. Contrary to popular psychology, the dreamer does not acquire indigestion because he had a dream; he gets it because he has not. To Bion, then, dreaming and reverie (which could be seen as kinds of more consciously involved dreaming), are intimately related to alpha function. To Freud, a dream was an expression of a disguised wish – an attempt to conceal yet reveal; to Bion, a dream attempts to synthesize mental elements of the mind. Here we have an idea of mental content that can be subjected to thought processes and mental content that cannot. The idea that there is something in the mind that cannot be thought about and digested but can only be treated as something to be got rid of, is very important. Whereas according to Freud, something is repressed, suppressed or censored and is attempting to bubble up into consciousness, here we have something mental that can only become a thought if the environmental conditions internally (and externally) are conducive to thought. An analogy with digestion would say: 'is this mental stuff food for thought or is it an indigestible lump that causes the gut to go wrong and try to expel it, or worse, to become seriously incapacitated in its functioning?' Importantly, only some conditions are conducive to thought. It is not possible to be a superhuman therapist who can think no matter what; something that can lend itself to thinking has to come from the patient. This does not always happen, and I feel it is reassuring to realise that there is such a thing as an impossible situation.

Beta elements are the stuff of the impossible situation. Something is wrong, the patient complains of *it* - there is always lots of *it* around, rather than *I*. In music therapy, the instruments could be treated as noise-making objects or the music could have a meaningless and empty feel to it. The therapist would find himself overwhelmed or uncreative and possibly bored. This is an unpleasant stuck state in which thoughts have little mobility; mostly there is a feeling of wanting to get away. In more severe cases of schizophrenia there might be fragmented, splintered, incomprehensible material like bits of a picture; things sensed and remembered but not made up into a whole picture or story, or put together in such a way as to be incomprehensible. This state might be an indescribable depression or feeling of dread or deadness, or there might be a 'so what' feeling to what is said, as if the patient's expressions lack authentic emotion, or it might be a 'tale told by an idiot, full of sound and fury, signifying nothing.' The general theme is of non-evocative communication accompanied by severe narcissistic traits where the patient relates to space either as if the therapist does not exist or as if the patient him- or herself is too vulnerable to exist.

Alpha function lends a subjective quality to expression; there is lots of *I* and the communications are provoking of thought and reflective engagement in the other. The content is more rich and involving, perhaps more metaphorical with evocative images. In therapy, the atmosphere is feeling-toned and moving, and the therapist is free to think and let the mind float a little. In music therapy, the music will be more moving and involving and space will feel more shared. By contrast, beta elements are dealt with through evacuation, so the effect on the other is quite marked. Beta elements provoke emotional responses but without a quality of engagement. One is provoked to feel things like rage, frustration, confusion, coldness, fear, tiredness, disengagement; and it is hard to think reflectively. There is a pressure to act and to evade, and one's mind can feel overwhelmed or saturated, as if a mental space needed for reflection is closed down. The psychological means of achieving this evacuation and evasion is through projective identification. This is an unconscious fantasy, so it happens mentally but the mind might team up with bodily functions to achieve evacuation. The physical functions of breathing, facial expression and digestive functions can all be used in the service of getting rid of beta elements. Sighing, yawning, grimacing, vomiting, diarrhoea, urinating, and other means of 'discharge' such as swearing, shouting and most of all moods that seem to powerfully inject feelings into one, can be used as evacuation functions. Bion's laboratory was the consulting room and it is here that he made his discoveries about how minds interact, and it is in the consulting room that alpha elements and beta processes become understandable in terms of their status as growth potential or non growth products.

Example

Mrs A had been working with J for some time. He was a very quiet and withheld young man and she felt it was hard to get to know him. When he played music he became loud and dominating and Mrs A often felt bullied and controlled by him. To her, his playing seemed mostly superficial and verging on noise making. Mrs A was struck by the asymmetry J insisted on: it was impossible to talk together or play together. She realised that something important was being communicated by her feeling that she was always put in the 'not related to' position. She stayed with the feeling of the projection and realised that J was showing her how it felt to be cut off from and bullied and helpless. Mrs A began to think that J was bullying the communicative side of his personality in a similar way; only when she was able to interpret to J his use of her in this way did things begin to shift.

Example

Mr T was working with a patient who was obviously finding it very hard to think. She had been seeing him for many years and Mr T felt that she was emptying her mind because there was invariably a feeling of blandness, confusion and disorientation in him in the sessions. Any thoughts he had seemed easily arrived at and a bit 'off pat' with little emotional depth. Some evasion was going on and the relationship lacked emotionality but he had no idea how the patient was doing it. His supervisor pointed out that he said 'I don't know' a lot in his supervision sessions, then suddenly with something that Bion calls a flash of the obvious he noticed that his patient said 'I don't know' almost every other sentence, and had been saying 'I don't know' for years. Mr T offered the patient his thought that her use of 'I don't know' was a technique she relied on to evacuate a build-up of uncomfortable feeling in her mind in the session. She was very cross, but did stop saying it. As a result, Mr T noticed a clearer sense of the discomfort that she struggles with – mostly around feelings of intense shame; but there is feeling of relief and sincerity too that getting more in touch with herself brings.

Alpha function is the container at work; it allows space for reflection, and there is a feeling of collaboration, of working together, and of letting the mind become visible. There is some feeling of wanting to know and to understand in both participants. Exploration can only really go on when alpha function is present in sufficient quantity and when some state of reverie can be maintained in patient and therapist. Problems in the therapist function appear most acutely when there is a prevalence of beta elements; usually a severe degree of anxiety in the situation that is possibly not felt consciously. The anxiety is inside the therapist and might be stimulated by the patient's projections or by the therapist's projections into the patient.

If the problem within the therapy process is more of a conceptual one, we might get help by simply reading something that helps us think theoretically about the patient in order to fit some aspect of them into a pre-existing pattern of ideas. However, the problem is most likely to be more inter-subjective and extremely related to the way the patient gets into the therapist. Patients inevitably try to impose their view of things on the setting, and use psychological force to maintain that view. In psychoanalytic work they are actually encouraged to impose their view so that it can be inter-preted. Hopefully, after a certain time when the patient has been affected by the therapist's own psychological pressure in the form of understanding, an alliance is formed and work proceeds. This feeling of being dominated by the patient can happen to students and 'experienced' therapists alike when we are faced with a particularly challenging phase with a patient, or an organisational pressure, or something in our personal lives. It all sounds like a perfectly normal part of being a therapist and hopefully can be encompassed into our understanding. Supervision can help the student gain insight into this process.

Being unsettled by the patient psychically is an occupational hazard, and very much a feature of working with narcissistic disorders where the patient has not yet acquired separation from an object. It is essential, as therapists, to retrieve a sense of self, and to not actually become destroyed. However, sometimes we remain destroyed and react by developing a therapist's false self in which we try to interpret or 'play our way' out of trouble. Reaching prematurely for a conceptual understanding is quite likely to help us feel better when the feeling of being destroyed is unbearable. This classic defence is one where we pretend to be a therapist when we are not really functioning as one. The reason we are not able to function as a therapist is because in this mental state our preconceptions are saturated and blocked and we are not holding the patient or containing our own anxieties.

Hopefully this is temporary and normal service is resumed, but in some cases the pretending is established as the mode of being a therapist. The patient is then subjected to a pseudo-maturity in the therapist and might react by unconsciously (or consciously) supporting the therapist in this idea of being a good therapist. This can feel very comfortable for both parti-cipants as it can wander easily into an illusion of ideal harmonization together. In this state, intuition is permanently blocked and not properly used and, I think, constitutes burnout in the 'experienced' therapist. As mentioned previously, this state can vary from patient to patient but I think it is something to watch out for through the supervision process. This is particularly the case for students because the anxiety that drives this state might be higher for them given other pressures on their containers, such as being assessed and other complex pressures in the training course that they have to juggle. It is important to recognise in student supervision that students might not yet have sufficient experience to learn the valuable lessons of waiting and holding in time. The pressure to get results to show in a presentation or in supervision is absolute 'death' to the processes I am trying to describe – the delicate balancing act between intuition and concept. The loss of the mental space between memory and desire where intuition is most sensitive can prevent the student from engaging with and sustaining the therapeutic process for the patient. Melanie Klein was once supervising a therapist who stated that the patient was projecting their confusion into her, to which Mrs Klein replied 'My dear, *you* are confused'.

Example

An acute music therapy group in a psychiatric unit began with an attractive female patient rather tartly stating that it made her feel that she was back in school. The male therapist felt rejected and devalued and reassured her that her participation was not mandatory. The patient withdrew sulkily and an opportunity to explore feelings of shame and humiliation in the group was lost. The group trundled on in a lifeless way and ended eventually, to the relief of all concerned.

Example

An acute music therapy group began with an attractive male patient making a joke about being back at school and the group laughed – the female therapist noticed herself feeling rejected and devalued but considered that these feelings were being activated in her by the group. She remained thoughtful and later explored with the group feelings of humiliation and shame in relation to their present experience. An animated conversation ensued, followed by a thoughtful improvisation. The group ended with feelings of appreciation in the air.

It is important to acknowledge when the problem is in the patient and when it is in the therapist (or both!). This can often be central to the supervisory work. When the atmosphere in a supervision session is indicative of a preponderance of beta elements it is vital to try to discern how much of the problem is with the therapist. The intersubjective field of the work makes careful examination of such things very challenging. In fact, I believe it is the single most challenging aspect of working as a therapist, and this means that the relationship between personal/self-analysis and supervision is very close. This can mean that the supervisor helps the developing therapist think about the uses of personal therapy and supervision, and encourages the supervisee to make connections with his or her personal material and the work with the patient, some aspects of which might need to be explored further elsewhere in personal therapy.

Countless observations of students and newly qualified music therapists have afforded an opportunity to witness the therapist-function in the personality developing strikingly over time. There is obviously a process in each individual where the function of therapist develops in conjunction with that person's identity as therapist. Personal analysis is essential in psychoanalytic work and is acknowledged as important in some music therapy trainings. From my perspective, therapists who use their emotional reactions to their patients as information about the patients will probably benefit from some personal analysis. In my view, psychoanalysis in its current evolution is the method *par excellence* for an encounter with oneself. It is interesting, however, that psychoanalysis has given to the world *two* new relationships: patient–therapist and supervisor–therapist. Neither of these relationships existed before psychoanalysis; it is as if once the psychoanalytic relationship between patient and analyst came into being there was then a need for the other relationship of analyst and supervisor. The need for the other relationship is obvious, and in essence it is because the unconscious really *is* unconscious.

Psychoanalysis is geared towards the interpretation of unconscious processes, and resistance is identified as a naturally occurring obstacle to the task. This resistance is variously conceived as operating as censorship, repression, narcissistic or schizoid strategies, the repetition compulsion and transference itself. It was recognised, too, that the practitioner also has an unconscious, which, despite personal analysis and experience, might still interfere with the task, especially if the analyst's own resistances are stimulated by the patient's material. The term 'experience near' has been coined for such correspondence between the patient's and the analyst's preconscious and unconscious issues.

Clinical supervision exists as a recognition of the value of a third party whose role is rather complex (see Chapter 4). Supervisors may add theoretical components to the work, which might help the therapist put the patient in a context by seeing where the experience fits into some other pattern of thought. They might also help the therapist bear and understand the intersubjective components of their relationship with the patient. Whether music therapists aim to be transference objects for their patients or not, there is always scope in supervision to look at the intersubjective part of the patient–therapist dynamic. This goes on not only in the contribution of conceptual understandings but also through the provision of an intersubjective relationship in which therapists can be both psychologically held and contained by their supervisor and their setting. My theory is that supervision, when working well, promotes the growth of the therapist's function in the personality. Supervision facilitates an expansion in the inner world of the therapist, of the capacity for both concept and intuition. In this way, returning to Bion, the therapist's alpha function can be promoted by supervision that is meaningful to the therapist. Also, as therapists develop they begin to trust their own capacity to respond spontaneously to patients and can tolerate the pain of negative capability. This confidence is the sign that a personal container has developed for use in therapy.

Conclusion

To Bion, psychoanalysis before Freud was a thought waiting for a thinker, Freud was the first practical thinker of psychoanalysis and I would say therapists who place a value on intuitively sensing the non-conscious parts of the patient and who make use of psychoanalytic concepts of projection and transference are working in that tradition.

The container/contained relationship in the mind and the capacity for alpha function are central to the natural processes of growth that exist potentially in each of us. Bion spoke of the psychoanalytic function of the personality and suggests that the human personality is constitutionally equipped with the potential for a set of mental operations that serves the function of doing truthful conscious and unconscious psychological work on emotional experiences (a process that issues in psychic growth). By calling it psychoanalytic he is indicating that this psychological work is achieved through the kind of thinking that is definitive of psychoanalysis – this is thinking that views experience from conscious and unconscious positions simultaneously, thinking that is tolerant of doubt and thinking that has a certain faith in the capacity for the mind to grow. It is thinking that makes use of concept and intuition. Dreaming and art-making are creative processes that can very strongly manifest this capacity of mind – the 'dreaming with the patient while awake' experience of working in music therapy puts us slap bang in the middle of the space where we view our experience consciously (conceptually) and unconsciously (intuitively) simultaneously. Music therapists, probably through their own personal use of music for shaping and regulating their own emotions, are well placed to respond intuitively to the emotional aspects and expressions of their patients, and indeed it is impressive how music therapy trainees often seem able to engage their patients on this emotional level. However, to work as a therapist the music therapist must be able to reflect on what the emotional transaction is about; this means having some idea of how the patient is using the mind of the therapist and what the patient is using it for. To understand the relationship and, if appropriate, to express or interpret the relationship to the patient, therapists need to link their thoughts to their emotions and to form the realisations into something that makes sense conceptually. They need to find and use a set of concepts that make sense to them and which act like a map that helps them orientate to the patient's inner world as it manifests in the relationship. However, the concepts must never saturate their mental space so as to create a mass of presuppositions into which the patient is squeezed. The relationship between concept and intuition is a subtle but strong one and, when working well in the mind of the therapist, it holds the patient in a therapeutic process; when blocked or malfunctioning, the therapy suffers and so does the therapist. The optimising of the dynamic relation between concept and intuition is the hallmark of the evolving therapist, the therapist's reflective processes, which, if held in the right dynamic tension, become the single most potent factor in the healthy working of the therapist functioning on behalf of their patient.

References

Bion, W. (1962) *Learning from experience*. London: William Heinemann, reprinted London: Karnac, 1984.

Bion, W. (1970) *Attention and interpretation*, London: Tavistock Publications, reprinted London: Karnac, 1984.

Bion, W. (1994) *Clinical seminars and four papers*. London: Karnac.

Coltart, N. (1992) *Further psychoanalytic explorations*. London: Free Association Books.

Eliot, T.S. (1943) 'Little Gidding' in T.S. Eliot *Four Quartets*, London: Faber.

Kant, I. (1781) 'The critique of pure reason', London: Dent Everyman Library, 1934, quoted in Coltart. N. (1992) *Slouching towards Bethlehem*, London: Free Association Books.

Klein, M. (1952) 'Notes on some schizoid mechanisms' in M. Klein, P. Heimann, S. Issacs, and J. Riviere (eds), *Developments in psychoanalysis*, London: Hogarth Press.

Richards, E. (2008) 'Whose handicap? Issues arising in the supervision of trainee music therapists in their first experience of working with adults with learning disabilities' in H. Odell-Miller and E. Richards (eds), *Supervision of music therapy: a theoretical and practical handbook*, London: Routledge.

Stitzman, L. (2004). 'At-one-ment, intuition and "suchness"'. *International Journal of Psychoanalysis*, 85(5), 1143.

Winnicott, D. (1960) 'The theory of the parent infant relationship' in D. Winnicott (1965) *The maturational processes and the facilitating environment*, London: The Hogarth Press.

Chapter 6

Music therapy supervision with trainees in adult psychiatry

Helen Odell-Miller & Nicolas Krueckeberg

This chapter focuses upon supervising trainees who are near the end of their training in the psychiatric setting. A case study approach is taken whereby the parallel process of a final-year supervisee and a supervisor will be examined from the inside. This internal perspective draws and reflects upon the supervisee's experience first hand, because the supervisee contributes vignettes from his own unique experience.[1] In particular, dealing with disturbances arising from group members who are psychotic, and the importance of understanding and accepting the negative transference through supervision, lie at the heart of the process described.

The relationship between the trainee therapist, clinical setting, supervision and the self

The importance of finding the right model, the clinical setting and experience for the supervisee, who is training to be a music therapist, is central to the ideas presented here. Edwards and Daveson (2004) comment in detail from the supervisor's viewpoint about the specific dynamics of trainees being supervised close to their final examination, taking a perspective that uses the parallel process of supervisor and supervisee. They emphasise the complex relationship between institution, supervisor (and potential assessor) and supervisee, who is reliant upon a good report to gain the final qualification. This complex relationship is relevant to the work presented in this chapter, which takes a clinical perspective. The clinical parallel process is examined within the supervision process, as is the importance of finding an appropriate model which reflects the setting and helps the supervisee music therapist trainee to work within a multidisciplinary team with severely mentally ill people. This supervisee perspective is unusual in the literature of music therapy supervision, which until now has focused more upon the supervisor's perspective (Forinash 2001).

1 Throughout this chapter the supervisee's contributions are in italics.

Central to this process is the understanding of the many layers of relationship involved, all of which must be attended to in order to help the
music therapy group function and have meaning. Many of the layers and
relationships relevant to the process are listed below, and highlight the
complex but enriching process of supervision, which the authors have called
context-based music therapy supervision. Focusing attention on some of
these layers might appear to detract from the desired focus, which is the
group members and the therapy process, but if any layers are neglected this
could lead to a difficulty of holding the process, and to a disintegration of
the group music therapy process itself.

Layers of relationship involved in the case

- Trainee and training institution (university).
- Trainee and health institution (mental health service).
- Trainee and clinical unit (main context).
- Trainee and relationship to music and music therapy skills.
- Trainee and attitude/relationship to self.
- Trainee and relationship to supervisor.
- Trainee and relationship to group members.
- Trainee and relationship to multidisciplinary unit-based team.

The clinical setting

It is important for any therapist to recognise that settings based upon a
therapeutic community model have their own culture, which will be a
crucial influence to the function of any therapy group within that milieu.
Trainee therapists are encouraged to spend time in the setting prior to
setting up therapy groups to inform and enhance their understanding.
Adults with severe mental health problems, who mainly have long-term
diagnoses of schizophrenia and bipolar disorder, and their multidisciplinary
teams, will need to feel ownership of the music therapist and of the session
itself for it to have most meaning. The induction period is crucial to this,
and to the building of trust in the teamwork. The reason for this is that the
people living in this setting are part of such wide networks, and are
dependent upon these for their day-to-day care, often owing to a lack of
ego strength, to severe illness and to disturbance. It is imperative for the
trainee supervisee to understand these features of the work, and to pay
equal attention to internal and external features, as discussed by Walshe
(1995) in his paper 'The external space in group work'. At first, this
emphasis upon working as part of a multidisciplinary team could be seen as
a boundary problem by a student coming from a training background
where individual psychoanalytic models are the foundation of theoretical
thinking. Likewise, many students find it threatening and do not feel

confident enough to work alongside skilled nursing staff and other team members with residents of the unit outside the music therapy session. In certain settings, the success or failure of the music therapy group rests upon the integration of the music therapist within the wider team or setting, be they trainee or experienced therapist, and this can be very hard for an inexperienced therapist as it involves:

- Professional elements of having to convince other staff members of the benefits of music therapy, if it is not well established on a unit. This type of unit, in my view, is not always suitable for a new trainee with no experience, and many students flounder in these situations in terms of external relationships before they have been able start the actual music therapy sessions.
- Personal resources of relating and building up a rapport with residents and staff. Here the supervision space is of paramount importance, but again, as suggested by John (see Chapter 5), the development of these resources relies upon the development of a sense of self within the trainee supervisee.

The supervisee and supervisor perspective raises boundary issues, which are discussed in detail elsewhere in this book (see Chapter 9). Boundary issues are important in this material, as the supervisee's training process, and the supervisor's training, clinical and research roles, resulted in changes in role (for example, between manager and supervisor, and between researcher and clinical specialist), which had to be negotiated or reflected upon. Different boundaries were held in different ways according to the role taken in the workplace at the time.

In the supervision session, clear boundaries were held, which ensured that the relationship between the therapist supervisee, and his clinical group, remained at the heart of the process and relevant to the task in hand. This chapter was written several years after the supervisor and trainee supervisee process ended, thus it has been possible to reflect upon the process retrospectively, having moved on from the roles of trainee supervisee and supervisor. This style of presentation is intended to be helpful for both supervisors and supervisees, particularly in a training setting.

Clinical considerations

Working in an institutional setting with people who have long-term severe mental health problems such as schizophrenia, presents particular issues for music therapists, especially when establishing a new music therapy group. The approach taken here is based on the idea that the community in which people live and are cared for should be central to any music therapy group work in this setting; otherwise a group on such a unit might not be useful for patients. The particular issues this raises for the trainee music therapist, and how supervision is used to address these issues, will be discussed. Clinical details have been changed and confidentiality protected, but the aim is to give a first-hand discussion and dialogue whereby the supervisor discusses approaches and guidelines for this work, and comments upon the process from her perspective, interspersed with the supervisee's vignettes, which form a reflective narrative. This provides both clinical and supervisory insights into such a process and suggests an approach particularly when musical material is not available as recording is not possible.

The supervision framework: Starting the work

On a training course, all trainees arrive with their own ideas and experiences of supervision and what it means. At the outset of a training course it is important to address this, and very often students are in a supervision group for their first case so that they can learn together and gain support from other students. For some, supervision might mean a person 'looking over your shoulder' to see if you are 'getting it right'. For others, supervision might have been academic and more about thinking and reflection, but with a focus upon text, literature and academic ideas.

Supervisee reflections: The trainee supervision group and individual supervision

One of the key elements of the first year of training was regular group supervision. On a weekly basis we would meet in small groups of three or four students. One of the course tutors initially supervised us in our overall experience of being on placement and helped us think about the different situations we encountered on our first explorations in care homes, schools or psychiatric units. Later on we proceeded to discuss our clinical work in this context and we generally took fortnightly turns in presenting material to the whole group. In this group situation we had become accustomed not only to the ever present peer-support of fellow students in the sessions but also to the slightly disjointed alternation between heightened scrutiny and temporary breathing spaces that was necessitated by our presentation rota. Starting individual supervision in the second year was a very different experience from the earlier group supervision space. Individual supervision struck me immediately as a more peaceful and focused space, with fewer interpersonal dynamics interrupting a train of thought, than had been the case when presenting in front of the whole group. I remember noticing that there were obvious connotations with personal therapy but the supervision space seemed differently calm and focused, had clear professional boundaries and for that reason made it safe to concentrate uninterruptedly on the clinical material at hand. Thinking back I also remember that this heightened degree of safety in the 1:1 situation was instrumental in relaxing certain defences and essentially

allowed me to bring up those daunting and vulnerable aspects of my sessions
that were in true need of supervision.

Supervisor reflections

Supervision is about joint reflection. It is about attending to the process of
the relationship with the patient, and it is also, whilst in training and
beyond, about learning from literature and from the supervisor. In the same
way that supervisees set up a relationship with their patients, they set up a
relationship with the supervisor and this will be crucial to learning. At
times, the reactions and responses from the supervisor will reflect upon
previous experience as well as drawing from the dynamics in the supervision
session, which will hopefully vividly reveal the clinical process between
supervisee and patient, and this will be thought about in a manner that
gives feedback and insights about the process, but that ideally does not feel
judgemental even when there is conflict and disagreement.

Some trainee supervisees expect to be told 'how to do it'. At times there
might be suggestions and directive comments from the supervisor, but it is
also important to get used to using conscious and unconscious reflections
and to realise that this might shed light on what is going on for the
supervisee and patient in the clinical work.

The main task is to help the supervisee work safely and to hold the
patient in focus at all times, working to understand the therapeutic process
between trainee therapist and patients. This might at times involve personal
material from the supervisee, but at the outset there will be an acknowledgement that we will also think about boundaries and what might belong
in personal therapy. Much of the material in the next section is discussed
and explained at the outset with the supervisees. A crucial factor in the
process is how the supervision process begins, and what the supervisor says
at the beginning is important. An example of what might be said at the
outset could be:

> Supervision is about reflection, thinking and discussing, and also about
> listening and experiencing. The focus is on how to understand the
> patients better and the therapeutic relationship as a whole. It is import-
> ant that you feel you can bring worries and experiences of 'not knowing'
> what to do or 'how to be' as well as work you are more certain about.
> The supervision may involve musical ways of role-playing situations, or
> even finding ways of exploring case material through music. It might
> also include using taped examples, and this is usually quite important in
> music therapy supervision.

This is an example of an introductory approach for trainees who might be
totally unfamiliar with this type of clinical supervision group. The aim is to

help them understand how to make use of the supervision, and how it is relevant to their clinical work and their own work in progress.

Group or individual supervision?

The supervisee reflections above suggest reasons why moving from group to individual supervision towards the end of the training was important for the supervisee, and for this case. It is interesting to note that, previously on this training course, students were supervised individually only for their clinical work, with some case discussions at the end of the training. Whereas this might appear to be a logical start, and a good model, the focus upon individual supervision at the beginning of training was experienced by many music therapy trainees as rather intense. So a more group-focused model was introduced, whereby trainees experienced group supervision for their first, longer case, at the time as also receiving individual supervision for shorter cases in their placement. Group supervision at this point in training, whilst potentially difficult owing to its more 'public' context, allows supervisee trainees to hear and learn from each others' experiences, and this is supportive and validating. It also introduces them to a variety of case material and leads to realisations such as 'I am not the only one struggling with a new case' and 'I am not alone in feeling diffident and not knowing'. It has also been crucial at the start of training for trainees to learn from others in struggling to find 'the right' musical resources, or to learn from others about holding a boundary in the face of hostile or disorganised multidisciplinary teams. Later in the training, individual supervision allows for more depth and intensity in consolidating an individual confident approach with one group or patient. In the case described below, the supervisee was already familiar with the supervisory relationship in general, through the initial trainee casework supervision group, but not with me in my role as supervisor, or with the particular dynamic of individual supervision. The nature of the supervisee's expectations, and response to the imagined potential for the supervision to be useful, were discussed at the outset, including the changes in role and boundaries that this presented for both parties.

Reflections on starting individual supervision

When my tutor told me at the end of year one that the head of the course would be supervising my upcoming music therapy group, I first of all did not know what to make of this piece of information. I immediately thought of the fact that the course head would be one of the tutors assessing assignments, sitting in on examinations and deciding over a final pass or fail mark. As a student in the midst of training, this initially filled me with a sense of slight unease. I think I had some general concerns about the way I could relate to her in her supervisory capacity. This feeling somewhat intensified during the first supervision sessions when I had been on my initial visit to the particular ward I would be working on. I had met some of the severely ill patients who would be prospective members of my group and realised just how lost I felt in the whole endeavour of setting up a new group in this difficult environment, whilst feeling certain that I had to show the head of training that I could manage all this by now. It was helpful at the time that the supervisor showed an immediate interest in these secondary anxieties and encouraged me to talk openly about my fears and fantasies relating to being supervised by her, and in particular how her role as course head might affect the work.

Through the open approach in addressing the complexity of our relationship, I got a sense that my initial impressions and emotional reactions, however trivial or ridiculous they seemed at the time, formed a vital part of establishing the supervisory support structure that would enable me to set up and run this group.

After some of my early anxieties had disappeared, I began to appreciate the fact that someone with a high degree of experience and knowledge had taken the necessary time to work through every possible aspect that could be thought of before I started the group.

Supervisor reflections

I had not supervised the trainee supervisee before and regarded him as competent and experienced, particularly in the learning disability field. I reflected upon my countertransference in preparing for the first supervision session, recognising that we might both have fixed, and possibly over-idealised, views of each other and that this would be in contrast to the fragile and sometimes violent disturbances in the setting. The dynamic of seeing me in my clinical place of work as opposed to in the university would be a change of role and situation for both of us. Above all, I had a sense that there would be much unknown material that would be challenging to the student, who might feel he had to keep a strong appearance and hide his vulnerabilities. Some of these issues were discussed in the first meeting and if there are such issues in any supervisory relationship my view is that these should be discussed at any point and acknowledged in order to allow the most conducive atmosphere for thinking and learning through the supervisory relationship.

Case material

The case material here written by the trainee supervisee, and myself as the supervisor, shows the setting-up of a group in a rehabilitation unit admission ward, where patients largely have long-term, severe, enduring mental illness, often with a diagnosis of schizophrenia, and where the milieu of the ward and relationship or 'fit' of the music therapy group to the milieu is crucial. We think that the stance taken is crucial for any clinical work, but particularly for the trainee or newly qualified music therapist. This stance is that the success of any clinical work with very dependent disturbed people in an institutional setting rests upon how well the music therapy model and the therapist themselves, 'fit' and 'understand' the milieu.

In working with this group, the above process was the first aspect of the case that challenged the supervisee's confidence. He was working in a field largely 'unknown' to him and, as a normally confident and reflective trainee, there was an initial challenge in being encouraged to explore and understand the setting and its meaning for the patients before starting the therapy group itself. The ward in question is based upon an adaptation of an earlier therapeutic community model (Clark 2004).

Supervisee's reflections on the initial sessions

Having finished the first year of the training, I started to think about the group I would have to set up and run for 3 months in the second year in a psychiatric setting. When the supervisor agreed to start seeing me during the summer break, I sensed a welcome opportunity to get this group under way and we arranged an initial meeting. I thought that after some preliminary discussions about practicalities and applicable group models, I could start the group after 2–3 weeks of 'setting-up' time. However, I soon realised that my imagined timescale did not match my supervisor's ideas about the time needed to establish a group in such a complex unit. As a matter of fact, we proceeded to spend the better part of seven supervision sessions preparing the group in every detail. We discussed my general observations and impressions gathered when visiting the unit, and reflected in depth on the many (as it seemed to me) bizarre encounters with clients on the ward. The supervisor also took much time in working with every last fantasy and anxiety about the people I thought could be prospective members of the group. I remember being encouraged to spend whole mornings or afternoons on the ward and to talk to the various clients about the music therapy group. By the time I finally started the group I thus felt reasonably safe in the ward environment and I knew most of the patients and staff members by name. Had I known at that point in time what awaited me later on in running this difficult group, I would not have judged my supervisor's very apparent 'clinical rigour' during the lengthy preparation stage with an air of impatience and overconfidence.

Musical considerations

As the case began, it emerged that taping music and videoing sessions might not be appropriate. From the outset of the clinical sessions, I suggested a narrative framework to the supervisee and asked him to write down the whole of what happened in the session as a narrative before then further processing it and bringing it to supervision. In terms of changing the emphasis of my role as course head to acting as individual supervisor, it was important to listen to and support the supervisee's anxieties about undertaking work with a client group that was unfamiliar and about whom he had some preconceived concerns in terms of how he would be able to cope with the disturbance of his patients in the group setting. The individual supervision relationship at this stage was important, particularly for facilitating a therapist stance in the supervisee that the feeling of 'not knowing', and the negative fantasies that this engendered, could be useful in preparing for the work and could be held and contained in the supervision sessions. This was particularly important for this supervisee trainee, who was used to succeeding and who had gained respect for his intellectual grasp of theory and for the relationship of this to practice in previous casework with learning-disabled clients. He had prior experience of working with people with learning disabilities before training and therefore felt more confident with that population.

Supervisor reflections

I knew as supervisor that the 'success' or 'failure' of the as yet mythical music therapy group would be influenced by the supervisee's ability to work within the particular ward milieu. Whilst realising he might experience the delay as frustrating, I also knew that that delaying the start of the group would, as he has described, enable the unfamiliar patient group, his responses to them, and the appropriate boundaries and practical arrangements for the group to be explored so that the work was grounded from the beginning appropriately.

The power of countertransference and how this was represented and thought about in the supervisory relationship, particularly in dealing with psychosis, was manifest in the supervision discussions. Exploring the effect of violent and sometimes perverse phantasies of patients in the therapy group towards the music therapist in a group setting became crucial to the function of the group, and these issues were often discussed in supervision. Examples of the type of events and how these were thought about and managed in supervision and subsequently in the music therapy group are discussed later in the chapter.

Supervision models and training

Whilst it is often thought that supervision of group work is most usefully carried out in groups, the authors argue that for music therapists starting out in this field working alone often as a 'sole' therapist, the individual supervision setting is crucial in order to deal with some of the powerful conflicts and disturbances raised in the therapy group.

At the outset of the supervision group earlier in the training, it is likely that supervisees were asked to discuss ideas and fantasies about what the supervision group might mean for them. In the same way, in clinical individual supervision at this point in the training I suggest not only that supervisees reflect aloud about their expectation of the supervisory relationship and what it means, but also reflect on the clinical setting they are about to experience and what that might mean for them. The reason for this is to help the individual supervisee reflect in depth about the clinical setting and patients he or she is about to encounter, in order to start to work with using countertransference and transference. Unlike in the supervision group earlier in the training, when the emphasis is more upon the students sharing learning and finding support from each other, the individual supervision process involves developing a robust, more independent 'internal supervisor' (Casement 1985). This can develop from the duet of the supervisee and supervisor if they spend time attuning to the clinical population and to how the supervision might be useful when reflecting upon this process.

The supervisor's encouragement, and the supervisee's response to spending time on the unit concerned prior to setting up the group is interesting, as discussed by the supervisee. Whilst, naturally, trainees are keen to 'get going', my impression was that being able to understand the issues for patients living there, as well as thinking with other staff in the community about the best way to set up such a group, helped in the final process.

The group

The result of the initial supervision sessions was the establishing of a group music therapy approach appropriate to the ward setting using an open-ward-based therapy model. The sessions were set up in such a way that patients could decide prior to the group if they felt well enough to attend. The group generally consisted of four or five participants, most of them suffering chronic schizophrenic symptoms and presenting in a very disturbed manner. In the first 5 weeks there was some fluctuation in membership as some members only joined once or twice. Three patients, however, came regularly and thus provided the group with some much needed continuity and consistency, as the sessions had initially been very chaotic and disjointed, lacking any reference to previous weeks. The regular attendance of these three core group members helped form a group identity that was also instrumental in maintaining certain ground rules, which soon had to be established, regarding acceptable behaviour, language and gestures. This arose from working in depth in supervision with the supervisee's countertransference in relation to the 'attacks' on the group, which threatened to obstruct its purpose but which, through understanding and managing, helped to further the group process.

Supervisee initial reflections

One patient, suffering from chronic schizophrenia and going through an acute phase at the time, joined the group right from the beginning. After taking a good look at my recording equipment in the first session he started shouting and pacing up and down the room, becoming increasingly distressed. When I asked him what was bothering him he explained that the cables from the minidisk player were wired to his brain and might allow certain groups of aliens to tap into his thoughts. He calmed down only once I had dismantled the recording equipment and taken it out of the therapy room. The same scenario repeated itself in the following session when I tried to introduce a video camera without obvious cables hanging from it. It became clear that I could not record my sessions in the usual way. My supervisor suggested a different approach and asked me to spend some time after each session writing down the narrative of the whole the session without starting to interpret any of the content. This actually turned out to be quite a cathartic activity, allowing me to record and externalise some of the difficult and disturbing emotions that had come up, immediately after the group.

Afterwards I read the script out loud in supervision, which allowed me, in a way, to chronologically 'relive' or 'act out' aspects of the session in one undisrupted 'swoop'. The technique of describing the improvisations and talking about the interactive subtleties of the patients' play or the musical qualities of the various pieces worked surprisingly well. As I had to 'recount' the music in supervision, I seemed to also develop a good memory for the improvisations, revisiting them in my mind during the hour of supervision and describing them verbally to my supervisor, who was listening attentively, as if there was music to be heard.

Supervisor reflections

This focus on the here and now, and attention to detail, allowed an analytic approach to be taken where the supervisee had to vividly 'bring alive' the music therapy group to the supervisor in the supervision session. This he managed to do by narrating each moment in detail and by describing the music and dynamics as he experienced them in detail. It was important in this approach for him to describe the patients' interactions and characters, and important interactions between him and the group, both generally and in the musical process, albeit without the actual music present in the room.

The theme of negative countertransference was a consistent feature in the supervision sessions, and attacks, suicidal gestures, and other violent moments had to be managed in order for the group to function. Reflections upon these influenced the structure of the group and enabled the 'internalised supervisor' to function, as in the following example where thinking in the moment was crucial. The example shows the supervisee asking a patient to leave a session; something he found unthinkable prior to this incident and had many subsequent thoughts about. It was important for me to listen and be attentive to his strong feelings relating to attacks and destructive aspects, and help him feel at ease with discussing some very difficult emotions arising for him, at the same time as using these to help understand patients' projections and also to enable him to literally manage the sessions.

Asking a patient to leave a session

One particular patient tried to sabotage the group on several occasions. In the third session he entered the room 10 minutes after we had started, slammed the door and sat down looking 'moody'. We were just in the middle of a musical improvisation but the spectacular entry of this patient had shocked/interested certain group members and the music fell apart shortly after. I felt slightly exasperated and decided to talk once more about the group rules we had jointly established in the first session. Patient X, who had not said a word since entering the room so noisily, was sitting with his eyes closed. There was a great element of tension in the room. Patient Y took the lead and accused Patient X of coming in late and ruining the music. In a moment patient X was on his feet shouting abuse at the others at the top of his voice. I asked him to sit back down and he resumed sitting on the chair with his eyes closed. I addressed him directly and reiterated what behaviour was possible and what not, reminding him that people needed to feel safe in the group. That moment patient X was on his feet again and with lightning speed had kicked over a large drum and shouted 'fuck safety I don't care', gesticulating wildly with both arms in the air. I got to my feet nearly instinctively and asked him in no uncertain terms to leave the group in order to calm down. He did go out of the door but burst into what seemed like 'mock' tears and hung on to the door handle when another staff member tried to accompany him to his room. In the next 2 minutes he attempted to re-enter the therapy room on two more occasions, shouting at other group members before he finally took off down the corridor. I was completely and utterly exhausted and remember that my pulse was even raised whilst reading through this particular session in supervision.

Supervisor reflections

First of all, I was acutely aware during the supervisee's narrative of this session that it was a terrifying experience. It was important for this to be recognised in addition to using the powerful negative countertransference described by him, and experienced by me in the supervision room, as a way of understanding the power of the negative projections and destructive impulses arising for this patient in the group. Through his experience, and as a result of previous discussions in supervision about managing clear boundaries, the supervisee felt clear about his role and what had to happen, which later he reflected upon in detail.

The internalised supervisor in difficult circumstances

I have described above situations where the speed of some group-members' attacks on me or on one of the other patients was seemingly too quick for me to consider a well-thought-through response. Often, it was simply about intervening and preserving safety and containment, especially in a group where verbal attacks 'out of the blue' had soon become the norm. In these difficult moments or confrontations I had to think on my feet and often I seemed to have a spontaneous notion or inkling of what the right intervention might be. Something about the space of aided reflection and analysis present in those many supervisions sessions seemed to give me an internalised sense of safety out of which I could 'respond' rather than simply 'react' to the swiftly changing climate of the group dynamics and actions.

Further supervisor reflections on narrative in supervision

In this supervisory model, with no tapes and where confidentiality and clinical culture make observation of the sessions by the supervisor inappropriate, such listening by the supervisor allows aspects of countertransference to be used as a source of meaning and understanding in the supervision session. Thus the style and nuance of the reporting in the session is assumed to be a re-enactment or representation of the dynamics present in the actual music therapy group, so a different kind of listening to the supervisee's narrative was brought into play. Included in this would be my acute attention to the detail of the reporting, including vivid descriptions of the music and when music and words began and ended.

The process of asking the supervisee to speak through his narrative usually involved me waiting until the end before commenting. Listening to my own responses was used to understand the unspoken nuances of the therapeutic relationship in the music therapy group. So, for example, on this occasion I was aware of the impulse to interrupt, and used this analogy at the end as a way of thinking about how the therapist and group members experienced the group. Listening to the narrative was parallel to imagining listening to the music in the group.

Taking notice of when I was tempted to interrupt in the middle of the narrative, and thinking about why, and whether I actually did or not further shed light on the relationship between the therapist and his group. This approach is similar to the work of Scheiby (2001), who describes analytical music therapy supervision and talks about identification of parallel processes. She writes about observation of the actual session, and listening to her own supervisor countertransference whilst oscillating between empathising and thinking more objectively, in order to help the trainee and patient/s. This approach is further described by the supervisee reflecting upon the supervision process.

Negative countertransference and the supervisee's perspective

One of the major challenges in supervision was to discriminate and analyse my own negative countertransference. The patients' regular verbal abuse, the attacks on one another or on my own integrity and above all the disturbing and perverted sexual phantasies that were often voiced unexpectedly during the group seemed to play havoc with my emotional reactions. I had never been in such extreme situations before and sometimes I felt very overwhelmed and confused. Every now and then there was no time to reflect as I had to intervene or respond to an attack or some displayed behaviour on the spot. Consequently, there were moments where I retrospectively questioned what motives had coloured or influenced my clinical judgements and decisions. Some unconscious phantasies and connotations were discussed and resolved in supervision, others were 'transferred' into my psychotherapy sessions. How my supervisor saw through the complex layers emerging in the group from week to week I did not comprehend at the time. Another mystery remained how she decided which aspect of the session to pursue and analyse in depth after my reading of the session script, considering the fact that the chosen avenue would usually lead straight to the main issue. Looking back now, I realise how much these supervision sessions taught me about distinguishing negative from positive countertransference. For the first time in my clinical practice during training, I experienced first-hand how my genuine emotional responses to the manipulations of the patients in the group, provided an excellent diagnostic indicator of the patients' maladaptive relational patterns. Supervision thus formed an essential part of my learning at this stage of the training.

Music and talking

Music therapy supervision usually involves listening to music as part of the supervision process. In the above examples this was not possible and so narrative description by the supervisee of the music was crucial to the process. The effect of this was that the making of the music was described, as well as the subjective experience of the music itself once made and listened to by the supervisee, who was sometimes participant and sometimes listener to the music whilst it was improvised by the patients. In this group, the use of the therapist's harmonic instruments, guitar and piano, were crucial to the holding together of some of the musical processes, and at other times the listening stance was important. As supervisor, my role was to help the supervisee reflect upon the meaning of the music, but more importantly to reflect upon his musical countertransference, defined by Odell-Miller (2001), within the music. The tension was around how much the therapist should musically lead and help structure the music and the supervision session was often a place for thinking about this.

Supervisee reflections: The musical dimension

The absence of music or video recordings in the supervision sessions presented us with an unusual circumstance and initially it left me feeling slightly perplexed. I could not imagine how the musical aspects of my sessions could be addressed in supervision if we did not have the chance to listen to any of the group improvisations. The idea of reliving and describing the music in detail in the supervision session seemed an absurd suggestion to me at the time. However, looking back now, I do not recall an unusually noticeable absence of music when thinking about these supervision sessions. On the contrary, I do remember talking about a specific scenario one day when towards the end of an improvisation I had continued accompanying a female client in the group who had kept playing the xylophone after all other participants had ceased to play their instruments. Being the only female client in the group that day it is important to add that she had been on the receiving end of some very derogatory and sexist remarks earlier in the session and, towards the end of this improvisation, I felt inclined to musically support her possible attempt at asserting herself in the difficult dynamics of the group. I remember describing the soft and nearly inaudible tones she produced to my supervisor, having felt in constant danger of drowning her music out with the steel-strung guitar I happened to play at the time. After a minute or two of this tentative nurturing, I remember her initially feeble xylophone sounds seeming to grow stronger and we managed to conclude the improvisation together and to her obvious satisfaction. Interestingly, no further comments were directed towards her by other group members for the remainder of the session. I must have taken great care describing this particular piece of music to my supervisor, as I could swear that we actually did listen to it in supervision.

For me, this turned out to be a very positive experience of the immense potential of improvised music in group therapy, especially as a trainee who had just about set out to understand, distinguish and work with musical transference and countertransference reactions in the sessions. I think one of the reasons why I now recall the narrative style of our sessions as an effective and memorable approach is the fact that I had to take a much more active and responsible stance in conveying my work to the supervisor because it essentially came down to me bringing the music alive in the weekly supervision hour.

Supervisor reflections: Imagination and hearing the 'unplayed music'

At first, the supervisee thought that listening and not being too dominant was important, and he was very allowing of chaos and musical dissonance. Despite the absence of music in the supervision session, it was very possible to imagine the experience of the group by the way in which he described the music, his affect and how flowing his narrative was. It was important sometimes for me to suggest actual musical techniques or approaches in terms of leading and providing structure, as well as validating his musical roles. Above all, it was important to provide a space for thinking about music that had not been played or made possible, or music that might have been annihilated or disallowed by powerful psychotic expression within the group. For example, a regular occurrence was that the group would play music that appeared to sound chaotic to the supervisee but was not necessarily experienced as such by the group. My role was also to help the supervisee feel that his creativity was always alive and not too annihilated by the often rather chaotic or 'stuck' musical improvisations. I also saw my role as drawing attention to literature about music therapy with people with schizophrenia in particular, which validated some of his experiences and gave an important reality and validity 'check', in addition to using the musical experiences to further understand and work creatively within the group setting for the group's advantage; furthering the process.

Supervisee's concluding reflections

Looking back now and assessing the impact of the described narrative supervision framework on me at the end of training, I think that the particular circumstance of not having musical excerpts to work with, did in fact provide the unique opportunity of in-depth work with the whole narrative of each week's group therapy session. As I have mentioned earlier, not at any point during this case did I come away with a feeling that the music had taken on a secondary role in supervision, even though we actually never listened to any of the improvisations. There was something very containing and appropriate about the supervision model described here, especially at the end of training when the stresses of writing papers and preparing for the viva examination start to have a more pronounced impact on the student's life and consequently on the student's clinical practice at the time. However, there was also the inherent dilemma of being supervised by the head of training in this final trainee case, whilst having to relate to the supervisor in a whole range of other capacities. Despite the efforts of working through these dynamics at the time, I maintain some reservations about this set-up at the very end of training, as it can complicate matters for student and supervisor, having to keep continuous checks on which 'hat they are wearing' in an array of possible daily scenarios and meetings, without jeopardising the fine-tuned and intimate relationship that might develop in supervision.

Having said this, the intensified work that supervisor and supervisee had put into making this particular set-up work seemed to pay off when the opportunity arose to present a live supervision session at a conference. I do not think that the supervisory relationship would have stood up to the test of 25 workshop participants observing the supervision of the music therapy group, had we not addressed the intricacies of our multilayered relationship so thoroughly at the onset of supervision. Maybe there was also an underlying desire at the time to present this model to other professionals in the hope that they might gain inspiration from an adapted and appropriate style of conducting supervision under the particular circumstances described above. Possibly this aspiration also encouraged us to write this chapter in the particular format of joint reflections on the supervision experience despite it being quite a few years ago now.

In conclusion, I would like to point out that the supervision of students' casework in psychiatric institutions during the final-year placement has the potential of confronting supervisor and supervisee with manifold challenges, some of which were addressed in this chapter. However, if a flexible and appropriate supervision model is developed to meet the complexities of this important phase in the student's training and development it can be a real window of opportunity, instrumental in preparing the student to eventually take the step into independent professional life and practice as a music therapist.

Supervisor's concluding reflections

Many trainees have less experience in the field of adult mental health than in other fields, which can lead to preconceptions, some of which relate to the possibilities of identifying with the illnesses and difficulties of the clients. Working with people with a marked learning disability that appears to have been there since birth seems more removed for many trainees from their own experience than working with mentally ill adults whose disabilities might be much less apparent on first meeting.

In this case, the supervisee was a naturally confident person and he had to be supported in his experience of not knowing and of feeling inexperienced and deskilled. He had a strong sense of himself and this is crucial to developing as a therapist, as described elsewhere in this book by John (see Chapter 5), who puts forward the view that a trainee can only work at his or her developmental level; that is to say, his or her identity as a person affects the way in which the role of therapist can develop.

In many cases, supervisees in training lack confidence in themselves, particularly outside of the musical domain, and this seems to come to the fore in the psychiatric setting, when fear of overidentification with patients can be an issue, often resulting in a lack of identification at all and an attitude of 'us' and 'them', which also does not result in a healthy developing therapist stance. So the task of the supervision sessions, whether group or individual, is in helping the therapist supervisee find a balance between healthy self doubt and an open attitude of willingness to learn, and a confidence in self.

The holding of the particular context, the acknowledgment of the multi-layered set of relationships involved in the work, the recognition of the trainee supervisee as part of the team, the complex nature of the musical relationships and the particular importance of individual supervision when addressing aspects of the negative transference are some of the many facets of the complex and creative process that facilitates such music therapy group work in the psychiatric setting.

References

Casement, P. (1985) *On learning from the patient*. Hove, UK: Brunner-Routledge.

Clark, D. (2004) The story of a mental hospital. Online. Available: http://www.human-nature.com/free-associations/clark/chap4.html [accessed 17 January 2004].

Edwards, J., Daveson, B. (2004) 'Music therapy student supervision: considering aspects of resistance and parallel process in the supervisory relationship with students in their final placement'. *The Arts in Psychotherapy*, 31, 67–76.

Forinash, M. (2001) *Music therapy supervision*. Philadelphia: Barcelona Publishers.

Odell-Miller, H. (2001) 'Music therapy and its relationship to psychoanalysis' in Y. Searle and I. Streng (eds), *Where analysis meets the arts* (pp. 127–152). London: Karnac.

Scheiby, B. (2001) 'Forming an identity as a music psychotherapist through analytical music therapy supervision' in M. Forinash (ed.), *Music therapy supervision*, Philadelphia: Barcelona.

Walshe, J. (1995) 'The external space in group work'. *Group Analysis*, 28, 413–427.

Chapter 7

Supervision in context: a balancing act

Sandra Brown

Introduction

An earlier version of this chapter was published as a paper in 1997 in the *British Journal of Music Therapy* (Brown 1997). In that paper, I drew together factors that need to be considered and held in balance within music therapy supervision, illustrating this with clinical 'vignettes' from my own supervision practice. On revisiting the paper, I have been pleased to find that, in general, I agree with myself. However, nine further years of supervision practice – and of life – necessarily encompass changing landscapes, both externally and internally.

On the external front, the structure of music therapy training programmes in the UK has changed and continues to do so, especially in relation to the demands of registration with the Health Professions Council, and I have brought things up to date.

An expanding internal landscape has widened my perspective regarding supervision, and has continued to increase my belief in the need for flexibility in supervision, with each relationship 'bespoke', tailored afresh, rather than being moulded to theory. Of course, models and theories provide very valuable concepts, which can give vital help in understanding and moving forward in supervisory situations, but danger lurks when supervision becomes dogmatically held in theory rather than in humanity, especially when this has political overtones.

In the original paper, I sense the undercurrents of my personal struggle with this in relation to a music therapy profession in which therapists often adhered to, and were identified with, rather polarised theoretical positions. Today, although I still very much endorse my Conclusion section, I would grasp this nettle more firmly, directly challenging the narrow vision and potential distortion that can be brought about by a refusal to reconsider rigid theoretical positions.

Where I have felt it important to clarify and/or revise my ideas, I have added these new thoughts and reflections in italics.

Supervision in context

Music therapy supervision means many things to many people, as indeed does music therapy itself. As I sat down to begin to explore and marshal my thoughts for this paper, I was struck by the number of factors that need to be taken into consideration, for example:

1. the supervisor's therapy training and background, and preferred therapy and supervision model;
2. the supervisee's therapy training and background, and preferred therapy and supervision model;
3. the stage of professional development of supervisor;
4. the stage of professional development of supervisee;
5. compulsory (e.g. as part of training) or voluntary supervision;
6. the immediate presenting therapy material/context.

All of these factors affect what will be most in focus in a supervisory context. This may bring different emphases on the centrality of the musical relationship, interpersonal factors and the 'therapeutic frame' (Gray 1994), which contains issues of time, money, boundaries, confidentiality, respective roles of supervisor/supervisee, etc.

It would seem that the vital and most difficult task of the supervisor is to find a way of working and a balance that can encompass the first five of these factors whilst doing the best for the sixth – the therapeutic relationship under consideration.

Aims of supervision

What are the aims of supervision? I see these as threefold: first, to enable the supervisee to develop their ideas and skills concerning clinical material, both musical and non-musical; second, to enable them to develop their own 'internal supervisor' (Casement 1985 p. 24) – not just a miniature version of the supervisor swallowed whole, but a gradual developing of the supervisee's 'own capacity for spontaneous reflection' and original observations. Casement states, with reference to training, but with relevance also to qualified therapists: '. . . students need to be able to develop a style of working which is compatible with their own personality; so there will be something essential missing if he or she becomes too much of a *pastiche* of the supervisor . . .' (Casement 1985 pp. 23–24).

The third aim of supervision is to provide holding and containment for the supervisee and client dyad – what Casement calls the 'nursing triad' (Casement 1991 p. 22) derived from Winnicott's vision that the 'good-enough mother' needs a supportive adult to hold and support her in her relationship with her child, especially in situations where the child begins to feel unmanageable, or where feelings of inadequacy or guilt arise for the mother (Winnicott 1991). Hawkins and Shohet (1989) note:

> This concept provides a very useful analogy for supervision, where the 'good-enough' counsellor, psychotherapist or other helping professional can survive the negative attacks of the client through the strength of being held within and by the supervisory relationship. Supervision thus provides a container that holds the helping relationship within the 'therapeutic triad'.
>
> (Hawkins & Shohet 1989 p. 3)

I would add that the 'negative attacks' on the process can also come from the therapist's internal issues and the needs of her/his own 'inner child', and this may also need to be contained and addressed by the supervisor.

First, although this analogy does have value, I now find it potentially limiting: the supervisory relationship is not as simply defined as suggested by this infantile model. In the same way that music itself is more accurately understood as 'non-verbal' rather than merely 'preverbal', the dynamics referred to here are part of and inform how we function and relate throughout all of life, not just in infancy, although of course in infancy the roots of both music and relational dynamics are most clearly seen and understood.

Second, on re-reading this, I was struck by the rather negative emphasis on the need for containment of attack and feelings of inadequacy or guilt. Perhaps it is indicative of a more personally optimistic internal landscape that, writing now, I would feel it essential to include in the supervisor's role the celebration of 'good holding' and the points of growth and development in the supervisee/client relationship as well as the containment of more attacking and 'negative' elements.

Supervision models

Hawkins and Shohet (1989) define two current models of supervision existing in the caring professions:

a) *developmental*, which advocates a gradual and monitored change of supervisory approach as supervisees progress through definable developmental stages;
b) *process*, where focus varies according to the need of the moment, from reflecting on the purely concrete content of the session to considering wider factors.

Hawkins and Shohet point out that the developmental stage of the supervisee, as described in the developmental model, obviously affects what is appropriate focus in the process model. However, this latter model also includes consideration of the effect of the supervisor's developmental stage and the interaction between the two supervisory parties.

Both these models obviously have relevance to my initial six factors and, indeed, to my own experience of supervisory work over the years. However, without doubt one of the keys to a successful supervisory relationship lies in respecting the paradox of what we need to balance both in musical improvisation and in life itself: the ability to build and maintain clear boundaried structures while simultaneously allowing for fluidity and flexibility according to the moment. We must be able to 'hold on to the general structure, but must also tolerate and adapt according to the circumstances . . . holding firm where needed, but simultaneously bending and changing with each new situation' (Brown 1994 p. 16).

Music therapy supervision

What then is the focus of the music therapy supervision session? What needs, interests, abilities have to be balanced? Figure 7.1 shows major areas for possible consideration.

As already noted, clinical material brought to supervision can be looked at in a variety of ways, depending on orientation and experience. In supervision within training the developmental model is inevitably more to the fore – the aim here is to balance a level of educational focus and teaching with encouraging students over the course of training to develop their own internal supervisor. There is no prerequisite for music therapy students to have had their own personal therapy before embarking upon training, and so the intra-/interpersonal factors of C-E may be novel and for this – or indeed other reasons – uncomfortable, resisted or welcomed with interest. One of the major tasks of supervision, especially in these first few months of clinical work, is to assess what can be meaningful to the student, how to present it and how to survive and make manageable the inevitable difficulties, projections and resistance within E!

Crick, writing as a psychotherapy trainee on the experience of being supervised, refers to the universality of the therapy student's experience of the 'adolescent position in relation to the training, the pains of learning, and the discomforts of being assessed' (Crick 1991 p. 236). Many music therapy students are professionals in their own right, and have a personal identity related to (and often dependent on) their previous musical skills and experience. Having to come to terms with the 'deskilling' of one's music use, and with the 'not-knowing' of the therapy process, after years of preparing precomposed music for the known goals and standards of exams and concert performance, can be an enormously painful and vulnerable experience. Inevitably, having further to expose oneself in supervision, with the implication of the judgement and control of the authority figure and the

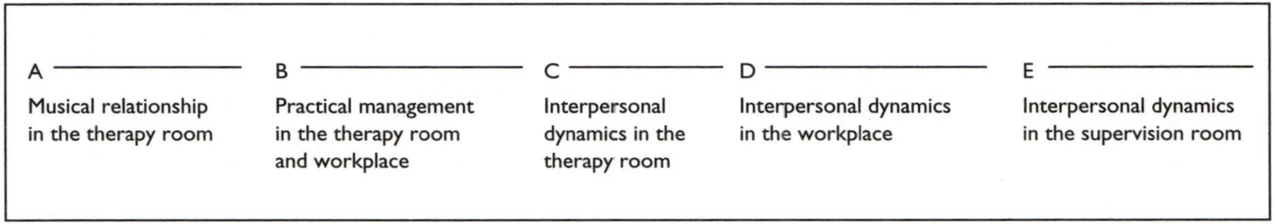

A	B	C	D	E
Musical relationship in the therapy room	Practical management in the therapy room and workplace	Interpersonal dynamics in the therapy room	Interpersonal dynamics in the workplace	Interpersonal dynamics in the supervision room

Figure 7.1 Major areas for music therapy supervision

actuality of ongoing assessment, causes the student therapist enormous anxiety, insecurity and often resentment and anger, as the basis on which s/he has built her/his self-esteem and identity no longer seems valued or even in view.

My own experience of becoming an analytic trainee after many years as an experienced music therapist and supervisor was very salutary in reminding me of this, and in bringing home afresh that there is no way of knowing how to 'get it right' next session, and indeed that supervision is always retrospective. Having to consider how so often one seems to have 'got it wrong' in the previous session, with no foresight as to what is to come in the next, brings huge vulnerability and the potential for the stirring up of shameful feelings.

The fact that supervisors are also assessors of students' clinical work can distort and disturb the supervisory process considerably, causing a desire in the student to monitor the material brought to a session, hesitation about disclosing personal issues arising within the therapeutic relationship, and suppression of negative or non-agreeing responses to the supervisor's perceptions, all of which may well limit therapeutic growth, both for client and student therapist. Understandably, it can be hard for a student supervisee to 'trust the process' and the supervisory relationship when vital assessment is involved. As stated earlier, the negative attacks resulting from this on both the therapy work and the supervision process need both containment and careful addressing by the supervisor.

In supervision work with more experienced therapists, some supervisees will always want to make area A their primary (and even only) focus; for others, consideration of C is what they see as crucial to their therapy practice. In my own practice, while holding A central, the need for personal supervision on issues of C (and D) became paramount while working with children with emotional and behavioural disturbance. With one child who would not play, who would often not come to sessions, and who was constantly physically abusive when he did, I was filled with an extraordinary apprehension before each session. With a sexually abused child, issues arising from sexualised behaviour and eroticism were central, as was the destructive and hostile multidisciplinary team dynamic directed my way on pursuing this child's disclosure to me of abuse. All of this required not only application of my own understanding of psychodynamics gained from my own personal analysis and reading, but also clear containing supervision in the psychodynamic arena rather than the musical.

Some therapists and supervisors are also interested in and find value in considering how the therapeutic process between themselves and their clients may be reflected in the supervisory relationship, i.e. E, and valuable work can be done in this way, as will be seen.

As a therapist who considers all of these modes of experiencing and thinking about the work not only valid but enriching, I would, as supervisor, hope to offer thoughts in all modes where appropriate and possible.

However, bearing in mind the needs of the six initial factors identified earlier, and in particular two, four and five, it is very necessary to hold a fine balance between offering one's own thoughts and listening, encouraging and respecting the supervisee's own developing focus and preference of style of working.

Inevitably, the final decider of this balance must be factor six – the material being brought, and the needs of that therapeutic relationship and that client. There are times as a supervisor when, although I may generally respect a 'preferred style' of considering the work, e.g. focusing on the musical interaction, or on interpersonal dynamics, sometimes the work cannot move forward without other areas being addressed. Here the client's needs are paramount, and the integrity of the work cannot be allowed to suffer because of issues and areas within the therapeutic relationship that the supervisee is reluctant to explore. In the following case material, drawn first from a supervisee in her first year of work, and then from work with students in training, the complex nature of this can be seen.

Case material

1. The first year of work

Here effective supervision work was generally held within consideration of the musical relationship and concrete 'external' happenings. This newly qualified therapist had little interest in looking at psychodynamic aspects of work, preferring to stay firmly focused on musical and more concrete and observable considerations; in general, the work was held more in A and B, and occasionally D, than in C and E. However, as you will see, there were points where circumstances dictated at least one, if not several, toes in the water of C.

The following extracts are selected from my notes of four of our first five supervision sessions. The nature of the supervisee's primary work situation, where she was employed both as therapist and teacher, and the constantly changing practical as well as therapeutic demands both in this institution and in her other places of work, very much dictated what was brought to sessions and looked at each week.

Session 1

This was very much an orienting session. We looked at what supervision might mean, and how Joan, the therapist, could best use it over our time together. We discussed at length the practicalities of how Joan could set up therapy work within a combined 'teaching/therapy' post, the need to create clear boundaries between different kinds of work, the need to negotiate with and to educate school staff about how many sessions practically she could offer in a day, and the need for time for listening back to recordings and the clinical analysis of sessions. There was also consideration of practical issues in preparing the room to be used for therapy, e.g. privacy, layout, etc.

We spoke of Joan's second place of work, where she works with a therapist from a different music therapy training. We considered how different their models of work are, and how working together might both be accomplished and become a learning experience. I also raised the issue of the potential difficulties for the children whose previous therapist has left, and who are continuing in therapy with Joan.

Session 2

General issues: Joan brought issues for us to look at to do with timetabling, selection of children for therapy and other organisational matters. She spoke of having to prepare for an Ofsted inspection, and I suggested that it might be useful to contact the Association of Professional Music Therapists' education secretary about the position of the confidentiality of music therapy sessions in relation to Ofsted inspections.

David (aged 9): Joan described David verbally to me, and spoke of his violence in this week's first session. We considered ways of dealing with this in terms of physical containment, when/if to stop the session if it all got too much, and musically what/how to play, for example meeting his strength with dissonance and volume if Joan was physically able to play at all, and the use of her voice otherwise. We then workshopped this practically, with Joan and I taking the role of David and therapist in turns, exploring ways of meeting David within the musical improvisations, and also how boundaries might be set behaviourally.

Susan (aged 6): Susan cried continually when brought to the session and did little when there but cry. On looking at video from the previous week's session, Joan was able to see how she was not supporting Susan's crying but trying to 'jolly' her out of it, both musically and non-musically. We considered the clinical possibilities of Joan's playing strong, harmonically structured music at the piano, using widespread hands, supportive bass and a slower pulse. We noticed how, in one place where Joan was playing more legato and slowly, without an implicit agenda for Susan to stop crying, Susan moved into interactive responses vocally. I spoke briefly of the need to consider the crying as a reflection of an inner state which needs to be acknowledged and met before change, if needed, can take place. This was also relevant to the work with David already discussed. I played Joan a section of tape from my own work illustrating crying–singing, and the use of widespread, harmonically structured music.

Session 3

General: Joan was very despondent – she was struggling with a heavy administrative and practical workload at her workplace and had many children in therapy who constantly cried, did not want to come to therapy, and were very evasive and resistant. I noted how she was finding it hard to hold on to a sense of self-value as a therapist – the final straw seemed to have been when she was deliberately urinated on by one child, Peter.

Peter: Joan spoke at length about Peter who, in the previous session, had pounded the cymbal for 15 minutes, after which Joan had put it out of the door as she couldn't find a way to deal with the onslaught of noise. She was not happy about this, and had returned it the following session, but with brushes; this was the session she played to me.

On listening, I was impressed by the wide range of musical resources Joan was using, often very appropriately and clinically. I suggested that she needed to note in the tape where there were connections, rather than noticing only the difficulties and evasions; and to try to see what might have contributed musically to these points of connection in order to give possible future direction. We discussed Joan having put the cymbal outside, the messages this may have given Peter, and how long one would continue to attempt to meet such overpoweringly loud playing. We considered whether physical intervention, for example the removal of the cymbal, ethically and clinically differed from musical intervention.

I pointed out that Joan did have a complex and difficult caseload, and that even a therapist with experience would have problems with it. I also spoke briefly about the therapist as 'container', as the person whom all the shit/pee was thrown at, who needs to be able to contain this without taking it on board as personal attack and signs of personal inadequacy – that this is part of the therapist's role and needs to be understood and worked with.

Session 5

Carol: Joan is about to begin therapy with Carol, who was the 'most difficult' child in her workplace A. Carol went everywhere with two helpers, who would also come to therapy and sit in the room. This felt very difficult for Joan, in that her work would be viewed and perhaps judged. She also spoke of Carol having to return to class afterwards, and her concerns that Carol might leave the therapy session in a 'non-calm' or disruptive state.

I felt that Joan was becoming caught up in the school's view and way of being with Carol. We spoke of the need for Joan to be 'in charge' in the therapy room, and of the potential confusion of crossed relationships with so many people in the room. We discussed clarifying to Carol's helpers the difference between how Joan works in class teaching situations (where they, Carol and Joan also meet), and strategies such as suggesting that the helpers sit at the side without being directly involved, with one helper being chosen as a primary one whom Joan could call on if necessary. I spoke of how music offers a new dimension, how Carol may present very differently, given half a chance, and how Joan must take the risk of really matching and being there for Carol, rather than trying to alter or control her external behaviour, as in the rest of Carol's school day. I also wondered if the 'viewing' of the helpers recreated the horror of the 'eyes in the observation booth' of Joan's student training supervision, and she agreed.

Peter: Joan spoke of how she remembered almost nothing of Peter's sessions afterwards, and how his playing at the time felt very confused. However, on listening to the tape, his playing seemed very clear, and she could not work out why she did not hear things, for example rhythmic patterns, at the time. Interestingly, Joan then could not find Peter's tape to play to me, although she was sure she had brought it. I commented on this in terms of 'everything about Peter getting lost'.

Joan described Peter's playing as 'very intense', and we discussed what qualities in his playing gave her this impression, what she meant by 'very intense', and what relationship this might have to the 'non-thought' of the session. I introduced analytic concepts such as projection, symbiosis and omnipotence, and we looked at Peter's need for Joan not to be separate from him, to be a part of him of which he was in total control. Joan spoke of her feeling that if she did not do what Peter wanted, she got a very powerful response (I noted 'being urinated on', in her case). I spoke of my own experience of being unable to think in sessions with one particular child, and of a psychotherapeutic paper which I found very helpful and would pass on to Joan.

2. Students in training

As I noted earlier, retrospective viewing and understanding of the process of therapy sessions does not mean that we have the answers to what we take into following sessions. This is particularly hard for student therapists, and it can be very necessary for a supervisor to be open to draw on all areas A–E as needed. The following vignettes are drawn from student therapists' work over the years.

Student 1. This student paralleled his client's continual crescendos and accelerandos with diminuendos and halving of note lengths, consistently moving to slower, legato, diatonic chordal music, often over a tonic pedal. This was understood by the student, but practice and efforts to alter this did not remove this tendency in the sessions.

Student 2. This student constantly made physical contact with a wheelchair-bound adolescent boy, although this meant that she ceased playing, and removed both herself and the child from the musical relationship.

Student 3. This student found it very difficult to hear or meet his young client musically. He commented that the child very much resembled photos of himself at a young age.

Student 4. This student, when working with a physically disabled child, consistently used a very narrow range of musical resources and keyboard register and was unable to change this, despite her awareness of the limitedness and inappropriateness of the music when listening to the session tape.

In supervision, student 1 came to see this mirrored his consistent reaction to any perceived aggression or lack of control in another person. His musical patterns were paralleled in his general life relationships by what he described as an automatic 'pouring oil on troubled waters', by always working to defuse situations out of fear of others' potential anger and destructiveness. He was able to make some change in the therapy situation following this awareness, but his personal unresolved issues in this area still remained limiting for him and the client.

With student 2, we looked at the child's need to engender physical touch and be 'baby-like', his resistance to autonomy, separation and 'growing-up', and the relationship of this to his wheel-chaired dependence and his subsequent clinical needs. The student then noted her own tendency to need physical contact to build relationship, and owned a lack of trust and belief in music (and particularly her own) to make an effective and 'good-enough' therapeutic relationship. This new awareness enabled her to move much more into a clinical–musical relationship with the child.

Student 3 found it an extremely harrowing experience to work with this child, and in supervision was able to see that he projected much of his own unresolved past on to the child. It was therefore difficult for him to find appropriate music, in general being either too intense emotionally, or overnurturing. The meeting of the child 'where he was' was therefore impossible, as the student was taken up with his own unmet needs.

When watching the sessions of student 4 live and/or on video in supervision, I consistently found myself becoming more and more rigid and hardly able to breathe. This was deeply uncomfortable, and I had to make conscious efforts to release myself. On more consciously noticing and imitating the posture and playing position of the student, with her rigidly held-in elbows, legs tight together, hands restricted to the two middle octaves of the keyboard, and her shallow, inhibited breathing, I felt that this was clearly connected to the difficulties of the profoundly physically disabled child she was working with. In supervision, the student experimented with 'letting the air under her armpits' when playing, although this was often enormously difficult for her – and for me as, third-hand, I experienced great feelings of risk and lack of safety, unfamiliarity and fearfulness, which seemed deeply and powerfully related to the fears this child was bringing into the room.

This consideration of the effects of countertransference on both student and supervisor (as in E in Figure 7.1), gave us a real sense of how difficult and risky musical activities and engagement could be for this child, especially those involving physically moving outwards. From this, the student was able to explore a much wider range of musical components, emotional colouring and keyboard register. She was also able to work physically with the child to enable a safe loosening and flexibility.

In all of these examples, powerful interpersonal dynamics were operating, and it was essential to consider what might be the student therapist's own issues cutting across the clinical work, and/or the client's issues as experienced by the therapist – and supervisor – in the countertransference. Again, an understanding of these processes reduced anxiety levels, and freed students to be more clinically appropriate in their musical improvising, as well as giving important insights into the experience of the client.

3. The experienced colleague

This replaces the original third piece of case material.

Alison, a music therapist – and supervisor – of considerable experience, has come for supervision for many years on a flexible basis. For some time, we met every 2 or 3 weeks, then this gradually and organically changed to Alison phoning to arrange a session when, through her own 'self-supervising', she felt that it would be helpful to bring a particular issue or client for us to consider.

The work with Alison and other experienced colleagues has led me over time to reconsider the three aims of supervision laid out in the first paragraph of my original paper: that is, to enable the development both of the supervisee's clinical ideas and skills and of an 'internal supervisor', and 'to provide holding and containment for the supervisee and client dyad'. In the meetings with Alison, I have not aimed to 'super-vise' – 'over-see' – Alison and her work; rather, we have considered together current clinical dilemmas arising in her work, drawing on both our experience, reflections, theoretical ideas, to create and develop ideas and understandings arising out of both of us. This certainly could fulfill the first and second aim, but for both of us, not just unidirectionally; and of course consideration of the third aim could be vital (with the caveats mentioned earlier). However, in general the experience has been of something much more 'level' and interactive between us than suggested in these three aims and in Hawkins and Shohet's two models referred to earlier.

I have wondered for some time if as a profession we need to redefine and refocus the term 'supervision' itself – the clinical needs of newly beginning student therapists are not the same as those of very experienced therapists. On this basis, I would now propose 'consultation with colleagues' as a mutually beneficial and bidirectional further stage in relation to the cited models of supporting and developing therapists' working practice.

Frame

I would like finally to consider what holds all this together – the different factors and areas of focus, and the aims and possible models of supervision.

I wrote earlier about the need for the supervision to manage the paradox of simultaneous fluidity and structure, and of how important it is to adapt one's supervisory style and focus to the supervisee's developmental stage and personal style. However, as with therapy, the adaptation and development of each unique supervisory relationship can only exist in relation to something solid and unchanging, which Gray (1994) has referred to as the 'therapeutic frame'. Here, something is negotiated and then fixed, for example time and cost of sessions, confidentiality, model of supervision offered. Through clarity and consistency, this 'frame' helps the supervisee to trust the situation, to feel safe, to bring delicate and difficult material, to feel valued, held and contained, as described by Hawkins and Shohet earlier.

Frames come in different shapes and sizes; some are very professionally measured with absolutely accurate right-angles and perfect varnishing. Others are more homemade, cobbled-together, a bit squint. What is important is that the frame continues to exist, and that its joints are strong enough to hold what potentially may go inside it, while not being too brittle, or too rigid, to accommodate the odd knock or bump.

Both from discussions with colleagues, and through the personal experience of being supervised by several different music therapists over the years, I am aware that what is understood by this frame can vary considerably. Some supervisors – and music therapists – find the concept of a frame outside the music unnecessary, particularly if their focus of work is totally in area A. The music itself is the therapy relationship, and is seen to provide the framework needed to contain and hold the therapy relationship: the supervision cannot mirror or duplicate this, being conducted in words, not music, and being focused totally on consideration of musical rather than personal processes. Thus, issues such as time, money, continuity, mixing of personal and professional relationships, are not seen to have particular relevance to, or effect on the therapist/client's therapeutic work or the supervision. For others, these issues are seen as of paramount importance to the therapy and supervisory process. One-off sessions are seen as unsatisfactory because of an emphasis on E as the core of the supervisory relationship; time and money issues are as relevant as in a therapy relationship; and a supervisory relationship would rule out any other forms of personal or social relationship, as in therapy.

As I noted earlier, I find consideration of both the musical and the intra-/interpersonal aspects of the music therapy sessions to be vital, and the holding and containing function of the symbolic frame very real. Both ethically and clinically I feel that, as a supervisor, it is an absolute necessity to hold a 'therapeutic stance', to be clear in myself about my role as supervisor within the framework of that hour. This would include striving for objectivity, containment of the therapeutic dyad, consideration of and dealing with the supervisee's and my own projections, idealisation, transference, social exchange kept to outside the supervision session, and so on. However, some supervisees need this frame held much more firmly than others, either from tendencies to push or disregard boundaries (which often reflects a lack of clarity in this area in her/his therapy work), or from feelings such as anxiety and insecurity. I find it is quite possible to supervise colleagues and friends, but it requires constant awareness of holding to the 'frame' boundaries by both parties, as well as considerable trust. I try to hold to a personal frame, which is clear in outline but made out of a rather flexible but firm substance, so that it can give and reshape a little in order to accommodate when necessary, but also maintain a very clear, firm and consistent shape when a particular supervisory relationship needs it. I would, for example, try to give extra time where possible if a supervisee arrived late after an unavoidable delay or if, at the official end-time, a place of some delicacy and therapeutic/supervisory importance had been reached. I would also endeavour to be flexible as far as fee is concerned, in cases of need, and offer a cup of coffee when circumstances pointed towards it.

On the other hand, a much less flexible frame would be held with the supervisee:

a) who is nearly always late;
b) who talks animatedly just beyond the session ending time, whose last taped extract is always longer than the ending time, who needs to make a final 'important point' after the ending time;
c) who asks about my work, my health, my social life in the session time, and delays bringing supervisory therapeutic material;
d) whose demand for a low fee does not seem to be related to need;
e) who constantly 'forgets' to pay.

In these latter cases, clear boundary stating and holding may be all that is needed, but often it can be valuable to bring these issues into discussion and to look at their relevance to the therapeutic process under consideration. Again, the depth to which this can be taken depends on the supervisee's willingness to consider these modes of working as relevant.

Clarity of frame may also need to be considered in drawing a defining line between supervision and personal therapy.

The supervisor may need to draw attention to the supervisee's personal issues and their effects on the therapeutic relationship under consideration. However, the supervisor is not the supervisee's therapist, and has a different purpose and focus. This can be a matter of difficulty, as a supervisee who is not in personal therapy may have nowhere else to take issues which are affecting the quality of their clinical work; or, if they are in therapy, then the negotiating 'what belongs where' in terms of supervision or therapy can be very difficult, and not at all clear-cut. There can be a tendency to split supervisor and therapist into 'good supervisor/bad therapist', or vice versa, thus clouding material brought to both relationships. The supervisee may also bring material from her own therapy to the supervision room, thus potentially 'acting out' and diffusing important therapeutic material.

As always, it is essential to hold in mind that the focus of the supervisory relationship must be to consider and facilitate the supervisee/client relationship. It is also vital to be aware of potential ethical concerns here – the music therapy profession does not have a code of ethics for supervisors, as do other bodies (e.g. the British Association of Counselling; see Feltham & Dryden 1994 pp. 130–137), and the code of ethics for music therapists does not offer much guidance on this. Clarification in this area, therefore, would seem to be essential in terms of our own professional practice, and the safe practice required of a registered health profession.

*I am less accommodating these days: I feel strongly that 'clarity of frame' and potentially uncomfortable issues **do** need to be considered, supervisees 'willing or not', if issues relevant to the advancement of the supervised work need to be addressed.*

Conclusion

Supervision, then, is no simple matter. Models, areas of focus and frame can vary greatly, depending on both supervisor's and supervisee's orientation and experience. However, at the centre must be held the needs of the therapist/client relationship under supervision; no one model, area of focus or frame has the answer to all situations. A rigid adherence to a preferred 'world view' by supervisor or supervisee may well seriously limit the work that can be done within the supervision context. Sandler (1988), quoted in Lanyado (1991), wrote about psychoanalytic technique: 'whatever facilitates the analytic process is therapeutic, and whatever moves us away from it is countertherapeutic.' (Lanyado 1991 p. 36). Perhaps this thought has something to offer us all for music therapy supervision as well.

*Today, I would tread less delicately in relation to others' theoretical toes, and would write '**will** seriously limit the work' rather than 'may well', as well as removing 'perhaps' from the beginning of the final sentence.*

References

Brown, S. (1994) 'Autism and music therapy – is change possible, and why music?' *Journal of British Music Therapy*, 8(1), 15–25.

Brown, S. (1997) 'Supervision in context: a balancing act'. *British Journal of Music Therapy*, 11(1). 4–12.

Casement, P. (1985) *On learning from the patient.* London: Tavistock.

Casement, P. (1991) *Learning from the patient*. New York: Guilford Press.

Crick, P. (1991) 'Good supervision: on the experience of being supervised'. *Psychoanalytic Psychotherapy*, 5(3), 235–245.

Feltham, C., Dryden, W. (1994) *Developing counsellor supervision*. London: Sage.

Gray, A. (1994) *An introduction to the therapeutic frame*. London: Routledge.

Hawkins, P., Shohet, R. (1989) *Supervision in the helping professions*. Buckingham, UK: Open University Press.

Lanyado, M. (1991) 'Putting theory into practice: struggling with perversion and chaos in the analytic process'. *Journal of Child Psychotherapy*, 17(1), 25–40.

Sandler, A.M. (1988) 'Comments on therapeutic and countertherapeutic factors in psychoanalytic technique'. *Bulletin of the Anna Freud Centre II*, part 1.

Winnicott, D.W. (1991) *Playing and reality*. London: Routledge.

Chapter 8

Supervision of music therapists working with children in schools

Amelia Oldfield

Introduction

I start this chapter by outlining my previous experience of giving super-vision, and then describe the approach I use and the thinking that informs it. I then include accounts written by music therapists I am currently supervising who work in schools, and my brief reflections on the super-vision work; I am very grateful to Andrea Casford, Dawn Loombe and Clare Rosscornes for taking the time to write these accounts. Finally, I reflect on common points outlined by the people I have supervised who work in schools.

Many music therapists in the UK work in special schools, and in recent years also in mainstream schools. The school environment is very different to a hospital or other NHS environment. As discussed by Amir (2001), in a school, the music therapist will have a different kind of role to that of most other staff members, who may have varying assumptions about the nature and function of therapy. As a result, the therapist might struggle to estab-lish a therapeutic stance with clear boundaries. In a setting mainly staffed by health professionals, by contrast, the music therapist may find much greater common ground with colleagues. Many of the rewards and chal-lenges of working as a music therapist in schools are intrinsically linked to the characteristics of the schools themselves and the special expectations and traditions of the school environment.

Supervising music therapists and reflecting on their work has been an important part of my professional life during my 26 years as a clinician. It is very interesting to be involved in the process of enabling music therapists to develop strengths and confidence in their own skills, to share frustra-tions, gain new insights and enthuse together about successful moments. Throughout the chapter I intentionally take a first-person autobiographical approach.

Supervising experience

My first experience of supervising music therapy students was in the early 1980s when I was working as full-time music therapist at the Ida Darwin Hospital, which was a large, long-stay institution for adults with learning disabilities. The music therapy students came from the Guildhall School of Music and Drama, on placement for 1 day a week for 12 weeks.

I do not remember being asked to provide formal supervision sessions or being given any specific guidelines in that respect by the course. The training course was grateful that I was taking a student on placement and it was assumed that I would 'look after' him or her. The head of the training course spoke to me on the phone before sending me individual students and I knew I could speak to her if I had any concerns.

In my new role as supervisor I was influenced by my own experience as a music therapy student. I remembered some excellent supervision sessions with a clinical psychologist while I was doing voluntary work in an adolescent psychiatric ward in Canada, before my music therapy training. I remember my supervisor taking time to listen; encouraging me, but also helping me to think clearly about what I said to the children I was working with. He helped me to reflect not only about the content of what the children were telling me but also about the feelings behind the words.

I began having my own formal monthly clinical supervision when I started working in child and family psychiatry, in 1987. It may seem strange that I had no formal supervision for my first 7 years of full-time work as a music therapist but in the early 1980s it was not usual for music therapists to have or give clinical supervision. At the time, I shared an office with a speech therapist, and the clinical psychologist worked in the next door office. We provided informal but invaluable support for one another on an almost daily basis and in some ways this support system made up for the fact that we did not have formal clinical supervision sessions. Perhaps that circumstance also strengthened the multidisciplinary team's capacity to develop its shared clinical thinking.

A few years later, in 1990, I became an approved supervisor for the Association of Professional Music Therapists (APMT) and began supervising other music therapists on an individual basis.

In 1994, after co-designing the MA Music Therapy training course at Anglia Ruskin University, in Cambridge, I started lecturing there. This meant that I was involved in teaching students, giving lectures, workshops and individual tutorials; I was immersed in thinking about training music therapists. There are many overlaps and similarities between teaching students and supervising qualified therapists, and the two experiences constantly inform and influence one another, as I explain in the next section.

Between September 2000 and July 2003 I ran a clinical supervision group for four or five music therapists working with children with special needs in the Cambridge area. I have described this group and some preliminary thoughts about individual supervision in a chapter on music therapy supervision in a recent book (Oldfield 2006). Here, I draw on material from those earlier ideas as well as from the experience of the three supervisees who have written specifically for this chapter.

At present, I continue to have music therapists on placement and my teaching role at Anglia Ruskin University is ongoing. I supervise five music therapists on a weekly, fortnightly or monthly basis and I am planning to set up another small supervision group in the coming year.

My approach to supervision

General points

In many ways, my approach to supervising music therapy students and then qualified music therapists, evolved in the same way as my clinical music therapy work. My thinking developed through practice and experience rather than through studying or learning about a theoretical approach and then applying learnt principles. I take a pragmatic problem-solving stance in supervision. Building the supervisee's confidence and drawing out the positive aspects of the process are crucial to the work.

By the end of the 1980s, I was beginning to have some definite thoughts about what seemed to be particularly important for students on clinical placements. In the early 1990s I wrote an article outlining these thoughts (Oldfield 1992). I identified three areas as being particularly important for the students: 'developing a relationship with the client', 'clinical improvisation' and 'developing group techniques'. I also outlined how each student was different and had very distinct strengths and difficulties, which needed to be carefully considered. Much of this thinking still underpins my approach to clinical supervision today.

It is interesting to note that, more recently, supervision approaches in placements described by the US music therapists Summer (2001) and Hanser (2001) discuss similar approaches. For example, Summer describes three focal areas as central. These are: 'to reinforce the therapeutic qualities inherent in each student's character', 'to evoke the student's musical character' and 'to address the preconceived notions about aspects of the music therapy process'.

When thinking what salient points underlie my approach to teaching music therapy students recently, I came up with several areas I felt were important. These included: 'remaining close to clinical practice', 'building on existing strengths', and 'continuing to be inspired by music or music making' (Oldfield 2006). These ideas are directly relevant to my approach to clinical supervision, and here I explain why.

Although supervisees will bring whatever material they choose to supervision, there is a shared understanding that most of our work will involve talking and discussing the supervisees' clinical music therapy casework, if possible using audio or video excerpts of their music therapy sessions. Sometimes we will talk principally about the difficulties that supervisees are experiencing with other staff, but usually the bulk of the work centres around casework. Indeed, there are times when it is helpful to remind supervisees who have become weighed down with 'political' music therapy issues, such as validating posts or convincing reluctant managers of the value of music therapy, to refocus on their clinical work. Most music therapists really enjoy their clinical work and find it helpful to reflect on this central aspect of it when other, more peripheral, aspects become overwhelming.

Music therapists have a very wide range of different skills, both clinically and musically. Some are naturally playful and lively and feel at ease working on the floor with young children. Others are more thoughtful and reflective and are quick to gain new insights into complex psychiatric cases. Music therapists play a wide range of different instruments. Some will be able to play anything by ear, others will be skilled at moving, playing and singing at the same time. During supervision, music therapists often focus on the skills they do not have, thinking their improvisations are boring or 'stuck', or fearing that others are more competent than they. I believe that it is important to help supervisees, particularly at the beginning of their music therapy practice, to recognise their own strengths and build their confidence from this recognition. Once supervisees begin to feel confident about some aspects of their work, it is possible to address those aspects that need developing, such as widening of repertoire or focusing on specific improvisation techniques. Increased assurance in those areas can then allow the therapist more internal space to acknowledge and reflect upon her countertransference experience.

Frequently, supervisees tell me that they need 'new' ideas with a particular client or group. They feel they have tried everything and do not know what to do next. In these cases I try to suggest one or two very different techniques or ideas. Sometimes I will remind supervisees of things they have done in the past that they have forgotten about, or I might suggest a textbook that can be referred to. In some cases it might be that supervisees do not need to think of 'new' approaches but rather of changing the way material is presented, perhaps taking more time, leaving more gaps and being confident about dwelling on individual improvisations in more depth.

Practical arrangements

I mostly supervise music therapists working with children and families, although sometimes if a supervisee is working part-time in several different clinical areas I will supervise their other work as well, but I make it clear that I am less experienced in these areas. I supervise music therapists on a weekly, fortnightly or monthly basis depending on what seems appropriate and possible.

I charge the same rate for all my supervisees, and use the APMT recommended rates as guidelines. Sometimes supervisees can be reimbursed fully or partly by their employers and, occasionally, their employers have negotiated contractual arrangements with my employers. I explain to all my supervisees that it is their responsibility to pay me the agreed rate. I am flexible about how frequently or when they do this.

I usually supervise at one of the places where I work, but occasionally supervise at home. Some supervisees prefer to come to the same place at the same time every week, or month. Others prefer to make different arrangements from one session to the next. Initially, I suggest that we should have around four trial sessions and then review our work to evaluate whether we think it is successful and helpful. This means that there is a planned opportunity to make changes or stop the sessions if necessary.

For the past 10 years almost all the music therapists I have supervised have trained at Anglia Ruskin University and have been students of mine. This means that they already know me well, and have insights into how I work and a good idea of what to expect from supervision. Similarly, I will know something of their past strengths and weaknesses and will be able to build on my previous experience of working with them as students. Nevertheless, I am always aware of the need to think of my ex-students as professional colleagues who quickly acquire their own specialist expertise. Sometimes we reflect on the differences between being students and being professionals, and explore how the relationship of student to teacher has shifted to that of supervisee to supervisor, which I see as a situation in which two colleagues are exploring and sharing aspects of clinical work together.

Accounts written by three supervisees

I asked three music therapists I am currently supervising individually whether they would be willing to write about their experience of supervision for this chapter. I gave them some brief guidelines and asked them to consider the following points, making it very clear that these ideas were only suggestions. All had been students of mine.

All the music therapists gained permission to video their clients and to discuss the work with me in supervision. For reasons of confidentiality, all names and details have been changed.

Points for consideration by supervisees

- Describe one or two cases or pieces of work you brought to supervision. Why did you bring the material? Was the supervision helpful?

What did you learn from Amelia, and/or from the process of discussing the case?

- How do you decide what material to bring to supervision?
- Have you felt different about your work as time has gone on? How?
- Has the way you felt about supervision or being in supervision changed? How?
- Is the supervision too formal/informal?
- Do you wish there were things you had discussed but didn't get around to after supervision has finished?
- Do you feel listened to?
- Things you particularly like about the supervision, things that you don't like, things you would like to change, add, develop?
- Why did you choose to ask me for supervision, rather than another music therapist, or another professional?
- Did it help/hinder that I taught on the MA music therapy training?
- Has your relationship with me changed since you qualified? Do I seem different?

Andrea

Andrea started coming to me for monthly supervision sessions 3 years ago, when she began working at a children's home. The children she was seeing were similar to the children I treat in my work in Child and Family Psychiatry.

What Andrea wrote about supervision

Andrea's first consideration when choosing a supervisor was to find someone who was experienced in the field she was working in. She also felt it was important to find someone she knew and she could trust. She wrote that it was a comfort to be supervised by 'a familiar face in a new working world'. In addition, she was looking for someone whose outlook and style of work she felt was interesting and inspiring.

Andrea summarised her thoughts about why supervision was important through the following bullet points:

- being able to share and discuss work
- receiving guidance from a person with much more experience working in the same field
- the opportunity to widen or focus on specific aspects of the work – gaining a perspective
- being able to discuss thoughts and receive help in exploring transference and countertransference issues
- practical help with suggestions for ideas in music therapy sessions

- receiving support from someone who has known her throughout her career as a therapist; this was especially valuable as she was working as a lone music therapist
- gaining greater insight.

Andrea felt that it was helpful that I had previously known her and worked with her while she was training, partly because I would be more aware of which areas of practice she needed to develop. She wrote that she was initially nervous about bringing issues to supervision that she felt she should already know about, but that she was more confident about this now. She felt that the difference between being a student and a supervisee was that as a student she was being taught new ideas whereas now she was exchanging ideas with me.

My reflections on supervising Andrea

Although the children that Andrea worked with were a familiar client group to me, the setting she was working in was very different. Her post was new and many of the staff did not understand what the purpose of music therapy was; she was employed for only a few hours a week and it was difficult to feel or be part of the team. Staff morale seemed to be low and some members of the team appeared to lack interest or motivation in their work.

The children, aged 6–14 years old, lived at the home and attended the school that was on site, because they had nowhere else to live. They were waiting for foster placements, residential schooling or court cases that would determine where they would go. They had a wide range of difficulties, including emotional disturbance, attachment disorders, conduct disorders, mild learning disabilities, post-traumatic stress disorders and substance abuse. They all had problematic relationships with their families and their length of stay at the home varied from a few days to several months, often with sudden, unpredictable arrivals and departures.

Andrea tried to organise a timetable, but the children distracted each other, walked in and out as they pleased, and brought their friends in when they felt like it. Andrea often found when she arrived at the home that the child she was scheduled to see had left. Nevertheless, she was clearly very motivated to go on working there. She travelled long distances to the home every week despite knowing she might encounter these difficulties.

When Andrea first started telling me about her work in this home, I struggled not to be overwhelmed with how difficult and distressing it was. The children were in crisis and mostly had histories of being completely let down by the adults around them. The setting seemed chaotic and unsupportive: how could Andrea possibly work there? Where should I start to enable this to become 'proper' music therapy work with clear boundaries, and incorporating appropriate music therapy structures such as 'hello songs' and prepared endings?

I then realised that Andrea was doing the one thing that most of the adults in these children's lives had not done: she was keeping going, trying her best and making a huge effort to be there consistently every week. I realised that it was my job to support her efforts and encourage her. So instead of criticising her work I told her that I thought what she was doing was remarkable and helped her to reflect on the positive aspects of her work and the reasons why she remained so committed. She reported that there were times when she had been able to make contact with a child and had been able to listen and respond non-verbally through musical improvisation in a way that she felt was possibly unique in that child's experience. At other times she felt she was able to interest children who had lost motivation in most other occupations, in creative music making and help them to regain a little feeling of self worth.

Occasionally, Andrea was obviously upset when talking about the children's very painful circumstances and I was often also very moved by what I heard. I reassured her that it was understandable that she was upset by the difficulties the children were facing and by the intensity of her countertransference experience, and that supervision offered a space for expression and containment of these feelings. It was clear, however, that Andrea was not overcome by emotion when she was in the room with the child.

Together we wondered whether the chaotic organisation and atmosphere in the home could be a reflection of the children's situations, and whether some staff had lost motivation and given up in the same way as the children. Thoughts such as these were helpful to Andrea in placing her own experience in the context of a wider emotional and organisational dynamic, and in deepening her understanding of how the children related to her and of other events in clinical sessions.

Gradually, Andrea established regular meetings with two senior members of staff, one of whom she saw every week. That supported Andrea in becoming able to be more boundaried about whom she was going to see, negotiating with children and staff at the beginning of the morning and subsequently writing out a clear list with specific times. She would then put this list on the door and block off most of the observation window to stop people 'peering in'. At the end of the morning she kept a space for people to 'drop in', because this was the only way some of the children were able to attend.

I continue to have great admiration for Andrea for doing this work. As a supervisor, it was particularly important for me to recognise the strengths that she was bringing to the work, and to recognise my admiration for it, rather than myself becoming overwhelmed by the extent of the difficulties and tasks I needed to help her with.

Dawn

Dawn qualified as a music therapist from the Music Therapy MA at Anglia Ruskin University, and had been working for 18 months. She has held a number of very different part-time music therapy posts throughout the area. Her work included sessions in residential homes with adults with profound learning disabilities and with older people with dementia, and work with children with special needs, both in a special school and a mainstream school. The following is drawn from Dawn's account after 11 monthly supervision sessions.

What Dawn wrote about supervision

Dawn asked me to supervise her because she strongly believed in my particular approach to music therapy, especially in relation to my work with children and families, and with children and adults with profound and multiple learning disabilities.

As a student, she had been influenced by videos of my work and by my belief in the value of music therapy. Dawn wrote that she left our supervision sessions feeling positive and motivated. She felt she benefited from an authentic, unpretentious style, which was neither too formal nor too informal, and that she felt comfortable and able to discuss any issue or area of her work with me. She wrote that she felt listened to.

Dawn also wrote that one of the reasons she chose to come to me for supervision was because she felt that we have something in common in that we are both working mothers, with teenage children in the same school years. Dawn felt that I seemed to understand the issues she had faced in undertaking a very intense training course at this stage in her life and, after qualifying, the process of setting up her own music therapy work in Cambridge. Our common life experiences added a level of trust and mutual intuitive understanding to our relationship.

Some examples of how Dawn used supervision

WORK WITH L

Dawn talked to me about L, a young, non-verbal adult with profound and multiple learning difficulties who no longer seemed to engage with the music or Dawn and would often look away or fall asleep, seemingly uninterested. After a few months, the work seemed to have become stagnant/stale. Dawn remembered that I had made the following suggestions:

- Making a list of key interactions/things that *had* worked (using an earlier video of her sessions) and building the session around them. It was important to keep these in mind, rather than focus on what Dawn saw as a lack of response/interaction.

- Using different types of impetus, e.g. listening, looking and 'doing'.
- Generally slowing down the pace and allowing L lots of time to respond.

We looked at a video recording of Dawn's work with L and this enabled Dawn to see many of the small responses from L that she could build on in her musical exchanges. We also discussed the idea of Dawn showing this video to other people working with L so that Dawn could generally discuss L's progress with them and get a sense from them whether they felt the music therapy sessions were beneficial.

WORK WITH D

Dawn initially struggled with how to engage D, an extremely isolated 5-year-old child. We talked about the importance of finding the right balance between structure and freedom; the key being to give the child space. We also explored the idea of having clearly defined geographical focal points in the room. Finally, we looked at providing a balance between activities that were directive and those where Dawn followed/played in parallel with D. Dawn thought that this last reflection helped her to 'break through' with this particular child. They were sitting in their 'corner' playing (in parallel) with the ocean drums. D suddenly noticed that Dawn was imitating his actions, lifting the ocean drum above her head and twirling it round, following his movements. They continued this for a while in a playful manner and then began what has become their 'trademark' interaction, which D now initiates every week. They held the large ocean drum between them and took turns to count '1, 2, 3 . . . Go!' and then shake the drum dramatically, vocalising loudly together until one of them shouts 'stop'. D really enjoys this interaction and races to find the ocean drum as soon as they have sung 'hello'. In recent weeks, Dawn has experimented with loud and soft versions (by counting very loudly or whispering the numbers very slowly and softly) that D has responded to, and although this is only a small, short connection, Dawn hopes this will allow other musical possibilities and interactions in future.

We explored the difficulty of being less directive in music therapy sessions than D was used to in the classroom. We agreed that D could manage two different sets of 'rules', which were specific to different rooms and different people. We also thought that it would be important to be clear with teaching staff that Dawn had a different approach with D in music therapy from that in the classroom, and that this was because the nature of music therapy is to experiment more freely with non-verbal musical interactions.

WORK WITH K

K was 9 years old and had emotional problems, which resulted in severe behavioural difficulties. Initially, K wanted very much to come and seemed to love playing music but at the same time worried that he would miss something the other children were doing. When K came into the room, he would play every instrument in turn, loudly and forcefully in a quite unstructured way. K's musical stories were very violent and usually family members and friends would die horrible deaths, involving lots of blood. The stories were often difficult for him to resolve and he would state dramatically 'to be continued . . .!' with a drum roll at the end. K seemed to be very 'boundary-less', making Dawn feel uncomfortable and that she was unable to contain him.

I suggested that K appeared to be behaving in the way in which one might expect an emotionally deprived child to behave. Whatever Dawn offered would not be 'enough', whatever he was doing would be difficult to enjoy because he might be missing something 'better', and any positive experience would need to go on 'for ever' because the opportunity to do it again might never occur. I encouraged Dawn to continue to provide a warm, caring, consistent approach, but to maintain clear boundaries. With the stories I suggested that it was important not to be judgemental in any way, and to give K opportunities to repair disasters if he wished to but without prompting him to do so. We explored the possibility of offering a clearer ending by saying: 'OK, so that's the end of the story for today', even when K insisted that the story 'was to be continued'.

We also discussed the importance of discussing K with his teacher and other key members of staff, in order that Dawn had sufficient information about his background and his emotional difficulties. It also seemed crucial to share with others that he was bringing very violent stories into the music therapy sessions, as this could be a reaction to experiences he had witnessed in the past.

My reflections on supervising Dawn

Supervising Dawn seemed to be a smooth continuation from supervising her work as a student in the weekly clinical supervision group at Anglia Ruskin University. The big difference was that I felt that it was often Dawn who came up with suggestions after presenting cases to me, rather than me coming up with completely new ideas. Sometimes I wondered whether I would have anything sufficiently 'original' to offer and was slightly anxious that I was not 'cost effective', but realised that it was the process of reflecting on work together as well as the actual advice or new insights that were important.

I have been impressed by how Dawn has managed to keep so many small pieces of music therapy work going, managing all the politics, liaison and paperwork around each separate and very diverse piece of work in a very thorough and efficient way. Because she has been so organised about these aspects of the work, we have been able to use supervision sessions to focus on the contents of the music therapy sessions, enabling her to develop her clinical music therapy skills.

As Dawn mentioned earlier, we are at similar stages in our lives, with our children being the same ages; sometimes we acknowledge that. This is an advantage in that I know from immediate experience what it is like to have your first child finish school and leave home, and can identify with the stress this causes and how it can impact on our work. Dawn and I enjoy exchanging stories about our children and it strengthens the bond between us. We are both good at being 'boundaried' about these exchanges, however, and do not let our personal lives interfere with the clinical supervision. In some way the bond between us in supervision is strengthened by our common experience; this does not mean that I necessarily share aspects of my personal life with all my supervisees, or that this special bond is necessary for supervision to go well.

Clare

Clare qualified as a music therapist from Anglia Ruskin University in January 2006. The following is drawn from Clare's account after five fortnightly supervision sessions with me.

What Clare wrote about supervision

For Clare it was important that her supervisor was an experienced music therapist who could shed new light on situations she was having difficulties with, reassure and encourage her when she was uncertain about her work, and bring clarity to her thinking when she was confused.

She came to me for supervision because of my clinical experience but also because she felt I was enthusiastic and could inspire her.

Clare gave an example of a 2-hour piece of work she was setting up in a school. The staff were very keen but there was some confusion about the sessions. Each week when she arrived at the school, something seemed to have changed, whether it was the number of children, or the number of sessions or the room that she would be using. Clare was beginning to feel a little frustrated by this and quite negative in terms of setting up the work. I recognised that the situation was confusing but pointed out that it was encouraging that school staff were so keen to have music therapy. Seeing it in that way, from a different perspective was very helpful. The next week she felt much more positive and arrived at the school with a clear agenda and an open and positive attitude making it easier to address the practical difficulties she had been experiencing. The staff at the school are pleased with how the music therapy sessions are going now and continue to be very supportive and helpful.

Deciding what to bring to supervision was one aspect that Clare initially felt challenged by. As a student on placements, she had experienced weekly 45-minute supervision sessions for just one or at the most three pieces of work. The leap from this to an hour's supervision every two weeks for 19 sessions of music therapy felt slightly daunting. However, Clare kept a notebook with her and when questions or difficulties arose, she jotted them down. Sometimes she found that issues resolved themselves before the next supervision session, either through her own thought processes or through peer support. Any remaining issues were brought to supervision.

One example of this was S, a boy of nine with autism whom Clare saw for individual music therapy sessions. Clare had found the first two sessions with him very difficult as he moved from one instrument to another very quickly. She felt exhausted after each session as she tried to support him by playing with him and sharing in his high levels of energy. Clare felt as though S was shutting her out and it was very difficult to engage with him. She brought a video of the session to supervision and I suggested that Clare could try giving him some space and perhaps not interact straight away, but rather sit near him, watch what he was doing, and relax and leave more spaces. In the next session Clare took these suggestions on board and it appeared to be helpful. S often chose the ocean drum and Clare sat near him as he played, rather than playing the piano as she had in previous sessions. Gradually, as she sat quietly he began to give very fleeting eye contact, the whole session generally felt calmer and there was a glimmer of interaction and contact between them. Since that session this contact has increased and they have shared some wonderful moments through the music, including laughter and some musical conversations. By taking a step back and giving S more space, the level of trust and interactions have increased providing greater opportunities in the work.

After five supervision sessions Clare has been surprised to discover that fortnightly sessions are enough and that she is increasingly able to process thoughts and difficulties arising from her work in between supervision sessions.

My reflections on supervising Clare

As Clare was starting out as a music therapist she clearly needed reassurance and encouragement to develop her confidence. On more than one occasion, I reminded her that in addition to being a newly qualified music therapist, she was also a qualified teacher with many years of experience, and that she should trust her own instincts and knowledge. Clare was very concerned about not taking on the role of a teacher in her therapy work. We often discussed this and I reassured Clare that I did not feel that this was happening. However, I also tried to help Clare to recognise the huge strengths and advantages she had gained from having worked as a teacher with children with special needs.

Another important aspect of supervision was helping Clare not to become overwhelmed by school politics or administrative inefficiencies. At times these issues seemed to dominate and it was important to get back to the actual music therapy processes to enable Clare to remain in touch with the central purpose of her work.

Reflections

It is obviously very rewarding for me to find out from these accounts that I am able to be helpful to music therapists in supervision. It is also interesting to compare these three accounts with those written by other supervisees in my previous chapter on supervision (Oldfield 2006).

In that earlier chapter (Oldfield 2006), I noted that most of my super-visees had initially been nervous about showing video excerpts of their work, and had only gradually plucked up the courage to show excerpts where they felt very unsure of what they were doing. This was not apparent in these three accounts. Indeed, Dawn particularly mentioned that although she enjoyed bringing videos of work she felt positive about, her first priority had been to share 'difficult' videos with me. An explanation for this change might be that on the training course, in recent years, I have been much more forceful about encouraging students to video their work and bring excerpts to supervision sessions, on a weekly basis. Recent advances in video technology mean that many students have their own personal video cameras with laptops to edit and show excerpts, making it much more straightforward to use this medium. Music therapists who have completed training in the past 5 years are therefore very used to using video excerpts and learning from them.[1]

The other 'typical' aspect mentioned by supervisees in my previous chapter (Oldfield 2006) was that it was helpful to be encouraged to focus on aspects of the work that are going well and not become overwhelmed by feeling inadequate about the difficulties encountered. This is also mentioned here by Andrea, Dawn and Clare, and ties in closely with the second point I mention in my teaching philosophy at Anglia Ruskin University 'building on existing strengths'.

---

1 Students follow rigorous ethical procedures and observe confidentiality procedures at all times. The clinical supervision groups on a training course are often seen as an extension of the clinical team.

When writing rough guidelines for Andrea, Dawn and Clare to use when writing about supervision, I added questions regarding their choice of supervisor, which I had not included in the questions to supervisees used in my previous chapter. It is clear that it is important to all three of them that their supervisor has experience in the field they are working in, and has a music therapy approach with which they agree. All three also mention that the personality and general outlook of their supervisor is important to them. These points are echoed by the accounts in my previous supervision chapter. As supervision involves being open about aspects of our work that we feel unhappy and worried about, it is not surprising that supervisees seek out a person who they feel they can trust and with whom they feel 'in tune'. Similarly, as a supervisor I would not take on a music therapist I did not feel I could work with, and I have great respect for the people I have supervised. As I mentioned earlier, I doubt whether I would have been brave enough to continue the work that Andrea was doing. I am uncertain that I could manage the large number of different jobs Dawn manages to do, and have great admiration for the management skills Clare brings to her music therapy work from her teaching experience.

As most of the supervisees' accounts I have gathered together are of work with children in special school settings, it is not easy for me to distinguish how supervision in this clinical area differs from supervision in other settings. Perhaps one feature is that, unlike specialist medical centres such as hospices, child development centres or psychiatric units, schools in general are familiar environments to us all, through our own school experiences and through those of our children or close relatives. This means that we all have preconceptions, and direct positive and negative experiences that we might bring to our work. We all have experienced 'splits' between parents, staff and children in school settings. As music therapists we often have to work hard in recognizing these divided loyalties in order not to become drawn into participating in the splitting or becoming overwhelmed by internal political agendas.

Another difficulty that some music therapists who have previously worked as teachers encounter is making the transition from being a teacher to being a therapist. This can be particularly difficult in a school setting, where many of the staff might struggle to make sense of work that has a therapeutic rather than an educational perspective. Many music teachers who choose to become music therapists will have chosen this new career path precisely in order to develop different ways of using music with children. When these music therapists then start working in schools it can be particularly difficult for them if they encounter resistance to a therapeutic stance amongst teachers. Supervision is an important space in which to reflect on these difficulties and to consider what may be needed to help the therapist maintain her professional identity.

For the past 12 years in Cambridgeshire, the local education authority agency whose main task is to provide instrumental tuition in local schools has also been responsible for employing music therapists in special schools and mainstream schools. It has been encouraging and exciting to witness the growing numbers of music therapists employed in this way. As one might expect with new appointments in a new organization, many issues regarding employment conditions have needed to be addressed. It has been a great advantage for me to be able to supervise this work from outside the system, as I am employed by the National Health Service. Not being employed by this agency myself has meant that it has been easier for me to encourage supervisees to focus on clinical aspects of their work rather than becoming overwhelmed with anxieties about organizational issues.

One of the central elements of all music therapy supervision, particularly at the beginning of music therapists' careers, is to enable supervisees to develop confidence and skills in clinical musical improvisation. This aspect of the work will be different for each person, but is the key to the success of the music therapy process. Once supervisees develop confidence in this area they will begin to develop their own clinical style and have the confidence to address other difficulties surrounding their work.

It is interesting to note that the majority of the people I have supervised have had to work in conditions that are much tougher than the clinical settings that I work in. It seems paradoxical that those music therapists who are starting to develop their confidence in the actual music therapy processes also often have to battle with difficult conditions, rooms where clients are easily distracted or disturbed, and lack of support from the schools they work in. As a supervisor, I often feel slightly guilty about the 'ideal' conditions I work in when I hear of the difficult settings my supervisees struggle with. However, I think it is also useful for music therapists to realise that usually, if they remain in post for long enough and continue to be clear about what they need, situations improve.

Having gathered information from nine of my supervisees [three in this chapter and six in Oldfield (2006)], it would appear that supervision is a useful process and that a number of elements are specific to supervision for music therapists working in schools. I would be interested in setting up some research in the future to look more specifically at how music therapists develop improvisation skills in clinical settings, and what part clinical supervision plays in this learning process.

References

Amir, D. (2001) 'The journey of two' in M. Forinash (ed.), *Music therapy supervision*, Philadelphia: Barcelona.

Hanser, S. (2001) 'A systems analysis approach to music therapy practice' in M. Forinash (ed.), *Music therapy supervision*, Philadelphia: Barcelona.

Oldfield, A. (1992) 'Teaching music therapy students on clinical placements: some observations'. *Journal of British Music Therapy*, 6(1), 13–17.

Oldfield, A. (2006) *Interactive music therapy in child and family psychiatry, clinical practice, research and teaching*. London: Jessica Kingsley.

Summer, L. (2001) 'Group supervision in first-time music therapy practicum' in M. Forinash (ed.), *Music therapy supervision* (pp. 70–86), Philadelphia: Barcelona.

Chapter 9

Turbulence at the boundary

Alison Davies and Ann Sloboda

This chapter is in three parts. The first is an exploration of boundary issues, drawing upon examples from both clinical work and supervision. The second part is a discussion of what might be called 'visible' and 'invisible' boundaries and of parallel processes in supervision. We have borrowed the idea of the 'visible' and 'invisible' from Agazarian and Peters; they use them in their book *The Visible and Invisible Group* (1981). They relate these two perspectives to group psychotherapy and the group process. We use these ideas to think of the visible and invisible in relation to boundaries. In the third and final part of the chapter we look at the specific boundary issues that arise in community music work, and music therapy in the community, in relation to the implications for the supervision process.

Some thoughts about boundaries

Boundaries and their meaning are central to the work of a therapist, and they should be central to the thinking of supervisor and supervisee as they work together.

Further complexities are potentially present for music therapists because they can find themselves working with both music and words. In this chapter we want to examine ways in which a thoughtful approach to boundaries can be maintained, exploring their meaning both in clinical work and the supervision setting. We discuss ways in which attending to boundaries might bring a deeper understanding of the therapy process, and how this in turn may throw light on a parallel process in the supervisory relationship.

The *New Collins Concise English Dictionary* defines 'boundary' as: '*Something that indicates the furthest limits as of an area or border*'. Some related words that spring to mind are 'perimeter', 'threshold' and 'edge'. One might think in terms of territory, checkpoints, frontiers or the clear demarcation of where one country ends and another begins. Boundaries can have a destructive element, representing barriers or divisiveness. The Berlin wall in the twentieth century is an extreme illustration of the separation of two regimes, that of a communist regime in the East and an isolated enclave of democratic capitalism in the West.

Taking a contrasting idea, let us look at the phenomenon of colour. When the primary colours blue and yellow are merged together they produce the colour green. A change has taken place where the boundary has merged or overlapped. Often, the most satisfying pictures are those where the image has been painted so that our inner eye and imagination go beyond the physical edges of the painting. The artist's vision can lead us through the frame to where we can see the picture in two ways, perceiving both what is painted within it and what is beyond the canvas and has to be imagined in order to make sense of the picture. Is there an analogy here in therapy? We have turned to these images to try to encourage a creative approach to thinking about the issue of boundaries in music therapy supervision.

In music therapy supervision, we have observed that clinical material that involves the disturbance or violation of boundaries can give us information as to what might be going on dynamically in the clinical practice or therapeutic relationship. This can help us to understand aspects of the internal worlds of our patients. At such times, therapist and supervisor need to attend closely to what is being communicated at the boundary edge in order to gain fuller understanding both of what is manifested outwardly and of what might be a latent, more unconscious communication.

Boundaries in groups

It is a common understanding in group analysis that a vital part of the work of a group conductor is to pay attention to events at the boundary. Noticing this and pointing it out helps group members to understand more fully what is going on. The struggle with boundaries can indicate the way in which members of a group are searching, often unconsciously, for ways to be together and to begin to trust and risk closeness with one another. Some examples:

- Am I important enough to be fully involved?
- I desperately want to be noticed but I will do everything to avoid exposing my vulnerability.
- I will come late or leave early in the hope that this needy and vulnerable part of me will not be addressed.
- If I stay on the fringe of things I will not have to divulge aspects of my family history or talk about things that might shame me, and I will not have to confront the reactions of others.
- If I play quietly or not at all I am less likely to be noticed.

These examples will be familiar to group music therapists and are also pertinent to individual work.

The musical dimension as an additional boundary in groups

In a music therapy session, how do we think about the boundaries between music, words and silence? How should events within individual or group improvisation be discussed or negotiated? If group members or those in individual therapy never comment on the music, should the therapist encourage them to speak? When do we allow the music to speak for itself?

We recognize that for some music therapists and in some therapy situations, the boundary between words, music and silence is less relevant. This may depend on the theoretical framework within which a music therapist might orientate herself. For some music therapists and in some contexts, the music might be looked on as a medium leading towards speech, whereas for other music therapists and in other contexts, only functional speech, such as the words of a song, might occur within the music. However, the issue of how group members communicate with each other within the music they create is relevant to all.

Consideration of musical boundaries in supervision

Music therapy supervision frequently involves detailed analysis of musical material. However, some supervisees choose not to bring recordings of clinical material to supervision, but discuss the process of their clinical work, describing both musical and non-musical aspects in words. The boundary between apparent overdependence on, or neglect of, the recorded material is a particular issue for music therapy supervisors. Where supervision sessions involve a therapist presenting entire recordings of session, there might be concern that the supervisee is not developing the ability to listen and formulate ideas independently. On the other hand, if the supervisee never brings any recorded material, the supervisor's ability to help reflect on musical interventions is severely limited, and may need addressing.

Considering how and when music is used in clinical work highlights an important but less clearly defined boundary that needs to be addressed in supervision. The use of music presents another arena where the boundaries need to be creatively observed, and which music therapists will recognise as familiar territory.

A supervisor hearing a musical extract for the first time can sometimes hear new things, or a fresh aspect of the musical exchange that is not apparent to the supervisee. This might bring a more objective view to what is being shared between patient and therapist and might be valuable particularly if there is a feeling that the therapist is getting lost in his or her own music. The supervisor needs to bear in mind that only the supervisee and patient or group of patients were present in the clinical encounter. However, the insights of the supervisor through listening and commenting offer a useful additional perspective. The fact that music therapy involves the shared creation of improvised music by therapist and patient creates a particular challenge to the traditional idea of the psychotherapeutic boundary, which can be more striking in music therapy than in some other psychological therapies. The music therapist has to be available for an active musical response to the patient's music, whereas in verbal psychotherapy, for instance, the therapist would not be simultaneously active at the same time or in the same way as the patient. In a purely verbal group such as a group analytic session, interrupting another person or speaking at the same time as them could be considered aggressive and not normally acceptable.

The activity of the therapist in verbal psychotherapy would be an attuned and emotionally responsive act of listening, with subsequent reflection, interpretation or clarification. These qualities, necessary in verbal therapy, could also be present for the music therapist in addition to the musical response. The therapist's improvised musical response generally avoids planned interventions, unlike the contexts of composition or performance where the content of music is agreed, discussed and consciously worked on between both parties involved. However, we will discuss later in this chapter the therapeutic reasons in a particular institutional setting for this boundary to be thought of in a different way.

Examples of musical boundaries in supervision

Here are some examples of issues related to musical boundaries that are often brought to supervision.

Vignette

A student on placement in a community psychiatric unit reported that members of the group were prepared to improvise together but had great difficulty in ending their improvisations. It was evident that the responsibility for drawing a boundary indicating the end of the piece aroused great feelings of anxiety and uncertainty.

This illustrates a typical dilemma that a music therapist might be confronted with. In supervision it was useful for this music therapy student to be helped to pick up on the anxiety manifested by the group members in their playing and to look at the wider context of uncertainty that was in play for the individual participants.

Other examples of boundary dynamics between musical and non-musical activities that are commonly brought to supervision:

- Interrupting a verbal statement or discussion by playing an instrument/s.
- Interrupting a musical improvisation with speech.
- A group in which members continually engage in discussion or musical improvisation, allowing no silence.

Examples that particularly indicate a patient's struggle to be in a close relationship:

- The patient who plays non-stop and will not 'let the therapist in'.
- The patient who dismisses verbal reflection as being of no value.
- The patient who regularly attends music therapy sessions and speaks but will not play.

The 'shifting' nature of boundaries

Boundaries are rarely stable for long. We have observed with interest that when one boundary is secured, another issue around boundaries might appear. This is illustrated by the following example, in which there is also a dynamic parallel between clinical and supervisory issues.

Example

Two music therapists working in a psychiatric service jointly ran a music therapy group serving patients in a long-stay ward. Despite expressing interest when approached in advance of the session, hardly any patients agreed to attend the initial sessions. Ward staff, although reminded, did not seem aware the group was happening, arranging conflicting appointments for patients at the group time. For some weeks the therapists felt too demoralized to bring this 'failure' to supervision but eventually complained to their supervisor of the difficulty in getting any patients to attend. They felt ignored, useless and rejected. Their supervisor noticed the parallel process that caused the therapists to neglect bringing this 'useless' group to supervision. She explored the idea that their feelings might be projections from nursing staff or patients in this setting, who might also feel denigrated or ignored. This made sense to the therapists. They decided to pay closer attention to their relationship with the ward staff, spending more time on the ward talking to nursing staff before and after the group. Despite fluctuations, the attendance duly increased and the therapists noticed the positive effects of their attention to this relationship. Once the group was better supported by the ward staff, a more regular membership was established.

However, different boundary difficulties subsequently began to arise. These were a manifestation of the patients' own problems in trusting one another and the therapists. Some were unable to manage the boundaries of the starting time and duration of the group. At least one member usually arrived late, interrupting the first improvisation. One patient regularly needed to visit the toilet in the middle of the group, another had a tendency to attend fortnightly and a third insisted on leaving early. The therapists discussed this in supervision and recognised this as a communication from the patients. When they realised how enormously difficult and anxiety provoking it was for the members to commit themselves to being present for the whole session, the therapists felt less frustration and more empathy towards the patients. With this understanding they were able to formulate a verbal communication to the patients, who in turn experienced some relief. The nature of the boundaries changed at this point and became focused on the musical activity. There was a struggle in particular with the issue over who should play the piano. The therapists preferred to provide musical support and structure on the piano, thus limiting the chaotic nature of the music by exerting control over the central arena of harmonic direction. The therapists struggled to balance their leadership with that of relinquishing control by allowing the group members, several of whom wished to play the piano, more freedom and scope to use the creative space. As a result, the therapists needed to find resources to deal first with a more chaotic musical milieu and second with the resulting anxiety that events in the session could get out of control.

Once the therapists had established a compromise that ensured that both they and the patients had access to the piano, yet another boundary required attention, that of their clinical role. They felt considerable pressure to move into the role of teachers and performers. Whereas one patient continually asked the therapists to teach him how to play the piano, another wanted the group as a performance space for a wider audience. Grandiose ideas ensued of TV performances and record sales, which indicated a psychotic quality in the perceptions of some patients. It was important for this to be recognized and for the therapists to assert their clinical role and remind the group of realities: that the setting was a psychiatric hospital, the therapists were staff and the group members were patients. This refusal to collude was necessary for the therapists to continue to function in their clinical role.

This example, with its succession of boundary questions, is rather like the notion of an onion where one layer peeled off reveals another and so on.

Students on placement

The role of the placement supervisor can involve supervision of clinical work as well as overseeing the student's clinical practice within the setting; this can include dealing with colleagues and contributing at ward rounds. The supervisor holds some responsibility for a trainee's performance in the workplace. This could lead to transference and possibly to boundary issues that will need to be sensitively addressed or interpreted. The supervisee might feel that she is being judged and is not free to make mistakes and, in the same way, the supervisor might feel scrutinized by the training course. The boundaries between student, supervisor and course can create the potential for splitting. The experience of a placement supervisor can be complex as she seeks to fulfil her accountability to the supervisee, the training course and her own workplace.

Further thinking about boundaries brings to mind the interface between what is 'inside' and what is 'outside'. For our purposes, the 'inside' refers to interactions inside the room between therapist and patient or group members. What is 'outside' relates to material brought in for 'discussion' from outside the session. Yalom (2002 pp. 46–64) writes in terms of the horizontal 'here and now' that is present in the therapy relationship(s) and the vertical 'past, present and future', which is brought in from outside. The supervisee sometimes needs help to work from the vertical perspective to the more transferential 'here and now' of the horizontal. To put it another way, the supervisee needs to be directed towards looking at the dynamics inside rather than outside the room. This will have parallels in the supervisory relationship. Another aspect of 'inner' and 'outer' has to do with the so-called 'inner' world of the patient and the 'outer' reality of events. The interface between these worlds and how to manage this boundary is also an important dynamic to consider in supervision.

'Visible' and 'invisible' boundaries

The issues that have been explored so far can be usefully considered under the heading of 'visible' and 'invisible' boundaries.

The 'visible' in terms of boundaries

Behr and Hearst, in their book *Group Analytic Psychotherapy, a Meeting of Minds* (2005 p. 42), talk about 'dynamic administration'. They apply this to group analysis but it is a helpful concept for all aspects of therapy, and an especially useful one for music therapists. The authors look at what is required of a therapy setting or what has to be put in place for effective therapy to take place. This means creating a safe, 'holding', confidential space with care and thought about the environment. Depending on the client group, this might include letter writing and telephone communication, seeing parents (if appropriate) and, particularly for the music therapist, the care and management of musical instruments. Attention to the setting, sometimes described as the 'frame', allows for the therapy to be contained. This idea of a 'frame' returns us to our analogy of a picture.

The 'invisible' in terms of boundaries

This refers to the emotional or invisible boundaries linked to the pathologies of the patient or the group, ourselves and supervisees as clinicians and clinical supervisors. The arenas of 'visible' and 'invisible' need not be separate from each other but can overlap and relate. 'Visible' and 'invisible' boundaries are important to grasp, especially when working within a psychodynamic framework. These dynamics are also present in the musical interaction and might be evident in the parallel process that gets enacted in the supervisory relationship or the environment where supervision takes place.

'Visible' boundaries explored

The frame

Creating a 'holding' environment as a physical boundary, or paying attention to the 'frame', acts as a 'silent but necessary background to all analytic work' (Modell, cited in Nitsun 1996 p. 154). It is important to help supervisees to understand that a 'holding' environment needs to be in place for the patient to feel secure. For all patients, but especially those who are very challenging, emotionally and behaviourally, successful engagement in therapy requires and depends on secure holding boundaries. A careful balance is required to achieve this, depending on the pathology and the personal history of the patient. The boundary of the environment or setting should not be too loose; that would jeopardize the patients' sense of the therapy setting as a special place. On the other hand, a boundary that is too tight can be experienced as punitive and persecutory, restricting the patient's ability to communicate freely. This can be equally true of the supervisory relationship. Critical supervisors produce highly defended supervisees.

Like the therapy setting, the supervision setting should be a place of confidentiality where the supervisee feels that he or she is taken seriously. By maintaining a secure frame, the supervisor makes it possible for supervisees to open up and share their vulnerabilities, doubts, lack of skills or competency and, of course, the difficulties presented by clients. Supervision is often the only place for supervisees to have this level of honesty away from the workplace, where they might have felt a strong pressure to demonstrate their worth and usefulness to the service. This feeling can be internally exaggerated by the therapist's own insecurities (and may have some external reality, in a climate where so many services are in financial crisis).

In *Supervision and Being Supervised* (Weiner, Mizen & Duckham (eds) 2003) Gee presents a clear discussion of boundaries in the supervision of psychotherapists. Much of this is equally useful for music therapists. He refers to the importance of helping the supervisees to '. . . deal with practical issues in a straightforward way' (p. 150) and gives the example of managing the involvement of the parent of a client. He highlights the need to understand the attitudes, terminology and expectations encountered in different work settings.

In some workplaces, such as schools, group homes and some hospital wards, the concept of 'therapy' might be alien and handling of boundaries needs care. With help, supervisees can weather these dynamics so that they are able to work in a complementary way alongside teachers and care workers.

An example from a school setting

In a school for children with severe learning disabilities, the headmistress barges into a music therapy session on the pretext of showing a prospective parent round the school. She asks the child in treatment, if he could show the 'lady' how he plays the drums. The child is confused, and the music therapist is very annoyed both at the interruption and the nature of it. She does not know how to react. She feels in a difficult position, not wanting to appear un-co-operative yet knowing the importance of a confidential space for the child. She could respond in several ways, acquiescing to the demand or not. Whatever she does is going to be uncomfortable.

In supervision it is possible to look at the dynamics that are involved in this incident. The supervisor might help the supervisee to protect and keep to firm therapeutic boundaries, as well as to foster understanding of the particular boundaries dictated by the institution. Supervision might also help the supervisee to look at the dynamics from both sides, so that a greater understanding of one another's work (therapist and headmistress) can pave the way towards creating an optimal therapy environment and a mutuality that models difference as important.

For the supervisee to bring these boundary dilemmas to supervision there needs to be an atmosphere of trust. The supervisor needs to be both sympathetic and challenging in helping the supervisee find ways to maintain the therapeutic boundaries. For a music therapist to feel a 'bad' therapist because she has not managed a situation well is very demoralizing. The crucial thing is that the supervisee feels confident enough to bring these incidents to supervision. Supervision should be a place where curiosity is awakened in the service of improving music therapy practice and where a supervisee can renew her strength in the all too familiar 'battle' for suitable music therapy conditions.

Again, Behr and Hearst (2005 p. 46) are helpful in their approach to dynamic administration. They speak about the intrusion of the institution, especially when dealing with the setting of therapy, and draw attention to the possible splits going on when all is 'bad' outside therapy and all is 'good' within. This may emerge in an overemphasis by the patients on the bad 'goings on' in the institution in order to avoid looking at what dynamics might be going on internally within themselves, the group or the therapy process.

This dynamic may also have a parallel in the supervisory situation. Are the continual disappointments voiced by the supervisee covering up his or her feelings about other things? As supervisors, we might have to look at what is being projected out. Conversely, there is the potential for us, as supervisors, to collude with our supervisees, especially when we have sympathy for their dilemmas. However, collusive thinking can obscure objectivity, avoid challenge and result in supervision that lacks energy and rigor. This leads to two capacities we think crucial in a supervisor: to be empathic and to challenge.

Attention to the boundaries of time and space can begin to make the work feel safer for both therapist and patient. The professionalism that this shows can also result in the therapy work in the wider institution becoming gradually more respected. It is also worth noting here that, as the desire for sameness and envy of difference gives way to an appreciation of different practices and ways of working, a greater sense of mutuality can often evolve with colleagues and the institution as a whole. Fostering an interest in difference on both sides avoids the desire to enviously attack what is not the same.

Newly or recently qualified music therapists often find work in settings where they are the sole music therapist employed. This very often allows them to be marginalised, resulting in their feeling unsupported and vulnerable, and excluded from the central business of the organisation. The single music therapist in a school, for instance, whether newly qualified or not, might be the recipient of envious attacks by teachers who perceive them as having the 'privilege' of working individually or in small groups and being able to hand their child back to the classroom teacher at the end of the session. When this, often unconscious, envy is in play, then the maintenance of administrative boundaries, such as room availability or times of sessions can seem under attack.

Protecting the artistic or musical medium can often be a troublesome area as it can disturb colleagues. The requirement of specific spaces with designated equipment for arts therapies clinical practice is a genuine, pragmatic one. Nevertheless, it can be provocative to colleagues, who perceive the arts therapists as inflexible and territorial. Out of the necessity of having a suitable place to play music, their clinical areas may become less flexible for use by other colleagues.

Example

A small psychiatric unit, which was keen to develop arts therapies, created a music therapy post for 2 days a week, and provided G, the newly appointed therapist, with a budget for instruments. What was offered was a building with only one multi-purpose room for meetings and groups, and very little storage space. Whilst genuinely positive about the idea of music therapy, staff inevitably displayed a more ambivalent attitude to it, with dark remarks alluding to 'invasion' and 'take-over' in G's presence when a piano and several large drums took up residence in the meeting room. G was very upset. Her line manager, the Head of Therapies, had conflicting priorities when attempting to support her. Other staff in her team had complained that the instruments were a distraction for patients, who were unable to refrain from touching and playing them during another non-musical group. It was important that G did not take this situation too personally or as an attack on music therapy. With the help of her supervisor, she negotiated with senior staff ways to find a storage solution for the instruments, and an alternative and more permanent place for music therapy sessions.

Supervisees often need help to hold onto the confidence and commitment required to maintain a safe therapy space. Supervision can foster a thoughtful approach in exploring the complexities of boundary issues, which can in turn allow a less narrow view to prevail. Such an exploration might include the following issues:

- Avoidable/unavoidable situations in the institution that require tackling (as in the case of G above).
- Envy of the work of a music therapist.
- Other colleagues' failure to take the therapy seriously.
- The music therapist's difficulties in taking her-/himself seriously.
- The challenge to the music therapy space representing a disturbance in the workplace that is being played out in the arena of music therapy.

A further clinical example from psychiatry
A psychiatric unit had recently undergone an inspection. The inspectors were critical of the amount of time patients spent on wards, apparently not engaged in group therapy or social interaction of any sort. A small team of music therapists working in the psychiatric unit had struggled to establish therapy provision on a long-stay ward for patients with severe and enduring mental illness, and succeeded eventually in establishing a small music therapy group. This group, held in the music therapy room, served the most severely ill patients who, overcoming their lethargy and reluctance to interact, were able to leave the ward and attend the group with a regularity that was impressive for such 'difficult-to-engage' patients. Another group of clinical staff, in response to the review, had set up a 'social skills' group in an adjacent room. They complained that the noise of the music therapy group made their work impossible and insisted that it move. It was striking that this occurred in

a climate where cuts in service provision were imminent and professional groups were required to prove their worth and demonstrate it by patient attendance. In supervision, the therapists needed encouragement to listen to the 'opposition' and be thoughtful about others' point of view whilst retaining a strong belief in their own work. Considerable maturity of thinking was required for the therapists to recognize the rivalry and primitive anxiety in the atmosphere, and to take a balanced approach to the difficulty of this boundary. The music therapists experienced a sense of attack on their service, but the staff in the adjacent room felt their own therapeutic boundaries were compromised. Discussing this in both staff meetings and group supervision was useful. It helped the therapists to avoid getting drawn into a paranoid position on the issue, which would have intensified splits between groups of staff. They were able to consider alternative locations for their group and retain their confidence in the value of their work for this particular group of patients.

'Invisible' boundaries explored

'The arts sensitized me, and clinical experience confirmed, that the psychic boundaries are permeable rather than being firm structures' Rose (2004 p. 2) Psychic boundaries are those in the realm of interpersonal relationships and encompass ideas of unconscious processes and projective mechanisms. These dynamics, as in all relationships, are also present in the supervisory one. They also appear in the music that is played between client and patient.

Cox (1978 p. 239) writes of '. . . the creative potential of using the boundary between self and others as a "zone" for risk-taking and growth'. This could equally apply in supervision in the form of risk-taking for the supervisor through challenging the supervisee, and for the supervisee in presenting aspects of his work that might expose vulnerability. This could be especially pertinent when presenting music where our own internal judgement of ourselves or our proficiency might be at play. Mutuality is needed here where both supervisee and supervisor can dare to risk the exposure of these feelings.

The so-called 'invisible' boundary around the patient's pathology and that of the supervisee might well be something that arises in supervision. Transference and countertransference are the important mechanisms that help us understand this boundary and the emotional space where the therapist meets the patient.

Let us look at examples of this more personal boundary. How, for example, does the music therapist handle the patient's transference disclosures? How might the supervisor investigate that with the supervisee? It is easier to handle material about the 'outside' or the 'there and then', both in verbal communication and in the music, than material from the 'inside' and the 'here and now'. Transference and countertransference are phenomena particular to working psychoanalytically. It is more risky to address the present 'here and now' because of the personal feelings and interactions it evokes. However, if Cox is right, this needs to be done in the interest of furthering the growth of a deeper understanding of the inner lives of patients. Yalom (2001 p. 46) puts it like this:

> The here-and-now is the major source of therapeutic power . . . it refers to the immediate events of the therapeutic hour . . . to what is happening here . . . (. . . . in the in-betweenness – the space between me and you) and now in this immediate hour. It is basically an ahistoric approach and de-emphasizes (but does not negate the importance of) the patient's historical past or events of his or her outside life.

It is our understanding that if something in the 'here and now' boundary feels too difficult to say, then this is a clear indication that it needs to be said. Finding ways of addressing the difficulty, however uncomfortable, might be the only way to further the understanding of the work. This is true in both clinical work and supervision. The following example illustrates this issue as well as a parallel process going on in supervision.

Example

The therapist brings a patient that she is feeling bored with, whose loud, repetitive playing of music is making her feel cut off. She finds her mind wandering elsewhere. She feels the atmosphere acutely in the session but does not know how to address it in the 'here and now'. When this material is presented in supervision, the supervisor begins to lose interest, cannot seem to make an intervention and finds her mind wandering, unable to listen further to what seems like a relentless list of nothing happening in the therapy.

The questions here might be:

- How can the supervisee address and work at understanding this 'here and now' boredom with the patient and also understand her own countertransference feelings, which might evoke all sorts of inadequacies musically and non-musically within herself?
- What is not being addressed in the clinical session that is also not being addressed in the supervision?
- What intervention does the therapist need to make in her work that the supervisor also needs to make in the supervision?

We have found that pointing out what is going on in the supervision session as a parallel process to the clinical work can often awaken a new depth and aliveness, and can be a way of challenging issues in a more acceptable way. The supervisor then gives the supervisee the renewed energy to make an intervention in the therapy. Of course, this has to be done in a 'holding' way so that the supervisee can 'hear' in a way that energizes thinking rather than promotes negativity. The supervisory situation, like all relationships in life, will have an element of transference/countertransference present. If there is courage to explore this in supervision, an emotional space could be opened up throwing light on the work and allowing the patient to be reached at a greater depth.

Helping the supervisee to manage the patient's personal disclosure is another emotional boundary that speaks of the personal and the 'here and now' and is present in both the supervision and the clinical setting. Cox (1978 p. 190) writes:

> Rules may exist to be broken, and there are obviously moments in psychotherapy in which disclosure of the therapist's experience can have a profoundly catalyzing and therapeutic effect if it is used appropriately. But, as a general rule, it can be said that an 'optimal therapeutic climate' is fostered by the cultivation of reciprocity felt by the patient on the basis of minimal personal detailed disclosure on the part of the therapist.

He goes on to say, with a touch of humour (p. 191):

> Too little reciprocity in clinical work can result in the therapist being perceived as a cold, aloof detached professional who makes the patient feel that he is regarded as a 'card with bronchitis on it'.

There are times when, as supervisors, we need to help supervisees by giving examples of our own boundary struggles. However, care has to be taken here, as sometimes giving examples of one's own work can make the supervisee feel that the specificity of what they are bringing is not being attended to. It can seem to the supervisee that the supervisor listens and translates into her own experience. The supervisee then feels that what is said is not a true reflection of what is happening. The supervisor here needs the ability to be attuned to what might be helpful and enabling and what might be unhelpful and disenabling around disclosures of her own boundary experiences!

Boundaries around individual pathologies

Understanding in supervision of the boundaries of individual pathologies follows from this theme of emotional boundaries. Some patients demand an intense shared space in therapy where the boundary of communication/miscommunication feels overwhelming for the therapist and the sense of mutual separation and capacity to think on the part of the patient (transferred often to the therapist) is absent. There is an inability on the part of some patients to turn within themselves for solace or to be alone. Other patients, by contrast, have an experience of the world in which they do not connect with others or with society and have turned exclusively within themselves for comfort. An example here might be an autistic or psychotic way of being in the world. Perhaps paradoxically these two extremes are rather close to each other. Both have the fear of intimacy; one with the fusional fear of separation and the other the fear of being invaded. Both are struggling, from different ends of the spectrum, with the theme of abandonment. In this way, perhaps, we can help the supervisee understand the 'I am helpless' notice or the 'no admittance' notice on some of the patients they see. We might also need to be aware of these so-called notices on the supervisee. We can be of help by drawing their attention to an understanding of this boundary presentation both in their patients and within themselves. This may be especially true for student therapists and those just starting out when presented for the first time with patient pathology of this kind.

The music in relation to the 'invisible' boundary

Vignette

A supervisee presents a music therapy patient who leaves no gaps in his music, filling every moment with frenetic playing and allowing little or no space to hear or respond to the therapist's music. The therapist perhaps has a part to play in this. There is a musical battle going on in which neither therapist nor patient can arrive at any mutuality or creative response to each other. The therapist realises that the patient also repeats this dynamic outside the music with a barrage of verbal worries and the inability to leave any space for reflection. The supervisee does not seem able to see the dynamic that is between them but she does feel that there is a controlling element coming from both the patient and herself.

In the above case, supervision might draw attention to the notion of a defensiveness or fear in the patient, of falling into a chasm where he might sink for ever, abandoned without connection to another person, unable to access any personal solace or resources. The supervisee may then become aware of experiencing this acute neediness herself within the supervision, feeling devoid of any thoughtful resources to call upon. In turn, the supervisor notices a sense of pressure to 'feed on demand'. It is very satisfying for the supervisor when there is a sudden recognition on the part of the supervisee of what is happening in the music and then realizing how it connects with pathologies outside the music. Helping the supervisee to see this parallel process, that was clearly present in the music, can enable her in turn to think with the patient about the emotional space he occupies in life.

In connection with this notion of 'invisible boundaries', we can consider the seemingly opposite personality who turns exclusively within himself for comfort and allows no-one to penetrate this solipsism. An illustration here might be the isolation of the schizophrenic way of being. This closed circular system of autism or psychosis might be reflected in the same way in supervision, for example in a 'cut off' feeling between supervisor and supervisee. This might be observed through attending to the transference in the clinical work presented with special reference to the relationship in the music. A parallel process might again be experienced and unconsciously played out between the supervisee and supervisor. Musical role-play can be useful here, especially attending to the feelings that come up in the music between the supervisee and the supervisor. It might be reasonably easy to role-play the clinical setting but it might be even more illuminating to role-play what is going on in the supervision. Exploring in this way, and thinking together with curiosity, can begin to deepen the work and, in our view, allow it to become fascinating. Being aware of how these pathological boundaries present themselves both in the clinical work and in the supervisory relationship can be an important part of understanding in the supervision space.

The boundary between music therapy and community music

Where music therapy has entered into the arena of community music (Pavlicevic & Andsdell 2004), negotiations at the boundary between the roles of therapist/teacher, therapist/co-writer and therapist/accompanist, need consideration. In the case of performance this is particularly crucial. Although not all the community music therapy literature concerns itself with these tensions, they are looked at with rigour and sensitivity by Turry (2005), who discusses the countertransference complications involved in a piece of music therapy work that moved from a clinical treatment setting to a therapeutic relationship involving composition, rehearsal and ultimately performance of the patient's own compositions. The acknowledgement of the need to consider the impact on the relationship of the therapist being involved in performance with the patient was discussed at length. This included consideration of the pressures on the role of the therapist and the strong feelings that may arise; for example, if either therapist or client makes a 'mistake' in performance. Related issues, such as being asked to provide music for an event in the institution (an entertainment, school play or carol service), frequently arise in supervision. How the music therapist deals with the boundary of the clinical role in these circumstances will vary, but careful consideration of the therapist's role is required, whatever the decision.

It is generally understood that the music a patient plays in a music therapy session in which improvisation is used as the primary model can be likened to free association (Odell-Miller 2001). There is also an element of free association for the therapist but as a response to the patient, and this must be carefully adjusted in the service of the patient's music. This is a delicate balance. The music therapist has to have one ear available to respond musically in the service of the patient and the other ear providing an intuitive yet thoughtful response. This requires a greater flexibility of thinking when the boundary is open to institutional events.

In the following example, the balance between 'inside' and 'outside' therapy was negotiated therapeutically in an institution where flexibility was of the utmost importance.

Example

J, a music therapy student, was being supervised for his work with a group of difficult, school-refusing adolescents. These young people could barely tolerate each other and found it extremely difficult to be in the same room except in their chosen pairs or small groups. J was eager to work with this client group but found the work very challenging. He was, however, determined that something good might come out of attempting to find ways of bringing these clients together in a therapeutic way. The unit was putting on a pantomime. J, in the music therapy sessions, was able to use this 'outside' event to help clients to write songs and prepare for the musical part of this performance.

What he began to notice was that unlikely pairs of young people began to co-operate in such things as accompanying each other, commenting on performance, listening and appreciating others' expertise. These aspects of being together in a group, tolerating each other and with a lessening of negative assumptions, were all good therapeutic outcomes. With a more positive attitude to one another the young people in the music therapy group could follow through with a performance out of the session with the therapist taking part. J was helped through supervision to use Pavlicevic's idea (Pavlicevic 2004 p. 37) of community music where the 'inside' reaches 'outside' and the 'outside' reaches 'inside'. He used his therapeutic skills to be creative around the boundary in the service of helping these disturbed young people towards a more social way of being with each other through music and shared performance.

Conclusion

Managing what is being communicated at the boundary can lead to greater insight in the service of a fuller understanding of our work as therapists, as expressed by Clulow (1994), writing about the supervisory relationship:

. . . communication between supervisee and supervisor occurs not only in what is said, but what is enacted between them . . . Managing the supervisory boundary, as well as making links between what is happening in supervision and work contexts, provides opportunities for translating enactments into insight.

(Clulow 1994 p. 182)

Legitimising the feelings of supervisors and supervisees is a precondition to attending to what they might mean, and how they might be deployed to the benefit of the clients.

(Clulow 1994 p. 184)

In this chapter, we have demonstrated the centrality of boundaries when working in supervision. Thinking about both the 'visible', more obvious boundaries that clearly manifest themselves in the setting and administration and the more latent 'invisible' boundaries represented by pathologies, parallel processes and transference/countertransference is all part of the work of good supervision.

It is our view that 'turbulence' or difficulties at the boundary are invariably an indication that something important is happening clinically. The process of working through boundary issues in supervision to develop a deeper understanding of the complexities involved can lead us to an understanding of our patients at a deeper dynamic level. Above all, we would like to think that supervision could be an immensely creative place of mutual discovery both for the supervisee and the supervisor that provides a sense of 'vision' that cannot be reached by the therapist alone.

We would like to thank all the supervisees that we have worked with over the years. Material for this chapter has only come about through their wish to share their clinical work with us. Especial thanks to Jonathan Perkins for permission to include a recent piece of supervisory work with him.

References

Agazarian,Y. (1997) *Systems centred therapy for groups.* London: Guilford Press.

Agazarian, Y., Peters, R. (1981) *The visible and invisible group.* London and New York: Tavistock/Routledge.

Behr, H., Hearst, L. (eds) (2005) *Group-analytic psychotherapy, a meeting of minds.* London: Whurr Publishers.

Clulow, C. (1994) 'Balancing care and control: the supervisory relationship as a focus for promoting organisational health' in A. Obholzer and V. Roberts (eds), *The unconscious at work,* London: Routledge.

Cox, M. (1978) *Structuring the therapeutic process.* Oxford: Pergamon Press.

Gee, H. (2003) 'Boundaries in supervision' in J. Weiner, R. Mizen and J. Duckham (eds), *Supervising and being supervised: a practice in search of a theory,* New York: Palgrave Macmillan.

Nitsun, M. (1996) *The anti-group*. London: Routledge.

Odell-Miller, H. (2001) 'Music therapy and its relationship to psychoanalysis' in Y. Searle and I. Streng (eds), *Where analysis meets the arts*, London: Karnac.

Pavlicevic, M., Andsell, G. (2004) *Community music therapy*. London: Jessica Kingsley.

Rose, G.J. (2004) *Between couch and piano*. Hove, UK: Brunner Routledge.

Turry, A. (2005) 'Music psychotherapy and community music therapy: questions and considerations'. *Voices: A World Forum for Music Therapy*, 5.

Weiner, J., Mizen, R., Duckham, J. (eds) (2003) *Supervising and being supervised: a practice in search of a theory*. New York: Palgrave Macmillan.

Yalom, I. (2002) *The gift of therapy*. London: Piatkus Books.

Chapter 10

Supervision of PhD doctoral research

Tony Wigram

Introduction

The most significant and important element in a doctoral research training is the level and quality of supervision researchers receive. This chapter focuses on the model of doctoral study that is quite common in Europe, where the production of a doctoral thesis stands at the centre (and conclusion) of the process, and every aspect of doctoral supervision and doctoral research feeds into this important product. Doctoral study in this model involves:

- Undertaking a rigorous research study that fills a gap in knowledge and stands as a significant contribution to the scientific literature.
- Writing up the research they have done in the form of a substantial thesis.
- Submitting the thesis for examination and successfully defending it.

To achieve the above objectives, it is not only necessary to find and engage with a supervisor who will guide you through the project that you are planning to undertake, but also to establish a good supervisory relationship so that expectations, on both sides, can be met in order to successfully train as a researcher. It is important to understand that a PhD study should be approached more as a training to be a researcher than an ambition to undertake a 'brilliant and groundbreaking' piece of research that will be talked about and remembered for years to come! The training to be a researcher should also encompass a process whereby the doctoral researcher not only learns his or her own research method from the study being undertaken, but also explores the multifaceted and fascinating world of research, learning about many other research methods and techniques in the process. That is why it is often helpful to engage in a research milieu where other students are also undertaking studies in a wide variety of areas and through an equally wide range of research methods.

This chapter is structured in a way that reflects the process of the PhD study and the role of the supervisor in that study. Consequently, I first describe the initial stages of the process, in which a future doctoral researcher is defining the objectives and boundaries of the study and trying to prepare a proposal that will be accepted and will form the framework and basis for the area of investigation he or she wishes to pursue. Following that, the next important aspect is defining and establishing a supervisory relationship. Once the process begins, the study immediately expands to include many different areas of investigation, and the doctoral student will realise how many potential ideas could be incorporated. So the first and second stages of the study often involve limiting and containing the ambitions of the research student. In the third stage, as the researcher begins to collect, analyse and interpret data, the supervision involves guiding and challenging the doctoral researcher. The last two stages to be addressed are the role of the supervisor in helping to write up the study and in preparing the doctoral researcher for defending the study.

In preparing for a PhD supervisors' course held in Denmark in October, 2005, I found myself constructing some general principles and guidelines that I believe form the basis of effective supervision of doctoral research. It is inevitable that people appointed to supervise doctoral research will rely heavily on their own experiences of supervision and also their own area of expertise and knowledge. However I consider, on the basis of my own experience over the last 20 years as a doctoral researcher and supervisor, that there are some important principles of supervision.

General principles of supervision (Wigram 2005)

PhD study is a training to be a researcher

Most doctoral students in the arts therapies have not necessarily studied research methods (as have, for example, psychology graduates). They might be beginning a doctoral study without having undertaken any courses in research design or statistics, and might be assuming that they can 'learn as they go along'. Studying research methods is essential, and three of the most useful books for this are the second edition of *Music Therapy Research* (Wheeler 2005) *Real World Research* (Robson 2002) and *Beginning Research in the Arts Therapies* (Ansdell & Pavlicevic 1998). Learning how to undertake research is part of doctoral study and supervision, and it must be anticipated by both the student and the supervisor that learning through experience involves learning from mistakes and misunderstandings. The learning process incorporates many different elements, including developing the theoretical framework, formulating method and a design, undertaking field work and writing abilities.

PhD study is a discipline whereby the 'student' changes from 'student researcher' to 'qualified researcher'

This principle is vital in determining the process of supervision, and the changing nature of the roles of supervisor and supervisee and the relationship between them. As the doctoral researcher becomes more experienced, more expert and knowledgeable in his or her area and more confident about how to explain the research, the less dependent he or she should become on their supervisor. This will be addressed particularly in the sections on guiding the study and writing up the study.

PhD study is isolating and lonely and there should be a milieu within which there is support and critique

In doctoral study, attrition can be quite high and many who begin doctoral studies never complete them. In a small discipline such as music therapy, it is difficult to find a large enough milieu where there are several other doctoral researchers. Three examples of larger settings are Aalborg University, Denmark, Melbourne University, Australia and Temple University, Philadelphia, USA. There are smaller doctoral programmes in Norway, Finland, the UK, the USA, Germany and Australia.

Principles applied to creative arts therapy research supervision

As all arts therapists have grown up in a tradition of creative, interdisciplinary thinking, there is a significant risk that when embarking on research, initial ideas can rapidly expand into multidimensional concepts. With this in mind, and considering that few arts therapists have undergone an academic training in research methods, some or all of these considerations may be necessary:

- The study is defined and agreed at the outset, and during conversion (elaborated proposal stage). Changes in direction should be kept to a minimum.
- The study should remain true to the research hypotheses or questions.
- The study should be restricted, and not allowed to expand beyond unattainable goals.
- The study should demonstrate a doctoral/philosophical level of thinking.
- The student's wishes are sometimes based on naivety, idealism, narrow mindedness or ignorance, and should be challenged.
- The student's intentions and assumptions are not always correct, and should be directed.

- Advice can be sought from advisors, specialists and consultants, but final decisions about any development or possible change in the research study must be discussed and agreed with the head supervisor.
- A secondary supervisor can be identified, with a proportion of responsibility (i.e. 20%–40%). Again, decisions about any development or possible change in the research study must be discussed and agreed with the head supervisor. This partnership can work, with some profit, providing there is adequate discussion between supervisors, and between supervisors and student.
- The supervisor's guidance is based on previous experience.
- The supervisor is not omnipotent, and can be challenged.
- The supervisor expects the student to take increasing responsibility for decisions and self-critique.

Although some of these points might sound unexpectedly limiting, there is a need for academic and scientific discipline if the doctoral study is to be successfully achieved, and initially this is the responsibility of the supervisor.

The practical aspects of supervision

Doctoral supervisors are hard to find, and they are frequently very busy with their own research, as well as usually having a heavy teaching load. Likewise, doctoral students can have a number of pressures, both in the area of their research and in their professional and personal lives, and it is worth paying attention to some boundaries and structure from the very beginning of the relationship to avoid problems arising; this will include defining meeting times, good preparation and meeting deadlines. There are obligations on both sides for ensuring a successful supervisory relationship.

Beginning the process – the initial proposal

My experience is that supervision starts before the student even becomes registered in a doctoral programme. Many future doctoral students send proposals to me that they would like to pursue in doctoral research and my first task is to help them to structure and organise these to develop a framework that is both realistic and relevant, can demonstrably fill a gap in knowledge and can show a philosophical level of enquiry. Any initial proposal needs to contain some essential elements:

- *The research statement and problem formulation*: an explanation of the reason why the research needs to be done and what gap in knowledge this will successfully fill. The problem formulation or research statement defines the scope and boundaries of the research that is intended to be undertaken.

- *The theoretical framework*: a small literature review needs to be presented, giving a theoretical framework for the study that is to be undertaken. Some evidence that there is a clinical and/or empirical basis for a study is necessary and if there is no previous research in music therapy to underpin the problem formulation, then clinical examples and research from other disciplines would be important as a context. At the end of this section, the provisional research hypotheses or questions should be specified in order to decide the method of the study. It is important at this stage to get a sense that doctoral applicants have thought through some options for method and design and can demonstrate that they have learnt something via research methodology from the some of the literature that is available (Ansdell & Pavlicevic 1998; Robson 2002; Wheeler 2005).
- *Practical considerations*: finally, the initial proposal needs to describe and define the expected research timeframe and contain a proposal for who might supervise the study. It would also be useful in the initial proposal for research applicants to define what additional training and courses they would hope to gain in order to develop their research ability and skills.

In my experience, this stage in the initial proposal is absolutely essential if individuals are to begin their doctoral studies with the right expectations and having thought ahead to what they are intending to do. I often find that it takes two or more drafts of a proposal before it is really ready to be circulated for peer-group review, prior to a university agreeing to register a candidate for doctoral study. Very typically, the following problems occur:

- The research statement is too broad and general.
- The research statement demonstrates that the proposed study is more service review or clinical audit than research.
- The literature review lacks evidence of previous research, or even of previous clinical or empirical substance, that will provide a good-enough foundation for the research.
- The literature review might demonstrate the candidate's limitations in writing style.
- The literature review might demonstrate a drift into areas that are completely unrelated to the research area proposed by the candidate.
- The research questions are often not well focused.
- The research questions might be too broad or actually too extensive, and might incorporate as many as 12–15 sub-questions.
- A research question is not formulated as a question that can be answered. There are many examples where people suggest they want to 'explore this . . .' or 'work towards developing a theory of . . .', consequently lacking focus.

- A method is inappropriately defined before the research question has been explicated and further questions or hypotheses developed.
- Research questions need to be limited and methods developed that can be achieved within the timeframe.

The beginning of the supervision relationship is going to involve a healthy and objective look at all these aspects, and some hard decisions early on. The supervisor knows how important it is to establish the correct focus and direction of research from the beginning, far better than the researcher usually does.

The supervisory relationship

A doctoral student will typically search for a supervisor who is both sympathetic to the area of research being undertaken and knowledgeable and expert in that area. From the perspective of the supervisor and the supervisee, it is important that they establish from the beginning a number of important criteria before agreeing to make a contract to supervise a doctoral study:

- *Level of expertise*: does the supervisor know enough about the subject area and have an adequate disciplinary background to guide the student through the process? The ideal supervisor might seem to be a person who is very expert in the area the doctoral candidate wants to explore. However, the 'expert' might actually not be very good at supervising, or could already be quite biased in his or her way of thinking, and might not allow the student to expand his or her thinking beyond that of the supervisor's own limitations. Conversely, one might find a very good supervisor, who knows a lot about research method and doctoral study, but is not an expert in the specific clinical or methodological area, and the researcher will need to enlist separate consultation and advice on specific or technical or clinical aspects on the area of study. The ideal would be a combination of both.
- *Level of interest in the study*: the supervisor and the supervisee need to agree that this is an area of enquiry that the supervisor has enough interest in to be motivated to support and promote the doctoral student's activities. This inevitably means that the area of enquiry should be linked to the supervisor's own research interests. But if not, somebody can nevertheless supervise well simply because they find the subject area very interesting.
- *Methodological expertise*: while it would seem logical that a supervisor should supervise within a research paradigm in which he or she has most experience (and this is normally the case), there are supervisors

with a wide range of experience who are eclectic enough to offer expert guidance within different paradigms.

- *Time commitment*: the agreement between supervisor and supervisee needs to take into consideration the timing of the study and the availability of the supervisor. Does the supervisor have enough time to give to the student, or at least that which is specified within the registration and enrolment requirements of the university?
- *Clinical perspectives*: many music therapy research studies are conducted as applied clinical research and therefore the supervisor will need to be well informed about the clinical area that is the focus for investigation. Understanding the needs and therapeutic interventions normally applied within different clinical populations can be an important, but not necessarily essential, part of the supervisor's expertise. A research supervisor can adequately supervise a study without having to be an expert within the clinical area. This is further addressed under the development of method.

The contract between the supervisor and the supervisee

For the co-understanding of both the doctoral student and the supervisor, it is sometimes advisable to formulate a reasonably structured but flexible contract to establish what is required and accepted. This should be treated as a professional contract rather than a prenuptial agreement! In the PhD supervisors' training course held in 2005 in Aalborg, Denmark, some elements that should be included within a formal, semi-formal or informal contract were discussed:

Issues relating to the relationship

- Supervisor's boundaries about consultation times.
- Setting a timescale (subject to review).
- Discuss your philosophy as a supervisor – about supervision.
- Cultural differences in expectations.
- Benefits for taking supervisory responsibility.
- Balance of interest between the supervisor and the supervisee in the study.
- Mutuality and collaboration.
- Apprenticeship – the doctoral study as a research training.
- How to promote growth.
- Platform of respect.

Issues relating to the contract

- Limit of hours, calculation of hours.
- Degree of expertise of supervisor.

- Boundaries of supervisor.
- University rules, regulations and obligations: defining boundaries.
- Responsibility of the researcher to plan meetings and propose topics for discussion in supervision.
- Supervisor's responsibility to monitor progress on behalf of the institution.

In music therapy research, the development of this relationship has special qualities, most particularly where the researcher is also the practising clinician in the study, and the supervisor a practising clinician within the same clinical field. There are expectations regarding the identity, role and areas of responsibility, and how much the supervisor is an adviser, supervisor or partner. There are also ethical issues for both supervisor and supervisee, where confidentiality (sharing problems in supervision in an appropriate and ethical way, respecting each other's privacy, and maintaining confidentiality about the work and the material) is present due to the sensitive material in focus.

I also have experienced the ease with which one can transfer into the role of a clinical supervisor, where the researcher's questions begin to focus more on the clinical approach, relationships with clients and therapeutic direction than research method. This might not actually be a bad thing, as the phenomena I have experienced in supervising a number of studies in child and adolescent psychiatry, developmental disability, adult psychiatry, oncology, autism and heart surgery involve addressing the therapist/researcher's clinical approach. This leads into a reflection on, and discussion about, the clinical procedures used, the therapist's style and relationship with clients, and the clinical applications of research outcomes, from both quantitative and qualitative studies. This is one of the most valuable side-effects of the occasional blurring of boundaries in the supervisory relationship. For example, establishing a clinical protocol, as was needed in achieving flexible but consistent therapeutic experiences in a study comparing music therapy with play for autistic children (Kim 2006), or exploring the therapist's methods in association with the client's response (De Backer 2005; De Backer & Wigram 2007; Elefant 2001) has proven fruitful in informing clinical practice, and in explicating therapeutic effect within the wider context of evidence based practice (Ansdell, Pavlicevic & Proctor 2004; Wigram 2002; Wigram, Pedersen & Bonde 2002).

The first steps – defining the study

The supervisory relationship shifts into a new gear when the enrolment and registration of the candidate are completed and the study has begun. In most PhD study programmes, there is a period of development of either 6 months (full-time) or 1 year (part-time) for the doctoral researcher to prepare an extended and elaborated proposal for the final doctoral thesis. An elaborated proposal or documentation for conversion will contain an extended (if not complete) literature review for the study and a well-formulated and elaborated method for undertaking the research. It may be that data collection has already begun at this stage, and some analysis may have been made that will add to the candidate's strengths for approaching this particular milestone in the study.

The research questions or hypotheses

During this stage, realistic, manageable and limited research questions that can be successfully answered, or hypotheses that can be effectively proven through the process of the research study are developed. This process is known as 'limiting the study', and also applies to the literature review and the method. The supervision process for this to be achieved will have required both boundaries and compromise! Often, the clinical versus the research issues arise at this stage. Music therapy researchers are primarily centred within clinical thinking and motivation.

Limiting the literature review

The literature review forms the theoretical framework for undertaking the study. Consequently, when candidates finally collect all their results and analyse them in preparation for the discussion, they will be expected to relate their findings back to the literature that they cited in this early section of their thesis. Doctoral researchers in music therapy might have gathered material from widely divergent areas, some only loosely connected with the primary research questions of the study. Consequently, it is important to limit the literature review.

I recommend, for a clinically applied investigation, the following broad headings for the literature review:

- Studies and clinical literature regarding the clinical population.
- General overview of the current treatment approaches with that population.
- Literature review of disciplines most closely related to music therapy that have investigated the population.
- A review of the clinical reports and empirical studies in the therapy field relating to the population.
- A review of any specific research studies in the therapy field that relate to the population.
- A review of specific research studies in the therapy field that relate to the research question or research hypothesis for this study.

This sequence of reviews enables the overall literature review and formulation of a theoretical frame to move from the more general, foundational literature to the most important and specific literature at the end (those research studies that have immediately preceded this study and relate to the research questions). Dileo (2005) provided excellent guidelines for reviewing the literature.

There are many variants of this model, and it can be adapted in many ways. The main principle behind it is to establish a sequence or flow of the literature from the general foundational literature to the most closely related. What is present in the literature review at the end of the first year of a full-time doctoral study should be enough to support the study; future additional literature that is published while the collection of data and analysis of results is taking place, can also be added into the discussion chapter at the end.

The method

In these first steps, agreeing the method is vital. This is an interesting area of discussion between doctoral researcher and supervisor. The doctoral researcher might have explored the literature quite thoroughly and read much about research method, but at this point it will be the supervisor who has the most experience and is therefore the most able to advise and make sensible decisions about method. Idealistic or overambitious plans to collect too much data and engage with too many subjects or, conversely, to collect too little data and base the study on one or two subjects, needs to be looked at very carefully in relation to the research questions. The method provides the most important element of rigour in the study, and it is on methodology that most doctoral studies can receive their severest critique if there is fault or lack of definition and focus in the way the study is designed.

Guiding the study

The middle period of the doctoral study is typically concerned with collecting and analysing data. Providing the study is well grounded in a good theoretical frame, and an adequate and manageable method has been developed, this part of the study can see doctoral researchers steaming ahead by themselves, with less need for the supervisor, except to report what is going on. During this stage, some typical issues are raised in supervision, and the supervisor needs to begin the process of devolving responsibility to the doctoral researcher for solving these, rather than taking personal charge of the decision making.

It is very much during this middle phase of the process that doctoral students start to feel in control of the study, and able to make their own decisions. It is a 'transition' by doctoral researchers from the feeling of being a 'student' to being a more autonomous researcher. The supervisor takes on more the role of adviser and guide, while keeping a watchful eye on potential difficulties in the collection and processing of data. A regression might occur in this respect during the writing-up stage when, again, the student will much need the advice, example and critique of the doctoral supervisor.

Another dimension specific to clinically applied studies in music therapy is the complexity of musical data. While many studies do still involve the use of non-musical standardised tools (Gregory 2000), the analysis of notated scores (De Backer 2005; Holck 2003; Lee 1995) and of the musical elements and musical style in both improvised and repertoire music (Bonde 2005; Elefant 2001; Grocke 2001; Skewes 2001; Wosch 2002), requires musical expertise from the supervisor. This type of data is highly enriching in supporting the findings. An increasing numbers of studies involve the microanalysis of video and audio material, too numerous to document. The techniques of analysis are currently being documented in an edited volume from a group of European, US and Australian researchers in order to provide the tools needed to both researchers and clinicians (Wosch & Wigram 2007).

Writing up the study

Constructing the thesis is a process that should go on throughout the doctoral study. The thesis represents the product of the research. In Greek, the noun '*thesis*' means a 'position' or 'stance', which in the context of research means that the thesis functions as a treatise of beliefs regarding the findings of the study. As such, the thesis is a document that represents the following important things:

- what the researcher has found out
- how this fills a gap in knowledge
- on what basis it was founded
- what it should link to in the future in the form of further research
- its relevance and applicability in the here and now
- the rigorous and effective production of a research study
- how it forms a significant and original contribution to the literature.

To fulfil these requirements, a thesis needs to be the product of a well-organised and well-structured process. I have already talked about the introduction, the literature review and the methodology chapter. The results chapter is normally a place where results are presented, explained and interpreted so that they can be clearly understood. In qualitative studies, there are examples where the discussion takes place within the results chapter. This is particularly relevant in case-study research, whereby a series of cases might be presented in the results section, where it makes sense to discuss the findings from each case rather than saving the discussion of all the cases to a final chapter. There would still be a final chapter, which concludes and summarises the thesis and establishes the links back to the initial literature underpinning the study. In quantitative studies, results tend to be presented, explained and interpreted, but discussion is left to a final chapter.

The discussion chapter is probably the most important and critical of the thesis. This is where doctoral researchers demonstrate their ability to develop theory, think philosophically, explicate and critique their own method and results, and consider the importance and relevance of their research. It is also where they are able to place their findings within their original conceptual framework and provide the platform for the next link in the research chain, the study that will follow their study.

In a doctoral defence, it is the material in the discussion section that will probably attract the most attention from the examiners in terms of determining whether doctoral researchers have achieved a level of doctorateness in their research education. Trafford and Leschen (2002) have explored in comprehensive detail the whole process of undertaking doctoral research and made a major contribution to the PhD supervisors' seminar that took place in Aalborg in 2005. They looked carefully at the process of examination (Trafford 2002; Trafford, Woolliams & Leschen 2002) so as to synthesise the main thrust of the types of question that emerged in doctoral vivas and how researchers were succeeding or failing in this process. In doctoral vivas, the patterns in the types of issues and questions that emerge from across disciplines can prepare candidates for what to expect (Winter, Griffiths & Green 2000). Doctorateness is demonstrated when the study relates the research results to theory, and presents a coherent argument for the thesis reflecting on the method, design and the concepts involved.

Supervisor's role in writing up

The extraordinary development of computer technology and e-mail has radically changed the face of doctoral supervision, resulting in a much faster and more effective process but also in a process that can overwhelm both the student and the supervisor. It is very easy to e-mail a latest version of a chapter to a supervisor, with full awareness that it will be received just a few seconds after you have sent it and therefore you hope, or look forward to, a rapid response! In the contract between supervisor and supervisee, these issues need to be very clearly discussed and agreed. The manual for postgraduate research study and writing a thesis in music therapy at the University in Melbourne (Grocke 2005) contains a section on feedback from supervisors that explicitly defines expected timelines. Grocke recommends as a guideline:

- A 'quick' question that the supervisor can answer without needing to refer to other documents to be answered by return e-mail.
- A question requiring the supervisor to access literature or seek advice from administrative staff to be answered between 24–48 hours.
- Feedback on written material will depend on the length of material, the degree of advice needed and the supervisor's workload at the time. Supervisors should indicate the likely timeline for the response.

This is particularly relevant when planning for supervision sessions. It is difficult for supervisors to offer considered advice and recommendations if they receive quantities of material between 24 and 36 hours before a supervision. In fact, it seems to suggest that the doctoral researcher is expecting their supervisor to put aside all other tasks in order to provide the appropriate responses in supervision and this is not always possible. Therefore, the more lengthy the material, the greater the need to send it in advance.

Some important factors need to be considered in writing up in order for the supervisor to provide the best guidance:

- *Style of feedback*: some supervisors will offer short comments on material they receive, perhaps offering critique such as 'this paragraph doesn't seem to make sense, could you try and work more on it' to 'the section you have written in this paragraph explaining how the findings from the study didn't meet the expectations of the research question, needs to be re-phrased and you need to offer more detail in order to explain this'. Styles are very individual and this largely depends on how much the supervisor feels the doctoral researcher needs 'educating' in the most scholarly and academic way of writing up their thesis.
- *Track changes*: a tool on Microsoft Word, Track Change has proven to be highly useful, in my opinion, in feeding back to doctoral researchers writing their theses. It enables the supervisor to illustrate how to express things by actually changing the text in such a way that the student can see the original version and the supervisor's recommended changes.
- Track Changes also allows one to enter comments in the margin with specific questions relating to sections of the text. It allows one to block and move text around and shows where text has changed.
- Track Changes allows a series of multiple changes to occur; each time a document is opened and new changes are entered into the text, it comes up in a different colour. This can get rather complex if more than two people are working on the text and a multicoloured version of the section in question appears!
- *Language*: when students are writing in a language that is not their mother tongue, the use of Track Changes for the supervisor to try and

exemplify how to express things is particularly useful. Many PhD theses are now written in English, as the international language of science. Doctoral researchers want their theses to be read, and will make that very big extra additional effort to write in English and publish in English. However, it is not at all easy to write a complex, philosophical research thesis in a language that is not your mother tongue. Consequently, I have always found it quite important to give a lot of additional help, structure and vocabulary to help somebody to present their thesis in the best way.

- This phase of the supervisor–supervisee relationship is both exciting and challenging. Invariably, I find that doctoral researchers 'assume knowledge' when writing up. Short statements or points are made that need further explanation and justification. I often hear myself asking (almost therapeutic) questions such as "can you say a bit more about that . . .' And '. . . why do you think that is so important . . .'. Typically, the response will be a lengthy explanation, or more detailed information, to which I then hear myself saying 'I think you need to write that down'. It is for this purpose that most of my doctoral students bring mini-disc recorders to supervision and record much of what we discuss, because later they find themselves saying 'what *was* it we said about that?!'

Defending the study – arguments, disagreements and challenges

The final version of the thesis is actually the product of both the doctoral researcher's thinking and the supervisor's. However, the doctoral researcher is responsible for what is written and has to be prepared to defend it. At the same time, the supervisor will be able to see much better than the doctoral researcher what has not been explained in enough detail, and will also look critically at the thesis with a view to its weaknesses and limitations in the face of the forthcoming examination by experts in that field. I see it as a clear responsibility to ensure that doctoral researchers go to the PhD examination, whether it is in a public forum or private viva voce, with the clearest understanding and best opportunity of how to defend their doctoral study.

The supervisory process during the writing-up stage, especially in the discussion section, is a vital and important part of developing the arguments in the thesis. Arguments might occur between the student and the supervisor, and there might be disagreement about what findings might mean or what conclusions should be drawn. This is a healthy part of the process and demonstrates the transition the doctoral researcher has made from 'student' to 'qualified researcher', whereby he or she is able to justify and argue the issues involved in philosophical work such as a doctoral thesis. Keeping the balance in the process, and in the relationship between the supervisor and the doctoral researcher, is of significant importance, not just during the process of building the research study but also in writing it up (Delamont, Parry & Atkinson 1998).

Assuming that the researcher is satisfied with, confident about, well prepared for and ultimately proud of the study he or she has completed, entering into the process of defence will be best undertaken with a positive mental attitude:

- The PhD defence is an examination where the researcher must be able to talk to the study and answer critique.
- The PhD defence is a forum for the researcher to demonstrate competence, knowledge and awareness of other research.
- The PhD defence is a forum for discussion, as well as presentation and answering questions.
- The PhD defence is intended to be a moment of triumph for the researcher to demonstrate his or her mental and practical research skills.

Resources

Universities invariably provide guidance and advice on undertaking both Masters level research study and doctoral study. An extremely good document, entitled *PhD handbook*, is prepared by Melbourne University (University of Melbourne 2005). This gives a comprehensive overview of choosing an effective supervisor, establishing a good partnership, agreeing expectations and working on a strong perceptual structure and research plan. It goes on to define the importance of writing up material early on in the study, keeping regular contact for feedback, involving students in a research milieu, and motivating and intervening when academic and personal crises emerge.

Various other texts, articles and books relating to doctoral study can be extremely helpful for a supervisor, as well as for the doctoral researcher. A text currently in its fourth edition is *How to get a PhD: A Handbook for Students and their Supervisors* (Phillips & Pugh 2005), which is a general guide to the process. Perhaps the most useful chapter is the one advising potential students on the importance of choosing and engaging with the right supervisor for their study! Bolker (1998) also offers guidance on writing a thesis, with the maxim 'fifteen minutes a day', supporting the principle of continuous writing up.

As stated earlier in this chapter, Trafford and Leschen (2002) have comprehensively explored the method involved in undertaking and completing doctoral study and have described this in a number of important articles and presentations. In their literature references, they have included many resources as good marker points for supervisors embarking on doctoral research supervision (Altheide 1996; Bryman 2001; Burnham 1994; Delamont *et al.* 1998; Denicolo & Boulter 2002; Hartley 1997; Hartley & Fox 2002; Jackson & Tinkler 2000; Newberry 1995; Phillips 1994; Trafford 2002; Trafford & Leschen 2002; Trafford *et al.* 2002; Winter *et al.* 2002).

Co-authorship

The guide to postgraduate study from Melbourne University also addresses the issue of co-authorship, as do Grocke (2005) and Wigram (2005). The supervisor will have invested much in the student's research, and also contributes intellectual property in the doctoral thesis. Consequently, the doctoral researcher should be planning on co-authoring at least one, if not two articles, together with their supervisor as second author.

Conclusion

Completing a doctoral study can often feel like entering a labyrinth, searching for a way out and never quite expecting to find it. In the experience I have had as a doctoral supervisor, I have only ever encountered one student who didn't want to finish! Most students, especially those who have undertaken doctoral study part-time over a number of years, can get quite fed up with their research study and lose motivation and interest in it. The finishing process is important but so is the whole process of doctoral study. I often find myself saying to the doctoral researchers 'you're supposed to be enjoying this . . . research is a challenge but it can also be highly satisfying'. Encouraging people to enjoy their doctoral study is vital, as they must start to believe in themselves as a researcher. This is perhaps one of the most important roles of the supervisor. To inspire and to guide, to be there at moments of difficulty and crisis, to challenge when necessary, to be responsible for supplying essential information, boundaries and validation are inherently part of the role. Doctoral researchers can experience a high level of critique of what they are doing and merely having the title 'researcher' invites them to be challenged and knocked down. Therefore the doctoral supervisor has an essential role in maintaining their self-esteem about what they are doing, complimenting them on the achievements they make and being very aware that this is very hard work, at a very high level of academic achievement and doctoral researchers are predictably quite dependent on the validation of their supervisor. Finally, we should perhaps remember that the way we supervise a doctoral researcher and the level of trust that is built up between us will inevitably be transferred by that student when they themselves become doctoral supervisors. We want to hand down a good model, a satisfying experience and a feeling that with the supervisor's help, the doctoral researcher has reached that level of doctorateness and quality that they wish to be recognised for and that the thesis represents a significant and important contribution to knowledge and to science.

References

Altheide, D.L. (1996) 'Qualitative media analysis' in A. Bryman (ed.), *Social research method*, Oxford: Oxford University Press.

Ansdell, G., Pavlicevic, M. (1998) *Beginning research in the arts therapies*. London: Jessica Kingsley.

Ansdell, G., Pavlicevic, M., Proctor, S. (2004) *Presenting the evidence: a guide for music therapists responding to the demands of clinical effectiveness and evidence-based practice*. London: Nordoff-Robbins Productions.

Bolker, J. (1998) *Writing your dissertation in fifteen minutes a day: A guide to starting, revising and finishing your doctoral thesis*. New York: Holt and Co.

Bonde, L.O. (2005) *Quantitative and qualitative investigation into the influence of Receptive Music Therapy with cancer survivors*. Doctoral thesis. Aalborg University, Denmark. Online. Available: http://www.musikterapi.aau.dk/forskerskolen_index.htm

Bryman, A. (2001) *Social research methods*. Oxford: Oxford University Press.

Burnham, P. (1994) 'Surviving the doctoral viva: unravelling the mystery of the PhD oral'. *Journal of Graduate Education* 1, 30–34.

De Backer, J. (2005) *The transition from sensorial impression to a musical form (proto-symbolism) in psychotic patients in a music therapeutic process*. Doctoral thesis, Aalborg University, Denmark. Online. Available: http://www.musikterapi.aau.dk/forskerskolen_index.htm

De Backer, J., Wigram, T. (2007) 'Analysis of notated musical examples selected from improvisation of psychotic patients' in T. Wosch and T. Wigram (eds), *Microanalysis: methods, techniques and applications for clinicians, researchers, educators and students*, London: Jessica Kingsley.

Delamont, S., Parry, O., Atkinson, P. (1998) 'Creating a delicate balance: the doctoral supervisor's dilemmas'. *Teaching in Higher Education*, 3(2), 157–172.

Denicolo, P., Boulter, C. (2002) *Assessing the PhD: a constructive view of criteria*. London: UK Council for Graduate Education Research Degree Examining Symposium.

Dileo, C. (2005) Reviewing the Literature in B. Wheeler (ed.) *Music Therapy Research 2nd Edition. Gilsin NH: Barcelona Publishers.*

Elefant, C. (2001) *Communication in girls with Rett syndrome through songs in music therapy*. Doctoral thesis, Aalborg University, Denmark. Online. Available: http://www.musikterapi.aau.dk/forskerskolen_index.htm

Gregory, D. (2000) 'Test instruments used by *Journal of Music Therapy* authors from 1984–1997'. *Journal of Music Therapy*, 37(2), 79–94.

Grocke, D. (2001) *A phenomenological study of pivotal moments in guided imagery and music*. PhD. Dissertation. University of Melbourne. CD-IV University of Herdecke, Germany.

Grocke, D. (2005) *A manual for postgraduate research study incorporating writing a thesis in music therapy*. University of Melbourne: Faculty of Music.

Hartley, J. (1997) 'Writing the thesis' in N. Graves and V. Verma (eds), *Working for a doctorate*. London: Routledge.

Hartley, J., Fox, C. (2002) *The viva experience: examining the examiners*. London: UK Council for Graduate Education Research Degree Examining Symposium.

Holck, U. (2003) *'Kommunikalsk Semmenspil i musikterapi. Kvalitative videoanalyser af musikalske og gestiske interaktioner med børn med betydelige'*. Doctoral thesis, Aalborg University, Denmark. Online. Available: http://www.musikterapi.aau. dk/forskerskolen_index.htm

Jackson, P., Tinkler, C. (2000) 'The PhD examination: an exercise in community building and gatekeeping?' in I. McNay (ed.), *Higher education and its communities*, Buckingham, UK: Open University Press.

Kim, J. (2006) *The effects of improvisational music therapy on joint attention behaviours in children with autistic spectrum disorder*. Doctoral thesis, Aalborg University, Denmark. Online: Available: http://www.musikterapi.aau.dk/forskerskolen_index.htm

Lee, C. (1995) *Lonely waters*. Oxford: Sobell Publications.

Newberry, D. (1995) 'A journey in research from research assistant to doctor of philosophy'. *Journal of Graduate Education*, 2, 53–59.

Phillips, E.M. (1994) 'Avoiding communication breakdown' in O. Zuber-Skerrit and Y. Ryan (eds), *Quality in postgraduate education*, London: Kogan Page.

Phillips, E.M., Pugh D.S. (2005) *How to get a PhD: a handbook for students and their supervisors* (4th edn). Oxford: Oxford University Press.

Robson, C. (2002) *Real world research: a resource for social scientists and practitioner-researchers*. Oxford: Blackwell.

Skewes, K. (2001) *The experience of group music therapy for six bereaved adolescents*. PhD dissertation, University of Melbourne.

Trafford, V.N. (2002) *Questions in doctoral viva degree examining*. London: UK Council for Graduate Education Research Degree Examining Symposium.

Trafford, V.N., Leschen, S. (2002) 'Anatomy of a doctoral viva'. *Journal of Graduate Education*, 3, 33–41.

Trafford, V.N., Woolliams, P., Leschen, S. (2002) *Dynamics of the doctoral viva: the postgraduate experience*. University of Gloucestershire: Summer conference, UK Council for Graduate Education.

University of Melbourne (2005) *PhD handbook*. Online. Available: http://www.sgs.unimelb.edu.au

Wheeler, B. (ed.) (2005) *Music therapy research* (2nd edn). Phoenixville: Barcelona Publishers.

Wigram, T. (2002) 'Indications in music therapy: evidence from assessment that can identify the expectations of music therapy as a treatment for autistic spectrum disorder (ASD): meeting the challenge of evidence based practice'. *British Journal of Music Therapy*, 16(1), 11–28.

Wigram, T. (2005) *General principles of supervision*. PhD Supervisors' Course, Aalborg University, Denmark, October 2005. Personal communication.

Wigram, T., Pedersen, I.N., Bonde, L.O. (2002) *A comprehensive guide to music therapy. Theory, clinical practice, research and training*. London: Jessica Kingsley.

Winter, R., Griffiths, M., Green, K. (2000) 'The "academic" qualities of practice; what are the criteria for a practice-based PhD?' *Studies in Higher Education*, 25(1), 25–37.

Wosch, T. (2002) *Emotionale Mikroprozesse musikalscher Interaktionen: Eine Einzelfallanalyse zur Untersuchung musiktherapeutischer Improvisationen.* Munster: Waxmann.

Wosch, T., Wigram, T. (2007) *Microanalysis in music therapy: methods, techniques and applications for clinicians, researchers, educators and students.* London: Jessica Kingsley.

Index